The Five-Minute Linguist

The Five-Minute Linguist

Bite-sized Essays on Language and Languages

Second Edition

Edited by
E. M. Rickerson and Barry Hilton

Published by Equinox Publishing Ltd.

UK: Unit S3, Kelham House, 3 Lancaster Street, Sheffield S3 8AF
USA: ISD, 70 Enterprise Drive, Bristol, CT 06010

www.equinoxpub.com

First published in 2006 by Equinox

ISBN: 978-1-908049-94-0 (hardback)
ISBN: 978-1-908049-49-0 (paperback)

British Library Cataloguing-in-Publication Data
A catalogue record for this book is available from the British Library.

Library of Congress Cataloging-in-Publication Data
The five-minute linguist : bite-sized essays on language and languages / edited by
E.M. Rickerson and Barry Hilton. — 2nd ed.
    p. cm.
    Cover title: 5 minute linguist
    Includes bibliographical references and index.
    ISBN 978-1-908049-94-0 (hb)--978-1-908049-49-0 (pb)
    1. Language and languages—Miscellanea. I. Rickerson, E. M. II. Hilton, Barry.
III. Title: 5 minute linguist.
    P107.A15 2012
    400—dc23
                                                        2011032446

Typeset by JS Typesetting Ltd, Porthcawl, Mid Glamorgan
Printed and bound in Great Britain by Lightning Source UK Ltd., Milton Keynes and
Lightning Source Inc., La Vergne, TN

'Wherever you are and whatever you do, language makes a difference!'

— The Five-Minute Linguist

The editors and publisher would like to thank the National Museum of Language and the Linguistic Society of America for their support in the publication of this book.

In memory of two colleagues who contributed to the first edition of this book:

Peter Ladefoged, 1925–2006

Frank Borchardt, 1938– 2007

Contents

Foreword

Bret Lovejoy

This book is for anyone who has a question about languages or the nature of language—which means just about all of us. But it's not just a musty academic text for specialists. While written by leading experts on the subject of language, *The Five-Minute Linguist* is a user-friendly exploration of the basics, a linguistic start-up kit for general readers. It assumes nothing on your part except interest in the subject. Its bite-sized chapters (no more than 5 pages each) give authoritative answers to the most frequently asked questions people have about language, and tell the story in a lively and colloquial style. It is a delightful read.

Although the main purpose of the book is to inform, it also aims to encourage the study of language and raise awareness of the nature and diversity of languages on the planet—which is why it is of special interest to us at the American Council on the Teaching of Foreign Languages (ACTFL). You may be aware that the U.S. Senate and House of Representatives designated 2005 as the 'Year of Languages' in the United States, to call attention to the importance—and the benefits—of language study. Throughout that year, ACTFL promoted activities aimed at jump-starting a sense of urgency about language. There were lectures and films at universities, poster contests in schools, billboards on highways, statewide language competitions, essay contests, folk festivals, cultural programs, national roundtables, and many other events. There was even established (at the college of Charleston in South Carolina) a new School of Languages, Cultures, and World Affairs.

One of the more ambitious projects—a radio series called *Talkin'*
About Talk—was broadcast on public, commercial and college
radio stations around the country. Members of the ACTFL Board
of Directors and staff took part in that project, and ACTFL supported it by posting audio files of the entire series on our national
website (www.actfl.org). The book you have in your hand is an
adaptation of that series: enriched versions of the original fifty-two
broadcasts, augmented by several new essays.

In addition to more lofty goals, there are some very practical
reasons to encourage language study. The U.S. is the only indus-
trialized nation whose children routinely leave secondary school
knowing only one language (the stereotype of the monolingual
American is not entirely untrue). The latest enrollment survey
tells us that only one American in three studies a foreign language
in school at all. Meanwhile, the government has great backlogs of
materials waiting for translation, a shortage of language specialists
everywhere, and a readiness level of only thirty percent in the
most critical languages. Beyond considerations of global commerce, in a post-9/11 world the lack of attention to languages
other than English has very serious consequences. Americans can't
afford *not* to study foreign languages and cultures at a time when
economic necessity and national security depend more than ever
on clear communication with trading partners, allies and potential
adversaries.

To increase its language capacity, the U.S. has to build a pipe-
line of students who start language study early in life and continue
it through college. There need to be language-learning opportunities for all students, especially in the elementary schools. State and
local officials need to look at priorities and put to rest the notion
that language is an 'extra' in the school curriculum, a frill that can
easily be cut when funding is tight. The paradigm has changed.
Every day 70 percent of Americans interact with someone whose
native tongue is a language other than English. In a global economy, no matter what job a student seeks, he or she will be just as
likely to do business with South Korea as with South Carolina.

Understanding what other people think, and why, helps us—Americans and others—to be better friends and better negotiators worldwide. And language is the key.

But to change the perceptions about the importance of language is not easy. Sadly, not much has changed since the first publication of this book, in 2006. The Year of Languages in the United States was a great first step. ACTFL has continued its attempt to educate the public through its ongoing *Discover Languages . . . Discover the World!* campaign, and Chinese classes have seen a large percentage increase in enrollment in the K-12 grades as well as college levels. But budget cuts in local school districts have resulted in closures of many other language programs.

Yet there is still cause for optimism. Growing numbers of parents understand that an education that provides not just 'exposure' but proficiency in a world language other than English will give their children an advantage in the global marketplace. The Department of Defense and other government agencies understand the critical nature of languages to our national security and they are supporting the expansion of language education. Increasing numbers of Americans are active on Internet social networks either talking about or learning another language. Language educators are seeking ways to connect with these supporters and ACTFL welcomes the role of facilitating the connections with the goal of curing American monolingualism.

Enjoy *The Five-Minute Linguist* and become a language advocate yourself!

Bret Lovejoy, Executive Director
American Council on the Teaching of Foreign Languages

Introduction

E. M. Rickerson and Barry Hilton

It's rare that scholarship is both informative and at the same time fun. Although it's the work of language experts, authoritative and full of facts, *The Five-Minute Linguist* is intended for non-specialists, an upbeat introduction to language and linguistics for general readers. The book's chapters are short (three to five pages), suitable for browsing or reading on the run, and its style is intentionally light—more like fireside chats than a textbook. In fact, it started its life as a series of radio chats called *Talkin' About Talk*, which in 2005 was part of a celebration of the 'Year of Languages' in the United States. The essays have an informal tone because of the on-air persona of the narrator, a knowledgeable and amiable guide whose task it was to de-mystify the sometimes complex subject of language for a wide range of listeners. Each week the narrator talked about a language-related topic in a relaxed, conversational style for *exactly five minutes*—thus the title of the book. The volume you hold in your hand (either in print or as an e-book) is the second edition, for which the essays were updated and the book expanded by five chapters to fill what we felt were gaps in the first version (published 2006).

Since the book's format ruled out in-depth coverage of any of its topics, the editors decided early on to limit its focus to a few guiding principles: What do people who are *not* in the language field want to know about language? What are some of their major misconceptions? What specific languages or language groups are of most interest to this audience? What do our readers want to know about *learning* or *using* languages? The resulting essays, each with a question as its title, are what we like to think of as a savory platter of linguistic *hors d'oeuvres*, something to whet your appetite and invite you to go on to a more substantial dish.

At the outset the editors had not planned to turn the radio series into a book; but neither did we know that the essays would be so warmly received. It turned out that they appealed not just to radio listeners, but to a variety of people with a personal or professional interest in language. The material was used in basic language and linguistics courses, introductory anthropology classes, pre-service training for language teachers, adult education centers, English as a Second Language programs, and classes for younger students in Language Arts. Secondary schools broadcast the programs through speaker systems to their student bodies, and a U.S. foreign affairs agency put them online for its employees worldwide. The American Council on the Teaching of Foreign Languages (ACTFL) posted the audio files on its website as a resource for language teachers. There was even an enterprising book club that started its meetings—well before this book existed—by playing the audio essays to stimulate discussion. The creators of *Talkin' About Talk* were especially honored when the series received the Linguistic Society of America's prestigious 'Linguistics, Language and the Public' award.

Let us be clear that there is no such person as the 'Five-Minute Linguist'. The radio voice and architect of the project was Dr. E. M. 'Rick' Rickerson, Professor Emeritus at the College of Charleston; but the 'Linguist' is actually a consortium of sixty experts from twenty-five U.S. states and the United Kingdom. They're an impressive array of talent by any measure, and we encourage you to read their brief biographies at the end of each chapter. Many have written highly acclaimed books of their own that discuss, at greater length and with narrower focus, the topics discussed in this book. Most are on university faculties or otherwise professionally engaged with language. They include what are sometimes called *scientific linguists* (linguistics professors, field linguists, philologists, phoneticians, psycholinguists and others primarily interested in linguistic theory and linguistic data); *language educators* (specialists in second language acquisition, and teachers of various languages); and *applied language professionals* (translators/ interpreters, language officers in government agencies, lexicographers, anthropologists, directors of resource centers and language programs, and members of advocacy groups or professional organizations). Despite their common interest in language, these three broad categories tend to occupy separate orbits. We believe it to be a unique feature of the book that its contributors represent the entire breadth of the language profession.

Keeping such a diverse group speaking with a relatively consistent stylistic voice—on the air and later in print—was the responsibility of a Review Board that examined, edited, and commented on drafts of each essay. At various times during the history of this project the Board has included the former president of the Linguistic Society of America, Joan Bybee, Distinguished Professor of Linguistics at the University of New Mexico; Frank Borchardt, Duke University Professor of German and specialist in language teaching technology; Sheri Spaine Long, Professor of Spanish at the University of Alabama at Birmingham, and Editor-in-Chief of *Foreign Language Annals*; Geoffrey Nunberg, professor at UC Berkeley's School of Information and featured presenter on the NPR show *Fresh Air*; Jill Robbins of George Washington University and trustee at the Museum of Languages; and the freelance writer and independent scholar Barry Hilton (co-editor of this book, along with Rick Rickerson). It should be noted that the Board's job was *not* to purge the collection of all contradictions or repetitions. (It's not unusual, in areas of lively academic research, for different inquiries to overlap, or for the same evidence to be interpreted differently by different experts.)

How to read this book

The Five-Minute Linguist does not have to be read from the beginning. Since the chapters are essentially free-standing, they may be read in any order. That does not mean, however, that each chapter is unconnected to the rest. Chapters may be related to adjacent chapters and to other parts of the book as well. To help readers pursue the connections, we have provided both an index at the back of the book and, after each chapter, a few suggestions for further browsing. For those whose appetite has been stimulated by the book's bite-sized essays and want to try something more substantial, each chapter is followed by a short list of relevant books, articles, and websites that are accessible to a non-specialist reader.

While the book is not formally divided into sections, you will see that adjacent chapters tend to fall into groups with similar subject matter. Approximately the first half of the book discusses language in general, from the perspective of scientific linguists. Topical groups include the nature of language (Chapters 1–14), language's relationships with brain function and thought (Chapters 15–18), the social context of language (Chapters 19–28), and the sounds of language (Chapters 29–31). In the second half, Chapters 32–37 address language learning and teaching. Chapters 38–44 are a miscellany of articles on language in the U.S. Chapters 45–50 discuss language 'applications' such as lexicography, translation, and forensic investigation. The last fifteen chapters are devoted to commentary on a selection of specific languages and language families.

Acknowledgments

It has taken a good many people and organizations to make *The Five-Minute Linguist* a reality. It should first be noted that this second edition of the book was jointly—and enthusiastically—sponsored by the National Museum of Language and the Linguistic Society of America. We are particularly grateful to Amelia Murdoch, President Emerita of the Museum, and members of the Museum's Board, who embraced the project from the start; to Paul Chapin, Secretary-Treasurer of the Linguistic Society of America; and to the dozens of LSA members who made contributions either to the radio series or the book, or both. And to Dr. Samuel M. Hines, Founding Dean of the College of

Charleston's School of Languages, Cultures and World Affairs, who provided resources and facilities at the School for much of the basic work on the radio series. Special thanks to Jill Robbins, who provided valuable input to the editors as a reviewer for the second edition.

We would also like to express appreciation to the language and linguistic organizations in the U.S. that so readily supported the project: to Bret Lovejoy, Executive Director of the American Council on the Teaching of Foreign Languages (ACTFL), for graciously contributing a Foreword to the book, and to Marty Abbott, Director of Education at ACTFL, who wrote an essay for the radio series and was one of the project's most consistent supporters. Other national language organizations that endorsed the radio project and encouraged us to carry it through included the Modern Language Association (MLA), the Center for Applied Linguistics, the National Foreign Language Center, the American Translators Association, the Joint National Committee for Languages, the Indigenous Language Institute, and the National Council of State Supervisors of Foreign Languages. The project also enjoyed the support of regional organizations: the South Carolina Council on Languages; a long list of foreign language teacher associations, including many of MLA's regional affiliates; and especially the Southern Conference on Language Teaching, which recognized *Talkin' About Talk* through a special 'Year of Languages' Award.

We are especially indebted to Professors Deborah Tannen of Georgetown University and G. Richard Tucker of Carnegie Mellon, internationally known linguists and authors who generously read and commented on the final draft of the first edition; and to Professors Walt Wolfram and Robert Rodman of North Carolina State University, two of America's most respected linguists, whom we think of as the book's godfathers. They were actively engaged in the radio project from its earliest days and gave it much-valued impetus and encouragement. Both contributed multiple essays to the anthology and freely shared their wisdom and experience to keep the project on track during the inevitable tribulations.

Finally, we would like to give special applause to the book's sixty distinguished contributors. The authority and clarity of the essays in *The Five-Minute Linguist* will be obvious to readers. Not observable, except to the editors, is the collegiality and selflessness that characterized the writing and shaping of them. Contributors joined the project voluntarily for the benefit of the profession, and did so without reserve. They embraced the project so wholeheartedly that the modest goal of raising public awareness about language and linguistics became, ultimately, a celebration of language itself.

1
Why learn about language?

Robert Rodman

Have you ever wondered which language is the oldest?
Or how babies learn to talk?

Language is universal, and each of us is a kind of expert in using the language we were raised speaking, but there's a lot more to language than what we use in everyday life, and it raises a lot of fascinating questions. Whatever happened to Esperanto? Can machines translate languages? Are some ways of speaking or writing better than others? The chapters of this book will address all these questions and many more.

Let's start with a big question: what is it that makes us human? Is it walking on two legs? Or living in society? Is it our ability to love and hate? To some degree, all of those. But none is unique to the human species. Birds walk on two legs. Ants live in society. And my dog loves me, and hates the cat next door.

It's language that distinguishes us from all other creatures. Whatever else people do when they're together—whether they play, or fight, or make love, or serve hamburgers, or build houses— they talk. We're the only creatures on the planet with the power of speech.

Every human being, rich or poor, is capable of language. Every child learns his or her native tongue, be it English or Zulu, just by being exposed to the talk around them. Most children are fluent before they're ten years old, sometimes in more than one language. Equally impressive is that as they grow up they master different styles of speech: everything from formal, job-interview talk to street slang.

Among the questions to be taken up in this book is how something as complex as language can be so easy for children to learn, yet so difficult for adults. We do know that certain areas of the brain specialize in language, and that children are born with a capacity to learn any human language to which they are exposed. Moreover, as will be discussed later, a child who is isolated from language while growing up may never learn to speak well as an adult. Based on that evidence, many scientists believe that the capacity for language is genetic, but that much of that capacity is lost by adulthood.

Our discussion pertains to spoken language. Learning to read and write—literacy—is another matter entirely. Writing—though it's closely related to spoken language and will be addressed in several chapters of this book—is a human invention, like the bicycle, and has to be studied. Talking is a biological trait, like walking, and comes naturally.

Something you'll see clearly in the course of the book is how much variety there is in the world's tongues, and how constantly they change over time. There are thousands of languages on the planet, all descended from earlier languages that spread and changed and split up into dialects as people moved. Given enough time, the separation of groups and the dialects they speak inevitably leads to the birth of new languages, the way French, Romanian, and Spanish grew out of the Latin spoken by the Romans.

You'll also read what linguists have discovered about how and when language began. What do you think? Was there a 'first language' spoken by some brilliant ancestor? Did musical grunts evolve into language around a campfire? Or did aliens from another planet teach our forebears to speak in the recesses of history? There's no shortage of theories, ranging from the supernatural to the imitation of animal sounds.

Do animals talk? Clearly, apes and other animals communicate with each other, and can be taught to do some language-related tasks, but they lack the linguistic flexibility of humans—our amazing ability to express new thoughts, without limits on subject matter.

And what about computers? In some ways they seem very clever. But can we teach a machine to speak and understand like a human? Not quite. Although they're capable of some flashy simulations of human-like skills, computers are limited in their ability to understand and produce meaningful speech. And they certainly lack the spontaneity and creativity of human language.

Think about it: almost every time you speak—except for a few set phrases such as exclamations of pain or anger, or words you recite from memory like poems or prayers—you're creating a sentence different from any other sentence you've ever heard or spoken. Each one is unique. And every day you create hundreds, or even thousands, of them! One reason language is special is that it's a universal form of human creativity. Happily, even without being great poets, authors or orators, we can be creative every day of our life when we speak.

There is no human trait more pervasive, or in many ways more valuable, than language. It's capable of expressing all of human thought, even thoughts about itself—which is what this book is all about. So start reading!

About the author

Robert Rodman is a UCLA-trained linguist who is currently a professor in the Department of Computer Science at North Carolina State University. He is co-author of a best-selling linguistics textbook, *An Introduction to Language*. Dr. Rodman is also a forensic linguist and consults with the judiciary in matters involving language and the legal system.

Suggestions for further reading

Fromkin, Victoria, Robert Rodman, and Nina Hyams. *An Introduction to Language* (Wadsworth, Cengage Learning, ninth edition 2011). This is a comprehensive book about language and linguistics written for persons with no previous background in languages. It is written in a light, readable style and makes copious use of cartoons, pithy quotations, poems, and song lyrics to make its linguistic points. More than one million copies of this book have been bought.

Pinker, Steven. *The Language Instinct: How the Mind Creates Language (P.S.)* (Harper Perennial Modern Classics, 1994; revised third edition 2007). This is a fascinating, witty treatment of the nature of the human mind as it pertains to language. It is well written enough to be a page-turner despite its technical subject. It's a must-read for anybody in the language field, and a joyful read for the linguistically curious.

2

You're a linguist? How many languages do you speak?

Paul Chapin

What is linguistics really about? What do linguists actually do, anyway?

Every profession has its cocktail party moment, the stereotypical reaction you get when someone finds out what you do. Economists are complimented on their ability to balance their checkbooks, psychologists are asked to refrain from analyzing fellow guests. For linguists, it's the question in the title.

Most linguists have trained themselves not to wince visibly when asked this. Their answers reflect a variety of strategies, some less polite than others. One linguist would say, 'One, I think.' Another, 'All of them, at some underlying level.' But the question is asked in good faith, and offers an opportunity to explain what linguistics is really about. So a good answer is something like the following.

People who speak multiple languages are called 'polyglots'. (You can learn more about them in Chapter 23 of this book.) That's an admirable skill to have, but it's different from linguistics, which is the scientific study of natural human language. Native-level ability to speak a language being studied is generally useful and sometimes necessary, but by no means always. This is good, because otherwise the number and variety of languages that linguists could work on would be vastly reduced.

So linguists mostly don't learn to speak languages. What exactly do they do, then? Well, language is a big subject, and the answer has to be broken down into parts. Let's look at some of them.

Many linguists work on describing particular languages. Every language has a structured system of sounds, called its phonology; a set of ways the sounds are combined into words: the morphology; a list of the words and their meanings: the vocabulary; and a set of rules for combining the words into sentences: the syntax. Describing a language means making a systematic report of all these components. If the linguist is not a native speaker of the language, he or she works with a native speaker as consultant. In these days when many of the world's languages are rapidly disappearing, as you will read elsewhere in this book, linguistic description is a particularly urgent task. If we cannot save all the endangered languages, we can at least try to document them.

Some linguists work at the more abstract level of linguistic theory. Most linguists today believe that all human languages have many fundamental features in common. Theoretical linguistics is the effort to identify those features and weave them together into a basic model of language, sometimes called a universal grammar. Contrary to what you might think, building a universal grammar is not a matter of somehow welding together all the grammars of all the world's languages. Any feature that's universal must appear in every language, so theoretical work often consists of very detailed analysis of a single language—just as modern genetics began with years of research concentrating on just a few organisms, such as fruit flies.

Language is spoken. The study of speech is a scientific field in itself, with two major components: phonetics and speech perception. Phoneticians study the various body parts involved in speaking and the intricate way they function together, as well as the acoustics of the sounds of speech. Speech-perception specialists study how the hearer translates the noises hitting the ear into meaningful messages. Since speech is a measurable physical phenomenon, unlike syntax or morphology, phoneticians are able to use the tools of the physical sciences in their research, including mathematics, the laws of physics, and sophisticated laboratory instruments. This gives their work an enviable rigor.

Language changes over time. Groups of people who start out speaking the same language, but are isolated from each other for centuries, eventually reach a point where they can no longer understand one another. Studying these processes of change, and reconstructing earlier stages of a present-day language by comparing it with other related languages, are the business of historical linguistics.

Because language is such a central aspect of being human, it is a necessary concern of other scientific fields that study human cognition and behavior. Interdisciplinary research is thus essential to understanding language better. Linguists team up with colleagues in psychology, neuroscience, child development, anthropology, or sociology, or become versed in those disciplines themselves, in order to explore the full range of what language is about. These efforts are sometimes called hyphenated linguistics, as in psycholinguistics, neurolinguistics, sociolinguistics, and so forth.

Psycholinguists study what goes on in our minds when we talk or read or listen to another talking. They have developed a number of very clever tricks for looking at this invisible process. What neurolinguists do can be described the same way, except substituting 'brains' for 'minds'. Research in neurolinguistics has advanced greatly since the appearance of new tools and techniques for brain imaging, especially functional magnetic resonance imaging (fMRI).

A fundamental mystery of language is how every child learns it so quickly and so completely, without any formal instruction, as easily and naturally as he or she learns to walk or recognize faces. Linguists interested in language acquisition have been studying this process for decades, and have learned a great deal, but there is still much mystery to solve.

Before the 1960s, language was generally considered a cultural phenomenon, so linguistics was a branch of anthropology. While the center of gravity of linguistic research has shifted to language as a component of cognition, it is still the case that language and culture are deeply interdependent, and anthropological linguistics continues to be a thriving enterprise. Anthropological linguists study how culture is expressed in language, and how language impacts culture. They used to focus primarily on pre-industrial societies, but today may apply their skills and perspectives in any setting.

We all know of other people who speak our language, whom we can understand and communicate with perfectly well, but who don't speak the same way we do. They may live in a different part of the country, or just elsewhere in town; sometimes they're of a different age. This variation in language is the central interest of sociolinguists. They have shown that social factors such as gender, ethnicity, and socioeconomic class influence linguistic variation profoundly. They have also shown that this variation plays a significant role in language change.

So now you know, when you run across a linguist, what not to ask. Ask instead, 'What's your specialty?' You will have an instant friend.

About the author
Paul Chapin received his Ph.D. in linguistics from MIT in 1967. After eight years on the faculty at the University of California at San Diego, he went to the National Science Foundation in 1975, where he became the first NSF Program Director for Linguistics. He retired from the NSF in 2001, and now lives in Santa Fe, New Mexico.

Suggestions for further reading
All the other chapters in this book. They give a good broad view of the whole field of linguistics.

See the list of current grants made by the Linguistics Program at NSF for a taste of what's going on right now at the frontiers of research in linguistics and the language sciences. Start at www.nsf.gov, click 'Awards' on the home page and 'Program Information' on the next screen. Write 'linguistics' in the box labeled 'Program' and click on 'Search'. A long list of grants will appear at the bottom of the screen. Click on any title that interests you to see a little more information about that project.

3

How many languages are there in the world?

M. Paul Lewis

How many languages are there? Who counts them?
Where are they spoken? Which have the most speakers?

How many languages are there? That's one of those 'it all depends'
questions: how you answer it depends on what you call a language,
and deciding what is and what isn't a language is not as easy as
you'd think.

Suppose your favorite breakfast food is thin round cakes of
grilled batter with butter and syrup. You call them 'pancakes'. Your
neighbor, who likes the same meal, might call them 'griddlecakes'.
If either of you travelled to a restaurant in a nearby town you
might find that you have to ask for 'flapjacks'. Now imagine that
chain of contacts stretching out further. After a few hundred
miles, even tiny differences along the way could add up to make
it hard to understand people. They might even say something like
'Wassup?' to mean 'Hello!' Where do you draw the line between
a dialect and a language? Where does one language leave off and
another begin?

Sometimes it's not hard to figure out. People in Iraq speak
Arabic; their neighbors in Iran speak Farsi, a completely unrelated
language. At other times, though, the linguistic differences are
small, and the answer becomes a matter of politics and sociology.

Swedes and Norwegians can understand each other easily. But they have different histories, customs, and governments, and they see themselves as two nations, speaking two languages, not one. The same thing, more or less, goes for Malaysians and Indonesians; or Macedonians and Bulgarians. Some groups go to great lengths to distinguish themselves from their linguistic cousins across a border: Serbs and Croatians understand each other's speech perfectly well, but they use two different writing systems. Other groups do just the opposite: a billion people live in China, with at least seven mutually unintelligible forms of regional speech. But they're reluctant to see themselves as separate nations, so they've clung to a unique ancient writing system that can be used any-where in the country and lets them think of themselves as united by a single language.

Another dimension that has to be considered is socioeconomic. Generally people with more education and economic opportunity adopt certain ways of talking. Those with less education and fewer opportunities often aren't able to learn the standard or prestigious forms. Frequently, educated folk have a difficult time understand-ing those who aren't part of their social class. While this occurs much more often in societies where social differences are clearly marked and strongly enforced, a certain amount of it goes on in any society. What you call a 'flapjack', someone else in your society might prefer to call a 'crepe'. Sometimes the differences in speech are so marked that people have difficulty understanding one another, and one or the other group in the society won't accept the variety they don't speak as being 'their language'. Also, some-times the less prestigious group reacts by adopting their linguistic variety as a marker of their identity, and they may insist with great pride that they speak a different language

So it's not easy to define what is or isn't a language, and count-ing is a matter of definitions. How many languages there are also depends on *when* you count them. Languages, like people, are born, they change and grow and sometimes have offspring, and they eventually dwindle and die. We'll never have an exact answer to the slippery question of how many languages there are, but among the most dedicated counters are the researchers at *Ethnologue*, a comprehensive directory of the world's languages that released its sixteenth edition in 2009. Their estimate, based largely on how well speakers can understand each other, is that a total of 6,909 languages are actively spoken or signed in the world today.

Some of those are just about extinct, with only a handful of speakers left. In fact, about *a quarter* of the world's languages have fewer than a thousand speakers and nearly 60 percent of the languages in the world have fewer than ten thousand. The median population size is 7,560. Many of those small groups are using their languages quite vigorously, but keeping a language alive is harder when there are fewer people to speak it with and when another language is being picked up and used for communication with outsiders.

At the other end of the scale is a group of very dominant languages. Over the next century they'll probably drive hundreds, or even thousands, of the smaller languages to extinction, just as superstores drive small shopkeepers out of business. The largest by far is Mandarin—nearly nine hundred million people in China speak it as a native tongue. Hindi, English, and Spanish each have over three hundred million native speakers. The other leading languages—all of which have between one and two hundred million native speakers—are Bengali, Portuguese, Russian, Indonesian, Arabic, Japanese, German, and French.

In addition to simply counting how many languages there are, it is interesting to observe how those languages are distributed around the world. We often think of Europe as a very multilingual place. And it does have 234 different languages. But it doesn't compare with Asia, which has 2,322—nearly a third of the world's languages—or with Africa, which has almost as many (2,110).

The number of languages in the world is constantly changing. And the *diversity* of the world's languages is amazing. Some people yearn for the days before Babel, when it's said that everyone spoke the same tongue, but that seems like a short-sighted view: *every* language is a window on the culture (and environmental setting) in which it's spoken and a window on the human mind as well. In addition, and perhaps more importantly, every distinct language represents an identity—a group of people who see themselves as belonging together and as having a shared history. There are good reasons not only to study them but to preserve what we can of *all* of them.

About the author

M. Paul Lewis is a sociolinguistics consultant with SIL International (a nonprofit faith-based language development organization) and the editor of *Ethnologue: Languages of the World*. Born in the U.S., he is the child of a multilingual, multicultural family with parents and grandparents born in England, Wales, and Argentina. He lived for nearly twenty years in Guatemala, where he studied and did research on the K'iche' language. He holds a Ph.D. in linguistics from Georgetown University. He currently resides in Malaysia with his wife. They have four grown children.

Suggestions for further reading

In this book

Various languages of the world are described in Chapters 52 (Native American languages), 53 (Latin), 54 (Italian), 55 (languages of Spain and Portugal), 56 (Russian), 57 (Icelandic), 58 (Hebrew and Yiddish), 59 (Arabic), 60 (languages of Africa), 61 (Chinese), 62 (Japanese), 63 (languages of India), 64 (Esperanto), and 65 (other invented languages). Also relevant are Chapters 27 (language death), 28 (language rescue), 38 (languages of the U.S.), and 50 (the Museum of Languages).

Elsewhere

Comrie, Bernard, ed. *The Atlas of Languages: The Origin and Development of Languages Throughout the World* (New Burlington Books, 1996).

Crystal, David. *Language Death* (Cambridge University Press, 2000). A good overview of the dynamics of language maintenance and death and related issues.

Grenoble, L. A. and L. J. Whaley. *Endangered Languages: Language Loss and Community Response* (Cambridge University Press, 1998). Looks at the ways in which various communities have responded to the endangerment of their languages.

Lewis, M. Paul, ed. *Ethnologue: Languages of the World.* (SIL International, sixteenth edition 2009). Also online at: www.ethnologue.com. Possibly the most comprehensive inventory of the living languages of the world.

4

What's the difference between dialects and languages?

G. Tucker Childs

Is it better to speak a language or a dialect?
Which do you speak?

Strange as it may seem, there is no generally agreed-upon way to distinguish between a 'language' and a 'dialect'. The two words are not objective, scientific terms, even among linguists. The lay community shares the same predicament, and people often use the terms to mean different things. As used by many people, language is what *we* speak and dialect is the linguistic variety spoken by *them*, usually someone thought of as inferior. In other contexts, language can mean the generally accepted standard, the variety sanctioned by the government and the media. Dialects, on the other hand, are homelier versions of the standard that vary from region to region and don't sound like the speech of radio announcers.

Language varieties, then, tend to be labeled dialects rather than languages for non-linguistic reasons, usually political or ideological. Dialects are spoken by people who don't run the country. They're generally considered to be not as 'good' as the standard language and consequently have little prestige. Oftentimes they're not even written. In short, the distinction is subjective. It depends on who you are and the perspective from which you judge the varieties.

From a linguistic perspective, no dialect is inherently better than any other and thus no dialect is more deserving of the title 'language' than any other dialect. A language can be seen as a group of related dialects. For example, the dominant position of the Parisian dialect in France is largely an accident of history. When the Count of Paris was elected king of France in the tenth century, the dialect of his court became the 'standard' French language. Other related varieties were disdained as well as other unrelated varieties (e.g., Basque in the southwest and Breton in the north). If things had gone differently, however, the dialect of Marseille or Dijon might have become the national language of France today.

Dialects can be *socially* determined, as Eliza Doolittle and the audience learn in *My Fair Lady*. In this play and film, as will be remembered, the snobby phonetics professor Henry Higgins wagers with fellow phonetician Col. Pickering that he can take an ordinary flower girl, change her speech, and make her presentable in high society. He succeeds, much to his own chagrin. (Higgins was based on the real-life phonetician Daniel Jones, no doubt a much more appealing person. Rex Harrison, who played Higgins in the film, was coached by the real-life phonetician Peter Ladefoged, who later contributed Chapter 29 of this book.)

Dialects can also be *politically* determined. The linguist Max Weinreich is often quoted as saying, 'A language is a dialect with an army and a navy.' His point was that political concerns often decide what will be called a 'dialect' and what will be called a 'language'. Powerful or historically significant groups have 'languages'; their smaller or weaker counterparts have 'dialects'.

Sometimes what are languages and what are dialects can be *arbitrarily* determined by a person or a government. In southern Africa an early twentieth-century missionary created a language now known as 'Tsonga' by declaring three separate languages to be dialects of a single tongue. Conversely, the government of South Africa created two languages by arbitrary declaration—Zulu and

Xhosa—even though there is no clear linguistic boundary between them. Instead, the two lie at the ends of what is called a 'dialect continuum', in which no two adjacent dialects are wildly different, but the dialects at the ends are mutually unintelligible.

Dialect differences are often relatively minor—sometimes just a matter of pronunciation ('You say tomayto, I say tomahto') or slight differences in vocabulary (Americans say 'elevator' and 'cookie', the British say 'lift' and 'biscuit'). Such differences are crucial to understanding George Bernard Shaw's famous quip that America and Britain are 'two countries separated by a common language.' But dialects can also differ so greatly from one another that they are incomprehensible. German speakers from Cologne and German speakers from rural Bavaria can barely understand one another, if at all. And although German is one of Switzerland's national languages, the Swiss speak local dialects of it that few Germans can understand.

One of the tests people use to differentiate 'language' from 'dialect' is mutual intelligibility. Many would say that if people understand each other without too much difficulty, they're speaking the same language; if not, they're speaking different languages. That seems like a good rule. So why are Cologne German and Bavarian German, which are *not* mutually intelligible, not considered separate languages? Or why are Swedish and Norwegian considered separate languages, when Swedes and Norwegians have no trouble understanding one another?

Such questions become even more unanswerable when speakers of Dialect A just don't *want* to understand speakers of Dialect B, and sometimes vice versa. One or both groups insist that they speak separate tongues, even though they are speaking—judged by relatively objective linguistic criteria—mutually intelligible dialects of the same language.

It is easy to conclude from all this that the terms 'dialect' and 'language' are politically and socially *loaded*. You might want to ask yourself whether you speak a language or a dialect. It's a trick question, of course, because ultimately, *all* languages are dialects. You speak both at the same time.

About the author

G. Tucker Childs is a professor in the Applied Linguistics Department at Portland State University in Portland, Oregon, where he teaches courses in phonetics, phonology, language variation, pidgins and creoles, African American English, and sociolinguistics. He and several of his students have done research on the dialects of Portland, realized as the 'Portland Dialect Study' (www.pds.pdx.edu). Dr. Childs also has interests in African languages, including the pidgins and new urban varieties spoken on the continent, his most recent book in that area being *An Introduction to African Languages* (2003). More recently he has been documenting dying languages in Guinea (www.ling.pdx.edu/childs/MDP.html) and Sierra Leone (www.pdx.edu/dkb). He has taught at universities in the United States, Canada, Europe and Africa, and has been a visiting researcher at France's National Council for Scientific Research (CNRS) in Paris, at Fourah Bay College (Sierra Leone), and at the University of Conakry (Guinea).

Suggestions for further reading

In this book
Dialects are discussed in Chapters 20 (English in Britain, America, and elsewhere), 30 (U.S. Southern English), 40 (New World Spanish), 44 (U.S. dialect change), 55 (languages of Spain and Portugal), 59 (Arabic), and 63 (languages of India).

Elsewhere
Alvarez, Louis, and Kolker, Andrew. *American Tongues* (Center for New American Media, 1987). Essential viewing—an entertaining video that illustrates the many dialects of American English with a sophisticated but straightforward (socio)linguistic message.

Lewis, M. Paul, ed. *Ethnologue: Languages of the World* (SIL International, sixteenth edition 2009). Online: www.ethnologue.com. A useful reference cataloging and classifying all known languages of the world, including some information on dialects.

Joseph, John E. and Talbot J. Taylor, eds. *Ideologies of Language* (Routledge, 1990). A collection of articles illustrating how power and ideology control the status of such languages as Afrikaans and French.

Trudgill, Peter. *Sociolinguistics: An Introduction to Language and Society* (Penguin Books, Ltd., 2000). An informed and accessible introduction to languages and dialects written for those with little knowledge of linguistics.

5

What was the original language?

Barry Hilton

When did language begin, and how? What language did the earliest humans speak?

Questions like these were easier to answer back when supernatural explanations were in fashion. You could just say that language was a gift granted to humans when they first appeared in the world, like their senses and their limbs. The answer to 'when?' was 'when Adam and Eve lived in the Garden of Eden'; and as for identifying that first language, Chapter 7 of this book describes some of the theories advocated during that era.

Beginning in the eighteenth and nineteenth centuries, though, a different way of thinking about the history of languages began to develop: the science of historical linguistics. As described in more detail in Chapter 6, its practitioners have identified relationships among existing languages and shown how they fit into 'family trees' reflecting thousands of years of changing and splitting from previously existing languages.

In many cases, these language genealogies point back to ancestral languages that no longer exist. Historical linguists have developed a method of reconstructing those long-dead languages from clues surviving in their descendants, and almost all of them believe it allows valid deductions about languages whose descendants have been separated for up to about seven thousand years.

Some think that it's possible to look, cautiously, even further into the past. Most, though, believe that languages separated for ten thousand or more years have changed too much for the method to be reliable; and modern humans have been around five or ten times that long.

This leaves a large gap to bridge: what happened to change wordless early humans, or near-humans, into the talkers that we've since become? And what was their speech like? There's been no shortage of speculation on these subjects, beginning in the late nineteenth century. Maybe, it was suggested, early people invented speech by imitating animal calls or other natural sounds and, over time, attaching meaning to them; or by attaching meaning to their own inarticulate grunts of emotion or exertion. Guesses like these are a legitimate step in scientific inquiry if they generate hypotheses that can be verified, but there didn't seem to be any way of finding relevant concrete evidence. Critics, even friendly ones, applied mocking names like the 'bow-wow' theory, the 'ding-dong' theory, the 'pooh-pooh' theory and the 'yo-he-ho' theory. For several decades, the Origin of Language was an unfashionable field of study.

Beginning around the last quarter of the twentieth century, though, increasing amounts of brainpower—and more and more *kinds* of brainpower—have been devoted to the question, and interest is picking up.

Paleontologists studying fossils and ancient artifacts have improved our chronology of humanity's early past, sharpening debate over *when* language is most likely to have emerged: with the first tool-using members of genus *Homo* some two million years ago? Or perhaps with the artistic flourishing that roughly coincided with the appearance of anatomically modern humans some fifty thousand years ago?

Other researchers have looked for modern analogs to the earliest human language origins: psychologists have intensively studied how infants make the transition from wordless creatures into talking children; primatologists have devised ingenious experiments to determine how much or how little human-like linguistic behavior apes can learn; and neurologists and anatomists are making clearer to us just how extensively human language is enabled and limited by the human body and brain.

The anatomists, in particular, have suggested that language was impossible until humans had both the right kind of vocal tract to produce speech sounds and the right kind of nervous system to control them. One physical distinction between modern humans and all other animals, even chimpanzees and earlier humans, appears to be critical: a lowered larynx. Your dog can eat his food in a few quick gulps, but he can't talk. You can talk, but you can also choke from food lodged in your larynx. The human ability to make speech sounds is not a bonus provided by the body systems designed for breathing, chewing, and swallowing—it's just the opposite: the lowered larynx (and associated changes in the pharynx and mouth) is a handicap to the usual animal uses of mouth and throat, but on balance this handicap is far outweighed by the great survival value in speech. You can talk—and participate in civilization—because you *can't* wolf your food.

It's unlikely that these multidisciplinary efforts will allow us to reconstruct what words our prehistoric ancestors said, or what their speech sounded like. But some interesting late twentieth-century research suggests that we may be able to know something about the *grammar* of the earliest languages—how words came together to form sentences. Within the past few centuries several new languages of a special kind have been born. European colonists arriving in the third world communicated with their local laborers using *pidgin* languages, a kind of adult babytalk using a hodgepodge of words from different languages, strung together with a rudimentary grammar. When children are raised speaking a pidgin as their native language, they turn it into a full-fledged language called a *creole*, with a broader vocabulary and a more elaborate grammar. Now here's the fascinating part: unrelated creole languages in places as far apart as Suriname, Haiti, Hawai'i, and Papua New Guinea have radically different vocabularies, but some researchers find their grammars very similar, suggesting that the human brain may be hardwired to create particular patterns of speech. Could this be a clue to how the earliest languages worked?

About the author

Barry Hilton is the Associate Editor of this book and was a member of the review board of the radio series from which it was adapted. He is a freelance writer/editor and independent scholar living in Maine and working as a marketing specialist for a small publishing company. He is an honors graduate of Harvard College who, after graduate studies at Cornell, Yale, and George Washington Universities and the Foreign Service Institute, has travelled extensively and lived in both Europe and Asia. In a variety of U.S. government assignments he has made professional use of Vietnamese, Chinese, Japanese, French and German. He describes himself as an 'armchair philologist and recovering polyglot'.

Suggestions for further reading

In this book
The origins and history of languages are also discussed in Chapters 6 (language relationships), 7 (the language of Adam and Eve), 8 (language change), 10 (pidgins and creoles), 51 (origins of English), and 57 (Icelandic).

Elsewhere
Kenneally, Christine. *The First Word* (Viking, 2007). A comprehensive and highly readable overview of the multidisciplinary investigations that are revitalizing the study of how language began.

Bickerton, Derek. *Roots of Language* (Karoma, 1981). A readable, serious presentation of the by-no-means-mainstream theory that evidence relevant to the prehistoric origins of language can be found in creolization processes observable today.

6

Do all languages come from the same source?

Allan R. Bomhard

What does it mean to say that two languages are related?
Are all languages related?

Have you ever studied German, or Spanish, or French? If you have, you were probably grateful for cognates: foreign words that sound and look like English words with related meanings. In German, your parents are your *Mutter* and your *Vater*. In Spanish, they are your *madre* and *padre*. In French, they are your *mère* and *père*.

These resemblances not only make language learning easier, they tell us something about the history of languages. English and German share some similar vocabulary because they are both descendants of a language called Proto-West-Germanic, spoken by tribes in northern Europe well over two thousand years ago. Over time, migrations split that language into dialects, and some of the tribes moved across the North Sea into the British Isles. Fifteen centuries of separate development turned the speech of the British Isles into varieties of English, while the language of the mainlanders turned into varieties of German. So we have two languages, obviously different, but also so alike that they are clearly part of the same language family.

Language families, like families of people, can be connected into larger and larger groupings, spreading outward in territory and backward in time, as our relatives do on a genealogy chart.

The Germanic family that English, German, and several other languages belong to has a cousin, the Romance family, which includes not only French, Spanish, Portuguese, Italian, and Romanian, but also several other languages that have Latin as their common ancestor; and there are other cousins as well.

Now let's look back a step further in time. The Germanic and Romance language families share a common ancestor called Proto-Indo-European. It was spoken by tribes living some six thousand to seven thousand years ago, probably in the steppes north and east of the Black Sea. From there, the tribes spread westward across Europe, and eastward and southward into Iran and northern India. As they spread and lost contact with each other, their language changed into Germanic, Romance, Celtic, Greek, Armenian, Albanian, Baltic, Slavic, Indic languages, Iranian languages, and several other languages that are now extinct. Taken together, they make up the Indo-European language family, the most widely spoken group of languages in the world today.

As different as the Indo-European languages were from one another, they all preserved bits of ancient vocabulary and grammar. Linguists have used these bits to figure out relationships and actually reconstruct the older languages. Sir William Jones opened the way at the end of the eighteenth century through a remarkable analysis of the classical Indic language Sanskrit, showing that Sanskrit was related to languages in Europe such as Latin and Greek. And now, even though no one has seen or spoken the original Indo-European parent language for thousands of years, we have a fairly good idea of what it may have sounded like. Moreover, by cracking the code of Indo-European, we have taken a big step toward answering the question, can all languages be linked in a super family tree that begins with a single ancestral language?

To find out, linguists have increasingly studied and compared *non*-Indo-European languages, asking: what families do they belong to? How far back can those families be traced? Clearly, many non-Indo-European languages can be grouped together. For example, Finnish, Estonian, and Hungarian, which are surrounded by Indo-European in the heartland of Europe, are not in the Indo-European language family. But they do group together with several other languages to form a non-Indo-European language family called Uralic. Similarly, there is a family called Turkic, which takes in Turkish, Azerbaijani, Uzbek, Uighur, Kazakh, and several other languages in Central Asia. In East Asia, the Sino-Tibetan family includes over two hundred and fifty languages, the largest of which is Mandarin Chinese. Linguists think that at least two hundred language families exist; the obvious next question is, are any of these families related to each other?

There are theorists who believe that we can lump all of the languages of the world—including even language isolates like Basque, which seems to fit nowhere—into a handful of giant families, called 'macrofamilies,' such as Nostratic, Dene-Caucasian, Amerind, and the like.

But maybe we can't go that far. The fact that the word for 'dog' in an Australian native language called Mbabaram is 'dog' does not mean that Mbabaram is related to English; it is just a random resemblance. The fact that Chinese calls coffee *kāfēi* does not mean that Chinese is related to English, either; the origin is a Turkish word that happens to have been borrowed by both Chinese and English.

Furthermore, we know that languages change continuously; new words join the vocabulary, while older words, including cognates, disappear, and the same has happened to grammar. After tens of thousands of years of change, can we reliably find a common ancestor? Do all languages come from the same source? The answer is: Maybe ... and maybe not. It's too soon to know.

About the author

Allan R. Bomhard is a linguist living in Charleston, South Carolina. His main areas of interest are distant linguistic relationship and Indo-European comparative linguistics. He has published over fifty articles and seven books.

Suggestions for further reading

In this book

Chapters on the history and origins of language include 5 (earliest language), 7 (the language of Adam and Eve), 8 (language change), 10 (pidgins and creoles), 51 (origins of English), 57 (Icelandic), and 58 (Hebrew and Yiddish). Chapters focusing on language families include 52 (Native American languages), 60 (African languages), and 63 (languages of India).

Elsewhere

Baldi, Philip. *An Introduction to the Indo-European Languages* (Southern Illinois University Press, 1983). An excellent overview of the Indo-European language family. Both beginners and knowledgeable readers will find much of interest here.

Bomhard, Allan R. *Reconstructing Proto-Nostratic: Comparative Phonology, Morphology, and Vocabulary* (E. J. Brill, 2008). Though fairly technical for beginners, this book is the most comprehensive treatment of the subject that has been published to date.

Comrie, Bernard, ed. *The World's Major Languages* (Oxford University Press, 1987). A comprehensive survey of the major languages spoken in the world today.

Fortson, Benjamin W., IV. *Indo-European Language and Culture: An Introduction* (Wiley-Blackwell, second edition 2010). An exhaustive, up-to-date, and accessible overview of Indo-European comparative-historical linguistics. Beginners should start by reading Baldi's book listed above before tackling this work.

Pedersen, Holger, translated by John Webster Spargo. *The Discovery of Language: Linguistic Science in the Nineteenth Century* (Indiana University Press, 1931). Though dated and lacking information about more recent scholarship, this remains the most comprehensive introduction to the history of the study of languages.

Ruhlen, Merritt. *A Guide to the World's Languages, Vol. 1: Classification* (Stanford University Press, 1991). Though this work is a comprehensive and reliable guide to the classification of nearly all known languages, some of the proposals regarding larger groupings remain controversial.

7

What language did Adam and Eve speak?

E. M. Rickerson

Does the language of Adam still exist? What language did God speak in the Garden of Eden? Did Adam and Eve speak Indo-European?

In the Old Testament story of the Garden of Eden, Adam was created as a fully formed modern being, with all the faculties of *Homo sapiens,* including the ability to speak. We can only guess what Adam might have said to Eve in their early chats, but we do know that both of them could talk. Eve had a fateful conversation with a persuasive snake, and one of Adam's first tasks on earth was linguistic: '... *and Adam gave names to all cattle, and to the fowl of the air, and to every beast of the field*' (Genesis 2:19). But what language did Adam use? Presumably it was the same one in which the serpent's words were couched and which the first couple heard when they were sternly evicted from Paradise.

It certainly wasn't English, which is a relatively young language, nor was it any of the world's languages that you might think of as 'old', such as Chinese or Greek. Leaving aside the question of how the first language-using people came into being, it is now fairly well accepted that humans were physiologically *able* to speak—that the vocal apparatus was ready to produce more than the calls or growls of our fellow mammals—as early as fifty thousand years ago, or earlier. Because we can trace languages only as far as their early written records, and because writing itself emerged only around five thousand years ago, we are left with a gap of thousands of years. And throughout those millennia, the language of the first human beings was undergoing constant and profound change. Therefore, whatever else we may say about the original language, it is clear that *none* of the languages currently spoken on the planet bears any resemblance to what may have been spoken in the legendary Garden of Eden.

That is the modern view, based on what we have learned about language since religious explanations gave way to the patient collection of linguistic data. But before the eighteenth century—from the earliest days of Christianity through the Middle Ages and Reformation—it was taken for granted that Adam spoke the first language, and that the *lingua adamica,* the language he used, still existed. For most of that time, the leading candidate for the honor was Hebrew, if only because it was the language in which the Old Testament was handed down. In the fourth century St. Jerome asserted that only the family of Eber had not been so foolish as to help build the Tower of Babel. As a result, when God destroyed the tower and scattered its builders, Eber's people—the Eberites, or Hebrews—were not punished, and continued to speak the original tongue. St. Augustine and other Christian church fathers accepted without question that Hebrew was the *lingua adamica* and, for the next thousand years or so, almost everyone agreed. I find it ironic that the scholarly discussion of this topic took place in Latin, which was as close to a universal language as there was in Europe during that time—yet no one suggested that Latin could have been the original tongue. The idea of Hebrew as the Adamic language had a firm hold on the imagination throughout the Renaissance, and even beyond.

The nature of Adam's language was an especially hot topic in the sixteenth and seventeenth centuries, when it was thought to be a divine or 'perfect' language, in which words coincided so harmoniously with the things they identified that people understood them without having to be taught their meanings. But not everyone accepted that this perfect language was, or had been, Hebrew.

With the Renaissance came a sense of nationhood in Europe, and the *lingua adamica* idea served as a way to build national pride. In Germany, people rallied to the language of Luther's Bible and asserted that German was closest to the language of Adam; some even claimed that Hebrew was derived from German. Linguistic nationalism also prompted a claim for Dutch or Flemish. The theory ran that citizens of Antwerp were descendants of Noah's son Japeth, who had settled in northern Europe after the Flood and *before* the Tower of Babel, so that Dutch preserved the purity of the Adamic tongue. Improbable arguments were also made for the divine status of Celtic, Basque, Hungarian, Polish and many other languages. This was the time when Sweden was making itself felt as a world power, so it is not surprising that Swedish too was proposed as the original language, again based on the story of Japeth. And that leads us to my favorite theory: the suggestion that God spoke Swedish in Paradise, Adam Danish, and the snake … French.

After the Age of Reason loosened the grip of religion on philosophical thinking, the divine origins of language became a lesser concern. In the eighteenth and nineteenth centuries it was gradually understood that words and the things they stand for are not magically connected, and that languages are not divinely given. They are created by human communities, not a heavenly force. It became clear that language was a matter of agreement that certain combinations of sounds would be used to mean whatever a community decided they should mean. Instead of theological debates, scholars in Europe used scientific criteria to compare known languages, and to figure out how they are related and how they developed over time. It is telling that when they discovered Indo-European, they made no claim that it was the original language. The discovery only made us realize that we cannot penetrate the linguistic past to its absolute beginnings. At that point the idea of an Adamic language became the stuff of poetry.

About the author

E. M. ('Rick') Rickerson is the General Editor of this book. He is Professor Emeritus of German, Director Emeritus of the award-winning language program at the College of Charleston (South Carolina), a former Deputy Director of the U.S. government's Center for the Advancement of Language Learning, and an Associate of the National Museum of Language. In 2005 he created the radio series on languages (*Talkin' about Talk*) from which *The Five-Minute Linguist* has been adapted. He is currently retired in the mountains of North Carolina. E-mail: rickersone@bellsouth.net.

Suggestions for further reading

In this book

The origins and history of languages are also discussed in Chapters 5 (earliest languages), 6 (language relationships), 8 (language change), 10 (pidgins and creoles), 51 (origins of English), 57 (Icelandic), and 58 (Hebrew and Yiddish).

Elsewhere

Rickerson, Earl. *The Lingua Adamica and its Role in German Baroque Literature* (unpublished Ph.D. dissertation, 1969; available at UMI Dissertation Services: www.umi.com/products_umi/dissertations). Chapters 1–3 provide an overview of how the Adamic language was viewed before the Age of Reason.

Eco, Umberto. *The Search for the Perfect Language* (Blackwell, 1995). A comprehensive and very readable history of the ways in which the idea of an original or perfect language occupied European thinkers for close to 2,000 years.

Olender, Maurice, *The Languages of Paradise: Race, Religion and Philology in the Nineteenth Century* (Harvard University Press, 1992). A scholarly discussion of ideas that underlay the comparative study of languages in the nineteenth century. Chapter 1 touches briefly on the *Lingua Adamica*.

8

Do languages have to change?

John McWhorter

Why is our English different from Shakespeare's?
What can English spelling tell us about language change?
What kinds of changes do languages undergo?
Can we stop English from changing?

Have you ever left a Shakespeare performance feeling worn out from trying to understand what the characters were saying? It wasn't just because Shakespeare's English is poetic, but because the English that Shakespeare knew was, in many ways, a different language from ours. When Juliet asked 'Wherefore art thou Romeo?' she wasn't asking where Romeo was—after all, he's right there under the balcony! *Wherefore* meant *why*. But we no longer have that word because languages shed words all the time. And they also take on new ones, like *blog*.

Languages are always changing. It's as inevitable for them to change as it is for cloud patterns in the sky to take on new forms. If we see a camel in the clouds today and walk outside and see the same camel tomorrow, then something's very wrong. It's the same way with languages—every language is in the process of changing into a new one.

In English, you can see this easily because our spelling often preserves the way the language was pronounced seven hundred years ago. The word *name*, for instance, used to be pronounced

'NAH-muh.' But we stopped saying the final /e/ and the AH sound (NAHme) drifted into an AY sound (NAYm).

Pronunciation is not the only area of impermanence: grammar changes, too. English used to be a language where verbs at the end of the sentence came. That is, a thousand or so years ago that's how you would have said that last sentence, with 'came' at the end. We also used to have more pronouns. *You* was only used to mean 'y'all'; the singular form you used, for talking to an individual person, was *thou*. And then for the 'generic' *you*—as in a sentence like 'You only live once'—the pronoun was *man*. Now we just use *you* for all those meanings.

This kind of change is why we face the task of learning foreign languages. If language didn't change, we'd still all speak the first language that popped up in Africa when humans first started to talk. But once the original band of people split off into separate groups, the language took on new forms in each new place—different sounds, different word order, different endings. The result was that Chinese has tones; some Australian languages have only three verbs; some African languages have click sounds; many Native American languages pack a huge amount of information into single words; and English uses the same word *you* whether one or two or many people are involved.

The only thing that makes it look as if a language stays the same forever is print, because print does stay the same way forever. We think of Latin as a dead language, because it was written, we can see it on the page, and we know that the particular language captured on that page is not spoken by anybody any more. But technically, the Latin we struggle with in classrooms was just one stage in a language that never died. It just drifted into several new versions of itself, like French, Spanish, and Italian. We don't think of the language of the opera *Don Giovanni* as 'street Latin'—it's a new language altogether. There was never a day when people in Italy woke up and proclaimed 'We were speaking Latin last night but today we're speaking Italian!' Latin just morphed along like cloud formations, which might look like a camel one day and like a weasel the next.

But within our lifespans, it's hard not to think of changes in our language as mistakes. There was a time, fifteen or twenty centuries ago, when Latin was the official language of the territory we now call France. The bureaucrats and scholars who lived there and spoke it heard the beginnings of French around them, but to them it sounded like just grade-F Latin, not like a new language in its own right. Gray zones are always tricky. So, when young people say things like 'She's all "don't talk to me like that" and I was like "you shoulda known anyway"', they're pushing the language on its way to new frontiers. It was through the exact same kinds of changes that English got from *Beowulf* to Tom Wolfe.

About the author

John McWhorter, a contributing editor at *The New Republic* who also teaches at Columbia, earned his Ph.D. in linguistics from Stanford University in 1993 and became Associate Professor of Linguistics at the University of California, Berkeley, after teaching at Cornell University. His academic specialty is language change and language contact. He is the author of *Our Magnificent Bastard Tongue: The Untold Story of English* (2008); *The Power of Babel: A Natural History of Language* (2003); and *Doing Our Own Thing: The Degradation of Language and Music in America and Why We Should, Like, Care* (2003). He has also written a book on dialects and Black English, *The Word on the Street* (1998), and two books on creole languages, *The Missing Spanish Creoles* (2000) and *Defining Creole* (2005). Dr. McWhorter has appeared often on radio and television programs such as *Dateline NBC*, *Good Morning, America*, *The Jim Lehrer NewsHour*, and *Fresh Air*, and he does regular commentaries for National Public Radio's *All Things Considered*. E-mail: jhmcw5@yahoo.com.

Suggestions for further reading

In this book

The origins and history of languages are also discussed in Chapters 5 (earliest languages), 6 (language relationships), 7 (the language of Adam and Eve), 10 (pidgins and creoles), 51 (origins of English), 57 (Icelandic), and 58 (Hebrew and Yiddish). Other chapters specifically focusing on language change include 10 (pidgins and creoles), 13 (grammar), 19 (prescriptivism), 44 (U.S. dialect change), 51 (origins of English), 53 (Latin), and 54 (Italian).

Elsewhere

McWhorter, John. *The Power of Babel* (Perennial, 2003). A book-length survey of how one original language became five thousand, with discussion of what dialects and creoles are and why writing slows down language change.

Bryson, Bill. *Mother Tongue* (Morrow, 1990). A great way to get a handle on how English became what it is after starting as a close relative of German (now a foreign tongue to English-speakers); witty and goes down easy.

Ostler, Nicholas. *Empires of the Word* (HarperCollins, 2005). A chronicle of the birth, spread and sometimes decline of languages of empire like English, Arabic, and Sanskrit, lending a nice sense of how language change is natural and eternal.

9

What are lingua francas?

Nicholas Ostler

Why are lingua francas needed? What are some examples?
How does a language become a lingua franca?
How does it stop being one?

Each of us has a mother tongue, which we speak within our own language community. But what happens when two communities that don't speak each other's language come into contact and need to talk? Sometimes they can learn enough of each other's language to get by, but sometimes that's not feasible—for example, what if there are three communities in contact, or five or more? In many cases they resort to a lingua franca, a kind of 'bridge' language that is distinct from the mother tongues of each group. An example from recent history is French, which was used from the seventeenth century until after World War I as the language of diplomacy in Europe. Written Classical Chinese served for an even longer period as a diplomatic lingua franca in countries bordering on China. Today's best example of a lingua franca is undoubtedly English, which supports international communication in fields ranging from aviation to business to rock music.

So how do lingua francas come about?

About ten thousand years ago, as agriculture and stock-breeding increasingly replaced hunting and gathering, human groups became larger and more hierarchical, and had more occasion to interact with neighboring groups that had different mother tongues. In some cases, perhaps, the groups were brought into contact by some dominant power—such as a regional strong-man, or an early empire. In others the contact may have arisen spontaneously, as networks of markets came into existence. Later on—since maybe five thousand years ago—another motive for intergroup contacts emerged: enthusiastic religious believers con-ceived it as their duty to pass on valuable knowledge of spiritual life to strangers. So imperialists, merchants, and missionaries have all been motivated to establish communication beyond their mother-tongue groups. A lingua franca is a technical fix that helps overcome language barriers across a set of groups that is too large—or too recently united—to have a common language. Performing that fix is the job of a new kind of specialist who must have begun to appear around this time: interpreters, who learned the regional lingua franca in addition to their mother tongue and used it to communicate with interpreters in other groups.

Sometimes a lingua franca replaces the mother tongues it bridges. Latin, for example, spread far and wide through the set-tlement of soldiers within the Roman Empire. It gradually became a mother tongue throughout western Europe (replacing languages like Etruscan and Oscan in Italy, Gaulish and Ligurian in France, and Tartessian and Celtiberian in Spain). But for Latin to remain a common language over so large an area, the groups that spoke it as a mother tongue would have had to remain in contact. This didn't happen. Germanic conquests after the fifth century broke the Roman empire into distinct regions that had little to do with one another, and Latin eventually broke up into distinct dialects and languages, like French, Provençal, Tuscan, Corsican, Spanish, Catalan, and Galician.

A lingua franca may be a language like Latin or Sanskrit, taught according to strict rules, and capable of surviving for many centuries with little change. On the other hand, it need not be a full-fledged language at all. An important subcategory of lingua francas is pidgins, which result when people who lack a common tongue make up a new one out of pieces of the languages they already know. The first language to be known specifically as 'Lingua Franca' was a medium of this kind. It was a kind of simplified and highly mixed Italian, used by traders and others in the eastern Mediterranean around the year 1000. Such a loosely structured language may change unpredictably; communication depends more on cooperative imagination and mutual good will than on a clear shared grammar and vocabulary.

Good will can't be taken for granted. Although lingua francas may be envisaged as neutral 'bridges' between the potentially competing groups they serve, they are a human phenomenon and subject to being drawn into the conflicts they mediate. They are typically used only by a skilled minority, whom other groups can perceive and resent as an unfairly privileged elite, out for its own interests. This was true of Greek-speakers in the eastern Mediterranean and west Asia at the end of the first millennium BC, and true of Latin-speakers, the educated elite in medieval Europe. It remains true for English-speakers today. The recent bloody civil war between the Sinhala-speaking majority in Sri Lanka and the Tamil-speaking minority grew out of legislation that suppressed Tamil language and culture. The same legislation also replaced English with Sinhala as the country's official language, because the Tamils were seen as being more skilled in English and drawing too many benefits as a result.

By definition, a lingua franca is not the mother tongue of most of the people it serves. People learn it deliberately, in order to achieve some purpose. This means that its fate in the long term is vulnerable to changes in the balance of wealth and power. It may survive as the mother tongue of the ethnic group that originally spoke it, but the purpose that has made people want to learn it as a lingua franca may disappear. Empires may be dissolved or conquered by other empires: hence Persian, which had been the official lingua franca in medieval India for almost a millennium, faded when the territory was taken over by English-speaking Britons. Trade networks may cease to operate for reasons of politics or economics, and their medium of communication may be forgotten: Sogdian, for example, for centuries the lingua franca for trade from Iran to China, ceased to be current after the decline of the Silk Road. Religions have been known to die out, and with them the need for a common language; for example, the use of Aramaic was largely lost in Asia in the first millennium AD, with the decline of Nestorian Christianity. Which brings us to the question: if storied languages such as Latin, Persian, Sogdian and Aramaic ceased to be lingua francas after hundreds or thousands of years, how long will English survive in that role? Changes can come very fast in the modern connected world, as patterns of influence surge and fade away.

About the author
Nicholas Ostler holds degrees in Greek, Latin, philosophy, and economics from Balliol College, Oxford, and a Ph.D. in linguistics and Sanskrit from the Massachusetts Institute of Technology, where he studied under Noam Chomsky. He is the author of *Empires of the Word: A Language History of the World* (2005), *Ad Infinitum: A Biography of Latin* (2007), and *The Last Lingua Franca: English until the Return of Babel* (2010). In addition to these three books, he has published, as author or editor, some five dozen scholarly articles, book chapters, book reviews, and general magazine articles on topics ranging from language history to language technology to general linguistics. He is currently the chairman of the Foundation for Endangered Languages, and lives in Bath, England.

Suggestions for further reading

In this book
Other chapters discussing languages that have bridged gaps between communities include 10 (pidgins and creoles), 20 (English in Britain, America, and elsewhere), 21 (language conflict), 53 (Latin), 58 (Hebrew and Yiddish), 63 (languages of India), and 64 (Esperanto).

Elsewhere
Ostler, Nicholas. *The Last Lingua Franca: English until the Return of Babel* (Penguin, 2010). A wide-ranging account of lingua francas and their role in history, with particular attention to the unprecedentedly powerful current position of English.

Crystal, David. *English as a Global Language* (Cambridge University Press, 2003). A historical exploration of the processes that have converged to expand the influence of English throughout the world.

Collitz, Hermann. 'World Languages' in *Language* 2.1 (1926), pp1–13. A classic article about international languages in history, by a German-born scholar who became the first president of the Linguistic Society of America.

10

Isn't Pidgin English just bad English?

John M. Lipski

What's a pidgin language? Is creole more than just food?
Are pidgin and creole the same thing? Are they real languages?

How una dé? Uskain nius? These two greetings, the first from
Nigeria and the second from Cameroon, both mean roughly 'Hi,
what's happening?' Both use words from English (like 'how', 'there',
and 'news'), but combine them in new ways. They're the kind of
language we're using when we greet someone by saying 'long time
no see', or when we invite a friend to come have a 'look-see', or use
'no can do' when something's not possible. When we do that, what
we're speaking is no longer English—it's a new language, based
on English words but with simpler grammar and vocabulary.
'Look-see' and 'no can do' come from a language once called *China
Coast Pidgin English*, which was used by sailors and merchants
throughout the Pacific. But what kind of bird is this 'pidgin'?

Imagine for a moment that everyone reading this article spoke
a different native language, and that the only English any of us
knew was the result of a year or two of limited exposure somewhere
earlier in our lives. If we all got stranded on the proverbial desert
island, we might well find that the only way we could communicate would be to use our bits of English with one another. As the
years went by, with no grammar books and no native speakers to
correct us or teach us new words, we'd all develop survival skills in

this way of talking, and we'd invent combinations that a true native speaker of English would barely recognize.

A language formed like this—among people who share no native language and are forced to communicate using elements of one that none of them speaks well—is what linguists call a pidgin. The word probably comes from South Sea traders' attempt to pronounce the word *business*. Most pidgins don't form on desert islands; they're created when speakers of different languages have to communicate with each other using bits and pieces of a language imposed on them—for example as slaves on plantations in the Americas, as contract laborers on South Pacific islands, or as itinerant vendors in urban marketplaces in Africa.

Pidgins start out as bits-and-pieces languages, but something happens when children are born to pidgin-speaking parents. Like children everywhere, as they grow they absorb the language they hear around them and make it their own. Unlike other children, though, as they learn their parents' language they expand and transform it from a makeshift jargon into a full-fledged new language. These new languages, spoken natively by the next generation in the family, are called *creole* languages by linguists (although sometimes the name 'pidgin' continues to be used in non-specialist contexts). There are dozens of creole languages scattered around the world, derived from European languages such as English, French, and Portuguese, but also from Arabic, Swahili, and other non-European tongues. English-based creoles are used in the South Pacific from Papua New Guinea to the Solomon Islands and northern Australia. Gullah in South Carolina and Georgia and Hawaiian Pidgin are creole languages native to the U.S., while Cape Verde Portuguese Creole in Massachusetts and Haitian Creole in Miami and New York are among the U.S.'s more recent immigrant languages.

Creoles and pidgins often include words and expressions that speakers of languages like English or French would recognize, but with very different meanings. For example, *beef* in west African Pidgin English refers to any animal whose meat can be eaten. So a pig could be a 'beef'. In Papua New Guinea the word *meri* (from the English name 'Mary') is a word for woman, any woman. The grammatical structures of creole languages are often simpler than the corresponding patterns in the source languages, but creoles can also express nuances not found in the sources. They're by no means simply 'light' or 'broken' versions of 'real' languages—they've earned their status as legitimate languages in their own right.

Creole languages have millions of speakers. They have grammar books, dictionaries, and written literatures. They're taught in schools and used in radio, television, and the press. They have their own names, such as Tok Pisin in Papua-New Guinea and Bislama in Vanuatu, and are increasingly serving as official or quasi-official languages in the Philippines, the Caribbean, South America, and elsewhere. The language used at the beginning of this article is spoken in much of west Africa. It's the language of African popular music and literature, including novels by the Nobel laureate Wole Soyinka.

Speakers of languages with long literary traditions sometimes laugh at creole languages, thinking of them—and their speakers—as inferior. But such views are not justified. Creoles are new languages, at most a few hundred years old, but they emerged through struggles similar to those that gave birth to many of the world's new nations, and they deserve the same respect.

Article 1 of the United Nations Universal Declaration of Human Rights, translated into Nigerian Pidgin English, begins: *Everi human being, naim dem born free and dem de equal for dignity and di rights wey we get, as human being.* Speaking a creole language with pride and dignity is one of those basic human rights.

About the author

John M. Lipski is Edwin Erle Sparks Professor of Spanish Linguistics in the Department of Spanish, Italian, and Portuguese at the Pennsylvania State University. He received his B.A. from Rice University in Texas, and his M.A. and Ph.D. from the University of Alberta, Canada; he has taught Spanish, Romance, and general linguistics, translation, language acquisition and methodology, Latin American literature, and a variety of language courses at colleges and universities in New Jersey, Michigan, Texas, Florida, and New Mexico. His research interests include Spanish phonology, Spanish and Portuguese dialectology and language variation, the linguistic aspects of bilingualism, and the African contribution to Spanish and Portuguese. He is the author of twelve books and more than 250 articles on all aspects of linguistics. He has served as associate editor of *Hispania* for theoretical linguistics, and is currently editor of the journal *Hispanic Linguistics* and a Georgetown University Press series on Hispanic linguistics. He has done fieldwork in Spain (including the Canary Islands), Africa, Brazil and all Spanish-speaking countries in Latin America, the Philippines, Guam, and many Spanish-speaking communities within the United States.

Suggestions for further reading

In this book
The ways languages begin and develop are also discussed in Chapters 5 (earliest languages), 6 (language relationships), 8 (language change), 13 (grammar), 44 (U.S. dialect change), 46 (dictionaries), 51 (origins of English), 53 (Latin), and 54 (Italian). Chapter 26 (sign languages) discusses the importance of children in transforming an invented language into a natural one.

Elsewhere
Todd, Loreto. *Pidgins and Creoles* (Routledge and Kegan Paul, 1974). A very basic book, still not outdated in terms of the general concepts.

Holm, John. *An Introduction to Pidgins and Creoles* (Cambridge University Press, 2000).
Romaine, Suzanne. *Pidgin and Creole Languages* (Longman, 1988).
Either of these books would be a good place for readers to pursue the topic of this chapter in greater detail. Holm is more accessible, Romaine more comprehensive.

Mufwene, Salikoko. *The Ecology of Language Evolution* (Cambridge, 2001). This book places creole language formation in a broader context of language in society.

11

How many kinds of writing systems are there?

Peter T. Daniels

How do writing systems differ? Which one is used the most?
Could we use a system other than an alphabet to write English?

Around the world, a little over thirty different writing systems
are in official or widespread use today (counting all the different
Roman alphabets, like English and French and even Vietnamese,
as variants of a single one; likewise for all the varieties of Cyrillic
and Arabic and so on). These systems, together with some used in
the past to write languages now extinct, fall into about half a dozen
different *kinds* of system that have been devised over the past five
thousand years.

Most familiar, and most widespread, is the *alphabet*. In an
alphabet, each letter represents one consonant or one vowel, and
(theoretically) all the consonants and vowels in a word are written down, one by one, from left to right. But since you read and
write English, you know that we are very far from that ideal! Why
should *though, through, tough,* and *cough* all be spelled with *o-u-*
g-h? Because we've been spelling pretty much the same way since
printing got started in England in 1475, while English pronunciation has been changing gradually over the centuries. Spanish and
Finnish and Czech do a lot better in keeping the spelling the same
as the sounds. The first language to be written with an alphabet was Greek—and to this day, Greek is written with the Greek

alphabet. Every other alphabet in the world is descended from the Greek! Russian and many languages of the former Soviet Union are written with the Cyrillic alphabet, and the languages of western Europe, with the Roman alphabet.

So, too, are many languages that have only recently started being written. Hundreds and hundreds of them, such as Massachusett and Maori, Zulu and Zomi, have had alphabets created for them, usually the Roman alphabet with maybe a few extra letters or some accent marks, by missionaries translating the Bible. These alphabets usually don't have much use outside the Bible texts and related materials. But sometimes they also get used for personal correspondence, newspapers, and even books and the Internet—and a literate culture has been created.

Before there were alphabets, there were scripts of the kind I call *abjads*. This seemingly simpler kind of writing can be seen in news photos from the Middle East. If you open a Hebrew Bible or a Qur'an, you'll see the letters surrounded by dots and dashes and curls, but if you look at billboards and placards, you'll just see the letters—Hebrew ones all squared up separate in a row, Arabic ones gracefully joined together to make whole words without lifting the pen. (These two scripts happen to be written from right to left.) The difference between the holy texts and the street signs, or ordinary books, is that ordinary writing in Hebrew and Arabic includes only the consonants; if you know one of these languages, you can fill in the vowels on your own as you read. But in holy books, getting the pronunciation exactly right is very important, and devout scholars in the early Middle Ages wanted to add helps to the reader. They wouldn't change the spellings they inherited, so they added in the vowels using dots and dashes around the letters.

The Greek alphabet developed out of the Phoenician abjad. The scripts of India developed out of the closely related Aramaic abjad—but with a difference. By the third century BCE Indian linguists had improved on the abjad by inventing a very sophisticated way of writing the vowels (I call the resulting type of writing system the *abugida*). For languages of India and its neighbors in south and southeast Asia, such as Sanskrit and Hindi and Bengali, Tamil and

Thai, you write a plain letter and it reads as a consonant plus 'ah'. If you want it to read as the consonant plus a different vowel, you add a mark to it; and if you want it to read as two consonants in a row with no vowel in between, as in *chakra* or *Mahatma*, you attach a piece of the letter for the first consonant in front of the whole letter for the second consonant. It *can* get complicated!

If we go back before the Phoenician abjad, back to the very beginning of writing, we find that the first writing systems are always *logographic*—instead of individual sounds (consonants or vowels), entire words (or word elements, called 'morphemes') are represented by a single syllable-sign. The one writing system based on the logographic principle that's still used today is the Chinese. Look closely at the characters on a Chinese menu. If you compare them with the English names for foods, you might see which ones correspond to 'kung pao' and which ones correspond to 'chicken' or 'shrimp'. With a logographic system you don't 'spell' words, because each character corresponds to a whole word or part of a word. It works very well, but it takes a *lot* of characters, since you need one or two for virtually every word in the language, and all languages have thousands of words. In the case of Chinese, you can read almost anything published in the language today if you learn about three thousand to four thousand characters.

Now look at a Japanese menu. Alongside the complicated characters that look like Chinese characters (in fact, they *are* Chinese characters, but each one stands for a whole Japanese word), you'll mostly see simpler characters. These represent the endings on the words, and each of these simpler characters stands for a whole syllable, a consonant plus a vowel. There are just fifty of these symbols, because Japanese syllables are just that simple: a consonant plus a vowel. *Su-shi, sa-shi-mi, ki-mo-no.*

Other languages are written with this kind of syllable-character, such as the American Indian language Cherokee and the Liberian language Vai. It would be hard to use syllable-writing for English, because English can make really complicated syllables, like 'strengths' and 'splint'. You'd need a lot of different characters to write them all.

What may be the best writing system ever devised combines the syllable approach learned from China with the consonant- and vowel-letter approach learned from India: Korean writing, or *hangul*. On a Korean menu, you'll see squarish shapes that look like simple Chinese characters—but look at them closely and you'll see just forty simple designs (the letters) combined into blocks (the syllables). A great deal of information in a small space!

Different types of writing system work more or less well with different languages; but languages change over time, while spelling systems tend not to, so over time a writing system works less and less well. You can find a glimpse of the history of writing in the next chapter.

About the author

Peter T. Daniels is one of the few linguists in the world specializing in the study of writing systems. He has published articles in a variety of journals and edited volumes, and contributed to several encyclopedias. He co-edited *The World's Writing Systems* (1996) with William Bright and was Section Editor for Writing Systems for the *Encyclopedia of Language and Linguistics* (2006).

Suggestions for further reading

In this book

Other chapters that talk about written language include 8 (language change), 12 (origins of writing), 58 (Hebrew and Yiddish), 59 (Arabic), 61 (Chinese), and 62 (Japanese).

Elsewhere

Diringer, David. *The Alphabet* (Funk & Wagnalls, third edition 1968).
Jensen, Hans. *Sign, Symbol and Script* (George Allen & Unwin, 1969).
These two books may take some effort to find, but each offers a very full history of writing. Diringer is more readable, Jensen more reliable and scholarly.

DeFrancis, John. *Visible Speech: The Diverse Oneness of Writing Systems* (University of Hawai'i Press, 1989). Stresses that all writing is based on the *sounds* of languages.

Daniels, Peter T., and William Bright, eds. *The World's Writing Systems* (Oxford University Press, 1996). A standard reference for facts about writing systems, past and present.

Gnanadesikan, Amalia. *The Writing Revolution: From Cuneiform to the Internet* (Wiley-Blackwell, 2009). A well-written, compact summary of the important writing systems of the world.

Rogers, Henry. *Writing Systems: A Linguistic Approach* (Blackwell, 2005). Preferable among the small number of textbooks on writing.

12

Where did writing come from?

Peter T. Daniels

When did writing begin? How did it start? Was it invented more than once?

Dozens of writing systems have been used over the ages around the world, in a bewildering variety. They're written from left to right or right to left or top to bottom or even from bottom to top. Their symbols come in many shapes and sizes. The origins of spoken language, tens of thousands of years before writing, are cloudy; but we have a very good idea of how and when writing began. Fragments of some of the earliest writing still exist, carved on rocks, so we can trace its evolution through time.

The invention of writing was almost inevitable when a society grew complex enough to need it. As long as people are in small groups, everyone knows who did what for whom. But when people settle in towns, commerce becomes more complicated. A potter makes pots, a weaver makes cloth, an administration collects taxes. At some point, there's a need to keep track of everyone's contributions. Records might be kept with knots in string, or with notched sticks. And everywhere, people draw pictures to represent things. In Stone Age caverns, we drew pictures of prey animals. In modern times, we make pictures of things we want people to *buy*.

A second condition for inventing writing is a certain *kind* of language, a kind in which words are likely to consist of only one syllable. The reason seems to be that if you don't already know how to read with an alphabet, you aren't able to break down a syllable into its individual consonants and vowels. And if the words (or morphemes) of your language are mostly just one syllable, then the picture you make to represent one of them is both a picture of its meaning and a record of its sound. That picture is useful when you need to write a different word, one that sounds similar but has a meaning not so easy to picture.

These conditions gave rise to writing at least three times that we know of, and probably more that have left no trace. Writing appeared over five thousand years ago in ancient Mesopotamia (now southern Iraq), representing a now-dead language known as Sumerian. A completely different writing system was created in China close to four thousand years ago for an ancestor of modern Chinese. And in Central America around the fourth century CE yet another system was developed to write down the Mayan languages. That system died a few centuries later with the Mayan empire. So all the writing systems in the world today can be traced back to just two places: China and Ancient Iraq.

Writing turns out to be a pretty useful thing to have. And once one group invents it, nearby peoples tend to adopt it. Japan adopted Chinese characters and started writing Japanese words with them. On the other side of the world, Sumerian writing was adopted for many languages between about 2500 and 1000 BCE, early in its history changing in form from pictures to easier-to-write abstractions. Sumerian inspired the Egyptian hieroglyphs we know from temples and tombs. And hieroglyphs became the raw material for the Phoenician abjad that gave the world its alphabets and abugidas. (See Chapter 11 for explanations of these terms.)

There are hundreds of such scripts in use today (now counting each variety of Roman alphabet, say, separately). Besides Europe and the Western Hemisphere, they're used across south and southeast Asia and on into Oceania. Most of them use twenty to thirty symbols. But they range in size from the alphabet used for a language of the Solomon Islands, with eleven letters, to the Khmer abugida of Cambodia, with seventy-four. They look as different as English, Russian, or Hebrew, but it's fairly easy to show that *every* abjad, alphabet, and abugida—those named above and many more—has a common origin: ancient Phoenicia on the eastern shores of the Mediterranean.

The Phoenicians brought their abjad to the Greeks, who (accidentally!) turned it into an alphabet and passed it via the Etruscans to the Romans, who gave our letters the shapes they have to this day. Greek was also the model for alphabets in eastern Europe, such as the Cyrillic alphabet of Russian and other tongues. Another descendant of Phoenician was the Aramaic abjad, from which came writing as different-looking as Hebrew and Arabic— and all the writings of India and beyond.

Writing originated from some pretty basic characteristics of human beings and human society. And yet it is not found every- where. Despite writing's obvious uses, fewer than half of the world's languages even have a writing system! Most languages are only spoken. But that's changing as missionaries and linguists spread writing—mostly the Roman alphabet—to developing nations around the globe.

Where would we be without writing? It's a remarkable part of language—and of human history. Without writing, you could reasonably ask, would history even exist?

About the author
Peter T. Daniels is one of the few linguists in the world specializing in the study of writing systems. He has published articles in a variety of journals and edited volumes, and contributed to several encyclopedias. He co-edited *The World's Writing Systems* (1996) with William Bright and was Section Editor for Writing Systems for the *Encyclopedia of Language and Linguistics* (2006).

Suggestions for further reading

In this book
Other chapters that talk about written language include 8 (language change), 11 (scripts), 58 (Hebrew and Yiddish), 59 (Arabic), 61 (Chinese), and 62 (Japanese).

Elsewhere
Diringer, David. *The Alphabet* (Funk & Wagnalls, third edition 1968).
Jensen, Hans. *Sign, Symbol and Script* (George Allen & Unwin, 1969).
These two books may take some effort to find, but each offers a very full history of writing. Diringer is more readable, Jensen more reliable and scholarly.

DeFrancis, John. *Visible Speech: The Diverse Oneness of Writing Systems* (University of Hawai'i Press, 1989). Stresses that all writing is based on the *sounds* of languages.

Daniels, Peter T., and William Bright, eds. *The World's Writing Systems* (Oxford University Press, 1996). A standard reference for facts about writing systems, past and present.

Gnanadesikan, Amalia. *The Writing Revolution: From Cuneiform to the Internet* (Wiley-Blackwell, 2009). A well-written, compact summary of the important writing systems of the world.

Rogers, Henry. *Writing Systems: A Linguistic Approach* (Blackwell, 2005). Preferable among the small number of textbooks on writing.

13

Where does grammar come from?

Joan Bybee

Does grammar change? What is grammar anyway?
Do all languages have it?

All languages have grammar, by which we mean those little function words (*the, a, will, some*) or prefixes and endings that signal meanings such as past, present and future. Grammar also includes the way we arrange words so effortlessly yet consistently in our native language; for instance, the fact that we say 'the dog is sleeping on the couch' rather than 'is dog ingsleep couch the on'. Although most of us are aware of words changing, we tend to think of grammar as more stable. But in fact, grammar is also constantly in flux.

The Language Police always deplore the loss of grammar—for instance, that we don't know when to use *whom* any more—but it's barely noticed that languages also develop *new* grammar. And yet they do! All the time.

For example, English has some old ways to indicate future tense by using *will* and *shall*. But these days American English speakers and younger Britons hardly use the word *shall* at all. A new way to mark future has evolved in the last few centuries from the expression *be going to* plus a verb. So when we say 'it's going to rain', we mean it purely as a prediction about a future event—it doesn't mean that something or someone is going anywhere at all.

In Shakespeare's time, on the other hand, if you used *going to,* it always meant literally that someone was going from one place to another for some purpose.

How did this change happen? It is a process that linguists call 'grammaticalization', through which a word or sequence of words like *be going to* may acquire a change of meaning and take on a grammatical function. Such changes happen very gradually, over long periods of time, and several things usually happen at once.

The change of meaning often starts when inferences get associated with certain phrases. For instance, if I say 'I'm going to visit my sister' I am telling you both where I am going and what my intentions are. After a while, the intention meaning becomes even more important than the movement meaning. From the intention meaning in turn you can make an inference about what will happen in the future. So eventually, we can use *be going to* to indicate future.

Humans are very interested in other people's intentions, so expressions of intent are a more important piece of information than expressions about movement in space. So when *be going to* began to be used for intention it was used more often. When phrases are used a lot they begin to lose some of their impact, and the original meaning seems to get bleached away. They also tend to be said faster, and pronunciation erodes: so when *going to* came into constant use as a main way to express the future, it started to turn into 'gonna'—a new bit of grammar. Not everybody has yet recognized 'gonna' as a future tense marker, but that is clearly the function it is serving, especially in spoken language. In another hundred years it will no doubt be firmly entrenched in our grammar books—until another way to express future develops.

Grammaticalization happens over and over, and in all languages. In fact, many languages use a phrase with a verb such as 'go' to signal the future. You can see it in Spanish, French, the African languages Margi, Krongo, Mano and Bari, the Native American languages Cocama and Zuni, the Pacific language Atchin, and many more. One of the reasons languages are similar is that they develop over time in very similar ways.

And it is not just markers of future time that develop this way, but all kinds of grammatical markers. For instance, it is common for the indefinite article *a/an* (as in 'a dog') to develop from the word for 'one'. In English, you can still hear the 'n' of 'one' in the 'an' of 'an apple'. Also, in Spanish, French, German and other European languages, the relation between the word for 'one' and the indefinite article 'a' or 'an' is quite clear. Spanish *un/una*, French *un/une* and German *ein/eine* all mean both 'one' and 'a/an'.

Or think about prepositions, those little words like *at, over, with, above* or *through* that link up with a noun to talk about when, where or how something was accomplished ('at ten o'clock', 'over the bridge', 'with daring speed'). They too are what we think of as part of 'grammar' and have undergone changes in their meaning and use. Our words *before* and *behind,* for example, are composed of an old preposition *be-* and the noun *fore* meaning 'front' and *hind* meaning 'the back part of a body'. While these prepositions started out with meanings having to do with space ('before the castle', 'behind the ramparts'), they are now also used for time ('before noon', 'I'm running behind schedule').

There are many features of grammar whose origins we don't know, but because the process of grammaticalization is so common, it's safe to assume that all words and parts of words that have a grammatical function came from other words.

And that helps us explain how the very first language got grammar. The earliest language was no doubt fairly 'telegraphic' in nature, a collection of individual words, supplemented with gestures to convey meaning. But soon after human beings could use words as symbols and join two words together, they surely used some combinations very frequently. With the making of inferences and inevitable changes in pronunciation, the development of grammar was put in motion. And that was a great thing, because—despite its bad reputation among those who struggled with it in school—it is the existence of grammar that makes fluent, connected speech possible.

About the author

Joan Bybee (Ph.D., UCLA) is Distinguished Emerita Professor of Linguistics at the University of New Mexico. At the University of New Mexico she has served as Associate Dean and Department Chair. In 2004 she served as President of the Linguistic Society of America. Professor Bybee is considered a leader in the study of the way language use impacts language structure. She has authored books and articles on phonology, morphology, language typology and language change. Her book *The Evolution of Grammar* (1994) uses a database of seventy-six languages to study the way in which languages spontaneously develop new grammatical structures.

Suggestions for further reading

In this book

Other chapters discussing grammar include 14 (universal grammar), 16 (animal communication), 25 (language deprivation), and 52 (Native American languages). Chapters 8 (language change) and 10 (pidgins and creoles) discuss how grammar changes over time.

Elsewhere

Deutscher, Guy. *The Unfolding of Language* (Henry Holt and Company, 2005). A lively popular introduction to linguistics from the point of view of language change.

Hopper, Paul, and Elizabeth Traugott. *Grammaticalization* (Cambridge University Press, 2003). A textbook for linguistics students about grammaticalization.

14

Do all languages have the same grammar?

Mark C. Baker

Is there a universal grammar that underlies all languages?
What do English, Japanese, and Mohawk have in common?

Probably nobody would claim that all languages have the same grammar. But many linguists believe that all languages have certain basic design features in common, and that it is worth looking seriously into a concept often called 'Universal Grammar'.

Suppose there did exist some set of rules underlying all languages. Might that help explain how children can so easily learn any language as their mother tongue—without graduate courses or government funds—even though language is one of the most complex systems of knowledge that any human being acquires?

Perhaps, but it's not easy to see what all languages might have in common—especially if we look beyond the western European languages, which have many similarities because they share a common history. Each language obviously uses different words, and it seems no less obvious that the rules and patterns for assembling words into phrases and sentences differ widely from language to language. Let's look at a couple of non-European examples.

In English one says 'John gave a book to Mary'; the Japanese equivalent is *John-ga Mary-ni hon-o yatta*. The words for 'book' (*hon-o*) and 'gave' (*yatta*) are different, of course, but so are their positions in the sentence. In English, the verb 'gave' is the second word of the sentence; in Japanese it is the last word. In English, 'book' comes after the verb; in Japanese it comes before the verb. In English the gift recipient 'Mary' comes after the preposition 'to'; in Japanese the recipient comes before *ni* (the equivalent of 'to'). To speak Japanese you need to learn not only a new set of words but a new set of rules for how to combine the words—a new grammar.

The Mohawk language differs from English in a different way. In Mohawk, the sentence 'The man gave a blanket to the baby' could be expressed as *Owira'a wa-sh-ako-hsir-u ne rukwe*. Word order is not grammatically important in Mohawk: you can put *owira'a* ('baby'), *wa-sh-ako-hsir-u* ('he-her-blanket-gave'), and *rukwe* ('man') wherever you like and still get the same meaning. What's crucial in Mohawk is the form of the verb: if you replace *wa-sh-ako-hsir-u* with *wa-h-uwa-hsir-u*, the sentence then means 'The baby gave a blanket to the man,' whatever order the words are put in. Stranger still, the direct object 'blanket' is not even a separate word in these sentences. It is indicated by *hsir*, which combines with the verb root *u* to make a compound verb ('blanket-gave')—something not usually possible in English or Japanese. Indeed, a Mohawk complex verb like *washakohsiru* can stand alone as a sentence: 'He gave a blanket to her.'

Despite contrasts like these, linguistic research is discovering that the grammars of different languages are much more similar than they appear at first.

The subject in Japanese is at the beginning of the sentence, as in English. Did you notice that apart from that, the order of the words in Japanese is the exact mirror-image of the English order? The recipient 'Mary' comes next to the word meaning 'to' in both languages. The direct object 'book' comes next to the word meaning 'gave' in both languages. Overall, the same kinds of words combine with each other to form the same kinds of phrases in English and Japanese. The only difference is a systematic difference in order—whether verbs and prepositions are put at the beginning of the phrases they form (as in English) or at the end of those phrases (as in Japanese). That's why it is right to say that the grammars are almost the same. After all, a picture and its mirror image are not completely different, even though none of the pixels match up. On the contrary, they are almost the same image—a truth we take advantage of when we brush our teeth or comb our hair.

What about Mohawk, where word order doesn't seem to matter? Such flexibility doesn't seem so strange if you've studied Spanish or Italian, where verbs change form to agree with their subjects; the subject can be various places in the sentence and you can still recognize it. But how about the way the direct object merges into the verb in Mohawk? Even this is not a completely alien feature. The direct object appears next to the verb in both English and Japanese, just as it does in Mohawk; the only difference is whether the verb and object combine loosely, into a verbal *phrase* (English and Japanese), or tightly, into a verbal *word* (Mohawk).

Indeed, even in English a verb and its object can sometimes combine to make a single word. Think of noun compounds like 'dish-washer' and 'man-eater', each combining an ordinary noun ('dish', 'man') with a noun formed from a verb ('wash', 'eat'). Notice that 'man-eater' refers to something (like a shark or a tiger) that eats a man, not to a man who eats things. That is, the noun 'man' is always the object of the eating, not its subject. This characteristic of English word-formation parallels what we see in Mohawk compound verbs, and in English and Japanese verbal phrases.

The fact that verbs always combine more closely with direct objects than they do with subjects is a good example of a general law of grammar, which seems to hold for all human languages. It turns out that there are many such universal laws. In fact, over the past several decades, linguists have uncovered dozens of them. The laws provide the basic skeletal structure of language, which individual languages then flesh out in various ways.

We are finding that once we dig beneath the surface, languages seem to have as many similarities in their structure as they have differences. So, while it is not quite true that all languages have the same grammar, it is much closer to being true than you might have thought.

About the author

Mark Baker was trained in linguistics at MIT under Noam Chomsky. He is now professor of linguistics and cognitive science at Rutgers University, where he specializes in the word structure and sentence structure of less-studied languages, especially those spoken in Africa and the Americas.

Suggestions for further reading

In this book

Other chapters discussing grammar include 13 (grammar in general), 16 (animal communication), 25 (language deprivation), and 52 (Native American languages).

Elsewhere

Baker, Mark. *The Atoms of Language* (Basic Books, 2002). A non-technical book-length discussion of the similarities and differences among languages, showing in more detail than this chapter how different-looking languages can be derived from almost the same grammatical rules.

Pinker, Steven. *The Language Instinct* (Harper Collins, 1994). Chapter 8 addresses the question of how languages differ, putting this question in the context of the overall view that language is an instinct hard-wired into the human brain.

Whaley, Lindsey. *Introduction to Typology* (SAGE Publications, 1996). An introductory textbook that gives some of the history and main results that come from comparing a wide range of historically unrelated languages.

15

How do babies learn their mother tongue?

Roberta Michnick Golinkoff and
Kathryn Hirsh-Pasek

When do babies start learning to talk? How do they do it?
Can babies learn any language they are exposed to?

Contrary to many people's ideas about 'baby talk', language learning starts well before babies utter their first words or babbles. As soon as babies in the womb can hear, they respond to sounds. They *jump* in response to noises, such as fireworks, and even before they're born they eavesdrop on every conversation their mother has. When they emerge, we can trick them into showing us that they recognize their mother's voice as well as stories and songs they've heard in the womb. (They consistently prefer listening to those sounds rather than rival sounds.) At first, language is only like a melody for babies, but they enter the world prepared to learn any of the world's nearly seven thousand languages.

With the melody imprinted, the first problem babies face is finding the *units* in the stream of speech that washes over them. Where does one word end and the next begin? (You may have had a similar problem as you began learning a foreign language and hearing native speakers talk a mile a minute.) They start finding unit boundaries by four and a half months of age, as they learn to recognize their own name. The first clue is its stress pattern

('IRVing' is clearly different from 'AnnETTE'), but very soon little Irving can distinguish his name even from other names with the same stress pattern (like 'Wilson'). Next, babies begin to recognize other frequently occurring words—like 'mama'—that can serve as additional markers in the speech stream. At six months babies can recognize a word they hear when it comes *after* their own name (but not when it follows someone else's name).

Having learned to find the word-like units in the stream of speech around them, babies need to figure out what these units *mean*. Naturally enough, some of the first words babies understand the meanings of are 'mama' and 'daddy'. Research tells us that by six months, even though they can't yet talk, they attach the word 'mama' to their own mother and not to just any woman. Likewise for 'daddy'. But as their internal vocabularies expand, learning what words mean can be complicated. Imagine yourself in a foreign country where you know very little of the language. A rabbit hops by, and a native says 'zoxil'. What might 'zoxil' mean? 'Rabbit' is a pretty obvious guess, but it might not be right. She could be saying, 'look', or 'hopping' or 'ears'. Picking up the new language this way, it'll take time for you to sort out the possibilities and add 'zoxil' to your vocabulary. Babies are in the same situation. But by twelve months, they seem to interpret words as labels for objects—usually whole objects (like rabbits) as opposed to parts (like ears) or actions (like hopping).

After babies find words and know some meanings comes the step that marks true language acquisition: they begin to learn how words go together to make sentences. They know more about their language than what they can say—just as you could understand more in a foreign language than you could speak. So while their first spoken words appear at around twelve months, they may already understand hundreds of words. By eighteen months, they can understand five- and six-word sentences when they may be saying only one or two words at a time themselves.

Picture an oversize TV screen, split between two moving images: on the left side, Cookie Monster is hugging Big Bird; on the right, Big Bird is hugging Cookie Monster. Babies watch the screen with rapt attention. When they hear 'Where's Big Bird hugging Cookie Monster?' they look more at the right side of the screen than at the left. This means that babies, amazingly enough, are already using *grammar,* the order of the words in English, to figure out who's doing what to whom—even if they aren't *saying* much at all.

So here's a paradox: babies can't tie their shoes or be left alone for more than thirty seconds, and yet they're like sponges when it comes to learning languages. The next time you're tempted to think of a newborn baby as a vegetable, think again! They're paying attention—and they learn languages better than their older and wiser parents!

About the authors
Roberta Michnick Golinkoff holds the H. Rodney Sharp Chair in the School of Education at the University of Delaware and is also a member of the Departments of Psychology and Linguistics. She directs the Infant Language Project, whose goal it is to understand how children tackle the amazing feat of learning language. Having obtained her Ph.D. at Cornell University, she has written over a hundred articles and chapters, and she lectures all over the world. The recipient of a prestigious John Simon Guggenheim Fellowship and a James McKeen Cattell Sabbatical award, she is frequently quoted in newspapers and magazines, and has appeared on *Good Morning America* and many regional morning television programs. She also serves as Associate Editor of *Child Development*. With K. Hirsh-Pasek, she won the Distinguished Service Award and the Urie Bronfenbrenner Award for Lifetime Contribution to Developmental Psychology.

Kathy Hirsh-Pasek is the Stanley and Debra Lefkowitz Professor in the Department of Psychology at Temple University, Pennsylvania, where she serves as Director of the Infant Language Laboratory and with R. Golinkoff, Co-founder of CiRCLE, the Center for Re-imaging Children's Learning and Education. Her research projects in the areas of early language development and infant cognition have been funded by the National Science Foundation and the National Institutes of Health and Human Development and have resulted in 12 books and numerous journal publications. She has appeared on *Today*, *20/20*, and other national television programs, and is often quoted in newspapers and magazines. She is a Fellow of the American Psychological Association.

Suggestions for further reading

In this book
Other chapters discussing language acquisition by children include 10 (pidgins and creoles), 17 (language and the brain), 25 (language deprivation), 26 (sign languages), and 36 (children and second languages).

Elsewhere
Golinkoff, R. M. and K. Hirsh-Pasek. *How Babies Talk: The Magic and Mystery of Language in the First Three Years of Life* (Dutton/Penguin, 1999). This is a fun read that reviews the latest research in language acquisition and offers tips to parents.

Hirsh-Pasek, K. and R. M. Golinkoff. *Einstein Never Used Flash Cards: How Our Children Really Learn and Why They Need to Play More and Memorize Less* (Rodale, 2003). This award-winning book shows how important language is for reading, expressing emotion, and succeeding at school.

16

Do animals use language?

Donna Jo Napoli

Do animals talk among themselves? If so, how? Do they have anything like human language?

Parrots talk. So the answer is yes, animals use language, right? Well, not so fast. There are two issues here, both interesting from a linguistic point of view. One is whether animals use language among themselves; the other is whether animals can learn human language. Before addressing them, we have to decide what should count as language.

Human languages have well-defined characteristics. First, they are *systematic*; that is, they all have rules that we call grammar. ('Chased dog the nasty a cat' is made of English words, but it isn't an English sentence—the words have been thrown together randomly, rather than according to the rules of English syntax.)

Human language is also *innate*. Children are born hard-wired to acquire language. No one needs to teach them. This ability depends on the plasticity of the infant brain, though: a child not exposed to accessible language by the age of five may never fully acquire it.

A third striking characteristic is what linguists call *displacement*—humans can talk about objects that aren't present, like the man in this sentence: 'The weird man you followed last week told me he's considering writing an exposé of existentialism.'

Still another feature of human language is its ability to talk about *abstract* notions—like 'weirdness', 'exposé', and 'existentialism'.

Finally, the 'weird man' sentence is one I never used before I wrote it just now. You probably never heard it before, either. All human languages have the ability to *create* new expressions.

Animals communicate with one another in ways that meet some, but not all five, of those criteria. Most language researchers agree that this means animals don't use language.

Bees have elaborate dances to tell other bees the location and quality of food sources. The paths and speeds of these dances clearly follow rules—the orientation of the dancer's head and the vigor of its waggle are significant. They are about food that isn't present (so we have displacement) and about how good the food is (so we have abstraction). And dancing appears to researchers to be innate. But creativity is lacking; the amount of information bees can pass on is extremely limited. They can't communicate, for example, that a new food source is near another well-known one, or that other bees are already approaching the source so that the hive had better hurry if they want any.

Birdsong has also rules. Robins, for example, use motifs that have to occur in a certain order (a kind of grammar) or other robins will find them unintelligible. The ability to sing is innate, and birds not exposed to song within the first several months of life never develop typical courtship-territorial song. Birdsong does convey emotion, so to that extent it refers to abstractions. We have no evidence, however, that birdsong allows displacement (birds never seem to tell each other that something scary happened to them on the other side of the barn, for example); nor do they make up new songs. Still, there are many species of birds and few of them have been studied.

Whales and dolphins sing and whistle. The form of their songs follows rules (the complex songs of some whales can go on all day long), and they can convey limited meaning (distress or warning calls), but there's no evidence of the novelty or creativity character-istic of human language.

Chimpanzees use grunts, barks, pants, wails, laughs, squeaks, hoots, and calls to alert others to the location of food sources, to announce a successful kill, to express alarm or danger, to identify themselves, or to express satisfaction. Their postures, facial expressions, and limb gestures play an even greater role in communication. But nothing so far has indicated that any of this follows grammar-like rules.

Turning to the second question, there have been many attempts to teach human language to birds, sea mammals, and primates. Alex, an African grey parrot that Dr. Irene Pepperberg of the University of Arizona worked with for thirty years before its death in 2007, had an extensive vocabulary. He could identify objects with English words, by their material, color, shape, and number. He could ask for food that wasn't present. He apologized when he misbehaved. He was facile at language and clearly understood the meaning of some words. But his verbal behavior was erratic in ways unlike even a very young human's.

Dolphins have been taught to respond to hand gestures and are able to interpret new utterances correctly. For example, dolphins who learned that the sequence of gestures PERSON SURFBOARD FETCH means 'bring the surfboard to the person' easily understood SURFBOARD PERSON FETCH as 'bring the person to the surfboard'—they recognized a system and used it.

Chimpanzees, gorillas, and bonobos have been taught to use and respond to sign language. The famous chimp Washoe, who learned a simple sign language from her trainers, adopted a baby named Loulis and reportedly taught him to sign. A gorilla named Koko is reported to have amassed a vocabulary of over a thousand signs. A bonobo named Kanzi learned to communicate using a keyboard with about two hundred symbols that represented words and actions. We are told he could understand over five hundred spoken English words.

And, most recently, border collies have been reported to respond appropriately to language, some showing recognition of over a thousand words.

Such experiments suggest that in laboratory settings or with rigorous training some animals can learn language-like behavior to some extent; but there's no sign that their real-world communication with each other makes any significant use of this capacity.

Could we be missing something? Could there be animals that achieve five-featured language-like communication with exotic means like seismic thumping, olfactory spraying, or electrical signaling? Nothing is impossible, but decades of research have not found anything among animals that is comparable to human language in terms of systematicity or creativity. Language remains the most profound distinction between animals and humans.

About the author

Donna Jo Napoli, trained at Harvard and MIT, is Professor of Linguistics at Swarthmore College. She publishes widely in theoretical linguistics, primarily on the structure of Italian and of American Sign Language. Her books include *Humour in Sign Languages: The Linguistic Underpinnings* (with Rachel Sutton-Spence, 2009), *Language Matters* (2003), and *Linguistics: An Introduction* (1996). She also writes fiction for children: www. donnajonapoli.com.

Suggestions for further reading

In this book

Chapters discussing grammar as a distinguishing feature of human language include 13 (grammar in general), 14 (universal grammar), and 25 (language deprivation).

Elsewhere

Anderson, Steve. *Dr. Doolittle's Delusion: Animals and the Uniqueness of Human Language* (Yale University Press, 2004). Clarifies the distinction between communication and language, and argues that while animals have the former, they do not have the latter.

Bradbury, Jack and Sandra Vehrencamp. *Principles of Animal Communication* (Sinauer Press, 1998). Discusses the range of communication between animals across the various senses.

Hauser, Marc and Mark Konishi, eds. *The Design of Animal Communication* (Massachusetts Institute of Technology, 1999). Studies how animal signals and responses to them develop, including methods of communication and ontogeny.

McGregor, Peter, ed. *Animal Communication Networks* (Cambridge University Press, 2005). Applies a network perspective to communication between groups of animals, with discussions of many group behaviors, such as chorusing and, in particular, eavesdropping.

www.cwu.edu/~cwuchci. The site of Central Washington University's Chimpanzee and Human Communication Institute, where scientists use ASL with chimps.

www.thegenieslamp.com/fun/alex.htm. An article by Kenn Kaufman about Alex the parrot and his communication with humans.

http://polarization.com/bees/bees.html. About bee dances.

17

How does the brain cope with multiple languages?

Henk Haarmann

Is there such a thing as too much language learning?
How does the brain deal with multiple languages?

Have you ever been faced with uncomfortable amounts of new or complicated information, and said something like 'I feel my head's going to explode'? Well, I don't want to blow anybody's head up, but one of the major aims of many of the chapters of this book is to encourage readers and their children to learn new languages. So in case you detect cerebral pressure building, let me offer some words of comfort about the magnificent flexibility of the human brain.

Researchers today compare the brain at birth to a kind of ready-to-assemble computer kit: it comes with working components, but they have to be connected before you have a fully functioning computer. In this view the brain comes with *readiness* for language in general, but acquiring the actual sounds, words, and grammar of a particular language means growing new connections between neurons, the individual brain cells. This connection-building is what happens as a toddler learns to associate the word 'dog' with a four-legged animal and 'milk' with what's in his drinking cup; or as another toddler learns the words 'perro' for the same animal and 'leche' for the same liquid.

But you may wonder, if a child is hearing *both* languages, will her brain mix them up and thereby hinder speech? Here's the comforting fact: the brain—especially in early childhood—has a huge, virtually inexhaustible capacity for making such connections. The more talk children are exposed to in the first three years of life, the better their language skills later. In fact, children exposed to more than one language grow not only the connections that build vocabulary in each language; they also grow connections that help them sort out which language to use in different situations.

They learn, for example, to ask their English-speaking mother for 'milk' and their Spanish-speaking grandmother for 'leche'.

In the past few years we've seen some tragic cases in which people adopted babies from orphanages in eastern Europe and found that, as they grew into childhood, they were handicapped in talking to their American mothers. That wasn't a result of being confused by hearing a new language. It happened because the orphanages were thinly staffed. People watching the babies gave them minimal care and had little or no time to talk to them. The babies were linguistically starved, and didn't have the verbal stimulation that leads to normal use of language. Hearing talk, lots of talk, in infancy and later is healthy activity for the human brain, and that seems to be true no matter how many languages are involved.

But the story gets even better. It seems that there are cognitive advantages in training oneself to keep two or more languages separate. A recent study found that brain regions important for fluent speech were better developed in bilingual speakers than they were in monolinguals, especially when two languages were learned early in life.

Here's why: when a bilingual child wants to express a word in one language, the brain also activates the corresponding word in the other language. To prevent the word in the other language from being unintentionally spoken aloud, the brain has to suppress it. By having to perform this kind of control, the developing bilingual brain gets a kind of exercise that the monolingual brain does not.

To repeat, learning two languages at an early age is *good* for the brain—and, you'll be interested to know, not just for learning to *talk*. Studies at York University in Canada suggest that early bilinguals also have better cognitive control in certain types of *non*-verbal tasks. And that was true not just for children but also for middle-aged and older adults. Bilingualism seems to protect healthy older adults from some of the negative effects of aging on the brain. That in itself is an excellent reason to be born into a bilingual family—or to start learning a second language while you're still in diapers.

About the author
Henk Haarmann is an associate research scientist at the Center for Advanced Study of Language (CASL) of the University of Maryland. He is a cognitive psychologist who has studied language memory through computer modeling and measurement of brain activity. He was born in the Netherlands. He received doctoral training at the Max Planck Institute for Psycholinguistics and the University of Nijmegen in the Netherlands, and post-doctoral training at Carnegie Mellon University. Contact: hhaarmann@casl.umd.edu.

Suggestions for further reading

In this book
The question of how many languages the human brain can absorb is also addressed in Chapters 22 (bilinguality) and 23 (hyperpolyglots). Other chapters discussing adult language learning include 31 (foreign accents), 33 (how to study languages), 34 (history of language teaching methods), 35 (study abroad), and 37 (language teaching technology). Chapters discussing children's language learning include 10 (pidgins and creoles), 15 (babies and language), 25 (language deprivation), 26 (sign languages), and 36 (second language learning in elementary schools).

Elsewhere
Bialystok, E., F.I.M. Craik, C. Grady, W. Chau, R. Ishii, A. Gunji, and C. Pantev. 'Effect of bilingualism on cognitive control in the Simon task: Evidence from MEG'. *NeuroImage* 24 (2005, pp40–49).

18

Does our language influence the way we think?

Geoffrey K. Pullum

How are language and thought related? Do you think the way you do because of the language you speak? What's the real story on Eskimo words for 'snow'?

Some of the remarks people make that seem superficially to be about language must, if you think about it, be intended as comments about thinking. You may say 'We don't speak the same language' when talking about someone you can't work with, but that nearly always means that the other person's *thoughts* run along different lines. 'I was speechless' nearly always means that I was astonished, not that my vocal folds seized up. And so on.

Of course, language and thought are quite closely related. Language helps us to represent thought explicitly in our minds. It helps us reason, plan, remember, and communicate. Communication with others gets most of the press when people talk about language. But could it be that the language we use actually causes us to *think* in certain ways? Could the language we speak make our internal representations of ideas different from those of people who speak a different language?

It's true that different languages phrase things differently. But does that mean it is possible to have thoughts in one language that can't be translated into another? Unfortunately, most of the people who answer 'yes' to this question turn out to have nothing in mind other than single basic word meanings.

It is pretty easy to find words in one language that don't have exact single-word equivalents in another. *Schadenfreude* in German is a famous example. It refers to a kind of malicious pleasure some people find in other people's misfortunes. But does the lack of an exact single-word English equivalent mean that English speakers aren't able to experience that feeling themselves or recognize it in others? Surely not. I believe I just explained in English what *Schadenfreude* means.

Another familiar example concerns color. Some languages have far fewer words than English for naming fairly basic colors. While some (like Greek and Russian) have more than one basic word for shades of blue, quite a few others use the same word for both 'green' and 'blue'. Some languages have hardly any color-name words. Does this mean their speakers can't physically distinguish multiple colors? Apparently not. An experiment in the 1960s found that members of a New Guinea tribe (the Dani) whose language named only two colors were just as good at matching a full spectrum of color chips as English speakers.

And lest we forget, I'd better mention the tired old claim that Eskimos (the Inuit and Yup'ik peoples of arctic Siberia, Alaska, Canada, and Greenland) see the world differently because they have some huge number of words for different varieties of snow. You may be disappointed to learn that there's hardly any truth to the linguistic claim: the eight languages of the Eskimoan family have only a modest number of snow terms. Four were mentioned in a 1911 description of a Canadian Eskimo language by the great anthropologist Franz Boas: a general word for snow on the ground; and words roughly corresponding to 'snowflake', 'blizzard', and '(snow)drift'. That was it.

Boas was making a point that had nothing to do with numbers of words or their influence on thinking. It was about the way different languages draw slightly different distinctions when naming things. But years of exaggeration and embellishment led to a seductive myth that people with no knowledge of Eskimoan languages repeat over and over in magazines and newspapers. They report with wonder that the Eskimos have some amazing number of words for snow, a number that differs wildly from writer to writer: some say dozens or scores while others say hundreds or thousands. They offer no evidence, and they usually ignore the fact that English, too, has plenty of words for snow—words like 'slush', 'sleet', 'avalanche', 'blizzard', and 'flurry'.

Do the vocabularies of Eskimoan languages really give their speakers a unique way of perceiving, unshared by English speakers? The possibility seems to have been grossly exaggerated. Some writers go as far as claiming that your language *creates* your world for you, and thus that speakers of different languages live in different worlds. This is conceptual relativism taken to an extreme.

The idea that our language inexorably shapes or determines how we think is pure speculation, and it's hard to imagine what could possibly support that speculation even in principle. For one thing, there is surely some thought (e.g., among animals) that is done without the aid of language. But notice also that in order for you to know there was a thought that was understandable for a speaker of (say) Hindi but not for you as an English speaker, you'd need to have that Hindi thought explained to you. If that couldn't be done, no Hindi speaker could convince you that the incomprehensible thought really existed.

In reality, things don't seem to be that way at all. Take as an example the Hindi word *kal*. It picks out a particular region of time: surprisingly, *kal* refers to both yesterday and tomorrow. You understand it whichever way is appropriate in the context. Does that give Hindi speakers a unique and special sense of time that you can never share? Surely not. Because I have just explained it to you perfectly well, so you can understand it after all.

Certainly, it is not impossible that your view of the world may be subtly influenced by the way your native language tempts you to classify the world; but that doesn't mean that your language defines a shell within which your thought is confined, or that there are untranslatable thoughts that only a speaker of some other language can have. If you find yourself trying to grasp a difficult thought, don't give up and blame your language. Just think a little harder.

About the author

Geoffrey K. Pullum is a linguist with broad interests in language. He was born in Scotland, and worked as a rock musician for five years before doing a B.A. degree in Language at the University of York and earning the Ph.D. in General Linguistics at the University of London. In 1981 he joined the Department of Linguistics at the University of California, Santa Cruz, where he served as a professor of linguistics and later as a dean. He was elected a Fellow of the American Academy of Arts and Sciences in 2003. After moving to the University of Edinburgh in 2007, he became Head of Linguistics and English Language, and was elected a Fellow of the British Academy in 2009. He has published about 250 articles and books on many topics in linguistics, including a major reference grammar of English, *The Cambridge Grammar of the English Language* (2002, co-authored with Rodney Huddleston), which was awarded the Linguistic Society of America's Leonard Bloomfield Book Award in January 2004.

Suggestions for further reading

In this book

Other chapters that suggest questions about relationships between language and mental processes include 15 (babies and language), 16 (animal communication), 17 (language and the brain), 24 (glossolalia), 25 (language deprivation), and 48 (machine translation). More information about Hindi appears in Chapter 63 (languages of India).

Elsewhere

Whorf, Benjamin Lee., ed. by John B. Carroll. *Language, Thought and Reality: Selected Writings* (MIT Press, 1964). Edited collection of the (fairly accessible) writings of Whorf, who was perhaps the most important popularizer of the idea that language shapes thought.

Martin, Laura. '"Eskimo words for snow": A case study in the genesis and decay of an anthropological example'. *American Anthropologist* vol. 88, no. 2 (1986), pp419–23. A critique of the absurdly exaggerated stories that have arisen concerning Eskimoan snow terminology.

Preston, John, ed. *Thought and Language* (Royal Institute of Philosophy Supplement 42, Cambridge University Press, 1997). A collection of serious papers on language/thought relations by some important modern philosophers.

Lucy, John Arthur. *Language Diversity and Thought: A Reformulation of the Linguistic Relativity Hypothesis* (Cambridge University Press, 1992). Major book-length study of the 'linguistic relativity' hypothesis that the grammar of our native language affects the way we think about reality; it contrasts English with the Yucatec Maya language of Mexico.

19

What's the right way to put words together?

Dennis R. Preston

Is there a 'right' way to use a language? What authority determines it?

The U.S. has no shortage of linguistic gatekeepers. Language pundits warn in the press, on the air, and even on the inside of matchbook covers that if we don't clean up our linguistic acts, the doors of opportunity will be closed. Fear of not saying things the 'right' way causes some of us to break out in a sweat when choosing whether to say 'between you and me' or 'between you and I'.*

What makes us so linguistically insecure? It's the idea that a language has only one correct form, and the fear that we're not in step with it. But let's remember that the choice of the 'best' or 'most correct' way of speaking is just a matter of history. Saying 'between you and me'—like not wearing sneakers with a coat and tie—is a convention, not a divine law. Power, money and prestige cause one variety of language to be preferred. In England, the focus of wealth, commerce, and government in London caused a variety of southern British English to be thought of as the best. In the U.S.,

---

* 'Between you and I' is said to be wrong by prescriptivists, who point out that the 'I' should be 'me', since it is the object of the preposition 'between'. They forget to tell us that such constructions have an ancient and glorious history. It was after all Shakespeare who wrote 'All debts are cleared between you and I.'

where there was no such center, the language of the well-educated, higher classes became the preferred variety. Over time, that variety came to be seen as the only acceptable way for people to express themselves.

There will always be people who prescribe how we should talk, and who point out what they see as flaws in other people's speech. Because they think the preferred language is the only one that's acceptable, prescriptivists try to prove that other varieties of language are deficient.

If you say 'I don't have no money,' for example, one of them may tell you that 'two negatives make a positive,' but even in simple arithmetic, minus two plus minus two equals *minus* four. Besides, does anybody really believe that people who say 'I don't have no money' mean that they *do* have some money? Are people who say such things frequently misunderstood? Not likely. The test of a language's effectiveness is not whether its arbitrary noises or scribbles meet a standard but whether it communicates. A speaker of impeccable English may say silly and illogical things; a speaker of a down-home variety may be logical and precise.

One must feel sorry for the watchdog pundits who try to tell us when to use 'whom' instead of 'who'. Such attempts are a losing battle, because how language will be used can't be legislated. Words and combinations of words don't have a 'real' meaning. They only mean what we agree they'll mean, and different groups may come to different agreements. Besides, language isn't a fixed system. It evolves. Some of yesterday's poorly-thought-of language may become today's preferred variety. You may deplore this if you're a speaker of yesterday's preferred variety, but most often, as language evolves, it adjusts in the direction of how lower-status speakers use it. That doesn't make it wrong or deficient. It's just what language does.

That said, another aspect of language is that it happens in societies, and societies always make judgments. It's a reality in English-speaking countries that speakers who use double negatives will earn disapproval from certain people, some of whom have power over what we hope for in life. If you're not a native speaker of the preferred variety of language, there are social and economic advantages to learning it, even though it's only a historical convention, no more logical or beautiful than the way you already speak.

Prescriptivists even want us to give up our native varieties. But we shouldn't let ourselves be bullied. Prescriptivism comes out of a desire for uniformity in behavior, in language as in other areas. It can lead to elitism, racism, and even silliness. When told not to end sentences with prepositions, Winston Churchill is said to have remarked, 'This is arrant pedantry, up with which I shall not put.' So should we all.

About the author

Dennis R. Preston is Regents Professor, Oklahoma State University and University Distinguished Professor Emeritus, Michigan State University. He has been a visiting professor at several U.S. universities and a Fulbright Senior Researcher in Poland and Brazil. He has served as President of the American Dialect Society and on the executive boards of that society and the Linguistic Society of America, and the editorial boards of *Language*, the *International Journal of Applied Linguistics*, the *Journal of Sociolinguistics* and others. His work focuses on sociolinguistics, dialectology, ethnography, and minority language and variety education. He is best known for the revitalization of folk linguistics and attempts to provide variationist accounts of second-language acquisition. His most recent book-length publications are, with Nancy Niedzielski, *Folk Linguistics* (2000), with Daniel Long, *A Handbook of Perceptual Dialectology*, Volume II (2002), *Needed Research in American Dialects* (2003), with Brian Joseph and Carol Preston, *Linguistic Diversity in Michigan and Ohio* (2005), with James Stanford, *Variation in Indigenous Minority Languages* (2009), and, with Nancy Niedzielski, *A Reader in Sociophonetics* (2010). He is a fellow of the Japan Society for the Promotion of Science and was awarded the Officer's Cross of the Order of Merit of the Polish Republic in 2004.

Suggestions for further reading

In this book
Other chapters touching on language standards include 8 (language change), 13 (grammar change), 20 (British and American English), and 46 (dictionaries).

Elsewhere
For non-linguists, the belief that there is simply a right and a wrong way to use language is a very strongly held notion. There are a number of excellent books that document the history of this prescriptivism and its current status. The ones recommended here should require no specialized knowledge of linguistics.

Battistella, Edwin L. *Bad Language* (Oxford, 2005). A catalog of how 'bad language' even gets its users labeled as 'bad citizens', highlighted in media reflections of popular attitudes to language.

Bauer, Laurie, and Peter Trudgill, eds. *Language Myths* (Penguin Books, 1998). Professional comment on twenty-one popular beliefs about language—all of which turn out to be false.

Bolinger, Dwight. *Language: The Loaded Weapon* (Longman, 1980). A book by one of America's most insightful linguists on matters of language and public usage. Bolinger tells you what bad language really is.

Cameron, Deborah. *Verbal Hygiene* (Routledge, 1995). A vigorous exposé of numbskull commentary on language use.

Finegan, Edward. *Attitudes toward English Usage* (Teachers College Press, 1980). A thorough investigation of the nastiness that ensued in the early 1960s when professional lexicographers dared to tell the public what was really going on in language.

Lippi-Green, Rosina. *English with an Accent* (Routledge, 1997). Use bad language; go directly to jail (lose your job, go to the back of the line, etc. …).

Milroy, James, and Lesley Milroy. *Authority in Language* (Routledge, 1985). Who gets to say what's right and wrong? Why?

Niedzielski, Nancy, and Dennis R. Preston. *Folk Linguistics* (Mouton de Gruyter, 2000). A survey and analysis of what real people (i.e. not linguists) had to say about language in America in the waning days of the twentieth century.

20

Is British English the best English?

Orin Hargraves

Is British English superior to other versions of the language?
How should we judge between different versions of a
language? Who owns English anyway?

Suppose you had the chance to record a sample of human language
for aliens to listen to. What language would you choose? You don't
have to make that choice, because someone has already done it:
when the Voyager space probes were launched in 1977, they car-
ried recordings of short greetings in 55 human languages—including English—for the benefit of otherworldly beings. But what sort
of English did they record?

You may be thinking, surely English today is one language: we
all understand the written form of it and we do reasonably well
with spoken varieties of it other than our own. English is written
with a single alphabet, and its basic grammar and core vocabulary
are commonly understood. But like any language, English comes
in a number of flavors, and a couple of flavors dominate the rest:
American and British. These two titans of English vie, in a very
refined and civilized way, for world domination, and the coming
decades will be crucial in determining which of the dialects is
going to come out on top.

In a sense, American English already has the upper hand. How
has it happened that the American dialect of English—one of the

many offspring of British English—should grow up to compete with, if not overwhelm, the island version of the mother tongue? The truth of the matter is that American English has gotten (yes: *gotten*) the upper hand by might, rather than by right. Great Britain gets the credit for successfully spreading English around the world during the glorious days of its empire. But the cultural and economic empire of the U.S. has since pushed the American dialect to the forefront. We read of people lining up on the docks in nineteenth-century New York to read the latest installments in the serialized novels of Charles Dickens. Today the situation is reversed: Americans who happen to be on the other side of the Atlantic will see a line (or rather, a queue) of people waiting for the premiere of the latest Hollywood blockbuster in London's Leicester Square.

American English has pretty much won the numbers game, but Britons are inclined to think that their strain of the language is the *purer* one: in other words, the New World may have won on quantity, but the Old Country still holds all the aces on quality. Is there anything to this argument? The British have been arguing for the superiority of their dialect since before the ink was dry on America's Declaration of Independence, but Americans have been just as vehement in insisting that their variety of the language is as worthy as any dialect to be the standard-bearer of world English.

Let's look at the canon: the British do have things that Americans can never take away from them: the King James Bible, Shakespeare, the romantic and metaphysical poets, the great tradition of nineteenth-century novelists. But despite British English's impressive credentials, Americans have never shown any sign of subservience to it. American English has gone its own way from the beginning. As one twentieth-century American writer observed, 'Why should we permit the survival of the curious notion that our language is a mere loan from England, like a copper kettle that we must keep scoured and return without a dent?'

The British, of course, take a different view of American linguistic independence and innovation. As one of their writers put it: 'The Americans are determined to hack their way through the language, as their ancestors did through the forests, regardless of the valuable growths that may be sacrificed in blazing the trail.'

Leaving aside the questions of quality and quantity, the question that remains is this: what is the future of these two dialects of English? It turns out that neither the Brits nor the Yanks will have the final say in determining that future. There'll be a wild card in the game, held by people around the world who will speak English as a second or foreign language. In a few years, that third group will outnumber the native speakers of English. And it turns out that those learners may not want *any* 'branded' variety of English; they just want a kind that they can use. Consider this: in 2000, a Chinese training program for steel engineers chose neither Americans nor Britons, but rather *Belgians*, to teach them English. The Chinese saw it as an advantage that the Belgians, like the Chinese themselves, were not native speakers. The Belgians, they thought, would have a feel both for the difficulties of learning the language in adulthood, and for using it with other non-native speakers.

Imagine, then, a conversation between a Belgian teacher of English and a Chinese engineer: if a pronoun fails to decline and there is no native speaker there to hear it, does it make a difference? The heyday of the big-brand dialects of English is probably over. In this century, the chief demand placed on English will be for an ability to adapt to the needs of the millions of speakers who use it as a second language.

And what about that clip recorded for the denizens of outer space? Well, the aliens lucky enough to decode it will hear the voice of a schoolgirl—who sounds to our ear as though she lives closer to Cape Canaveral, Florida, than to Sloane Square in London— saying, 'Greetings from the children of Earth.'

About the author
Orin Hargraves is a tenth-generation American of almost undiluted British Isles ancestry, and has lived for considerable periods in London.

He is the author of *Mighty Fine Words and Smashing Expressions* (2003), which explores the differences between British and American English, and also of *Slang Rules!* (2009) an ESL lesson book about American slang. He has made substantial contributions to dictionaries and other language reference works from publishers including Berlitz, Cambridge University Press, Chambers-Harrap, HarperCollins, Langenscheidt, Longman, Merriam-Webster, Oxford University Press and Scholastic. He now lives in Carroll County, Maryland.

Suggestions for further reading

In this book
The contrasts between different regional versions of languages are discussed in Chapters 4 (dialects and languages), 30 (U.S. Southern English), and 44 (U.S. dialect change); linguistic standards are discussed in Chapters 8 (language change), 19 (prescriptivism), and 46 (dictionaries).

Elsewhere
The author's book *Mighty Fine Words and Smashing Expressions*, noted above, is a good place to start exploring the subtle and pervasive differences between the two main dialects of English. Other suggestions:

Fiske, Robert Hartwell, ed. *Vocabula Bound* (Marion Street Press, 2004). A book of essays about English, one of which (a longer article by the author, entitled 'Who Owns English?') inspired this chapter.

Bragg, Melvyn. *The Adventure of English* (Hodder & Stoughton, 2003). An enjoyable overview of the subject.

McArthur, Tom, ed. *The Oxford Companion to the English Language* (Oxford, 1992). This book is the place to go for one-stop shopping concerning all things English.

21
Why do people fight over language?

Paul B. Garrett

Is language important enough to fight about? How do conflicts over language get started? What are the underlying causes?

The idea of fighting over language might seem strange, but it's all too common. Why do people sometimes feel so strongly about their language that they take up arms against speakers of another? How can language issues create tensions that last for generations? The answers to these questions lie in the close relationship between language and identity, particularly cultural and ethnic identity.

Many of us who speak only English may tend to think of monolingualism as the norm: in France they speak French, in Japan they speak Japanese, and so on. But worldwide, there are close to seven thousand languages—and only about two hundred nations. That means a lot of multilingual nations! And because languages tend to coincide with ethnic groups, it means a lot of multiethnic nations as well. Of course, some are more multilingual and multiethnic than others. At one extreme are countries like Japan, where the vast majority of people are ethnically Japanese and speak Japanese. At the other extreme are countries like India and Nigeria, each of which has hundreds of languages and ethnicities within its borders.

In many areas of the world, people of different language backgrounds interact on a daily basis. For the most part, things go smoothly enough. But sometimes tensions arise; and sometimes these tensions erupt into conflicts. This is especially likely when speakers of one language feel threatened or oppressed by speakers of another. When that's the case, language differences become powerful markers of social, cultural, and political difference. And wherever you find language conflicts, you're sure to find struggles over territory, religion, political power, and other issues.

The weapons used in these conflicts may be more than harsh words. Language conflicts can escalate into riots, insurrections, wars, even genocide. Conflicts over language played a major part in the separation of Bangladesh from Pakistan in 1971. What began as a Bengali language movement escalated into a nine-month war for independence in which more than three million people died and another ten million were displaced.

About a decade later, in Sri Lanka, the Tamil Tigers, a separatist group whose members were speakers of the Tamil language, took up arms against a government dominated by the Sinhala-speaking majority. Significantly, the government had passed a 'Sinhala-Only Act' in 1956, and then had banned Tamil books, films, and other media. In response to these and other forms of exclusion and oppression, the Tamil Tigers set out to establish an independent Tamil nation in the north and east of Sri Lanka. Their armed rebellion evolved into the Sri Lankan Civil War, which lasted until the Sri Lankan military finally defeated the Tamil Tigers in 2009. By then, more than a quarter-century of fighting had resulted in as many as a hundred thousand deaths, and several hundred thousand Tamil civilians had become refugees.

Elsewhere in the world, language is at the heart of ongoing conflicts. In Spain, the separatist group ETA has used bombings, kidnappings, and other violent tactics in pursuit of its goal of an independent Basque homeland, where Basque would be the national language. Belgium is deeply divided between the Flemish-speaking north and the French-speaking south. There has been no violence, nor is any expected, but many who live in Belgium fully expect—indeed, some hope—that the country will ultimately break in two. Meanwhile, in the U.S., the relationship between English and Spanish has become the focus of much debate and political action—some of it quite acrimonious—as Spanish-speakers (many of whom also speak English) from diverse backgrounds have become an increasingly influential part of the country's population.

Language conflicts don't always lead to violence, but they can create tensions that persist for years, affecting the lives of millions on a daily basis. Take the case of Canada—generally a peaceful place, but one that has its share of language conflict. Canada as a whole is officially bilingual, but most French-speaking Canadians live in the province of Quebec. Surrounded by English-speaking provinces, they often feel that their language and culture are under siege; and they feel particularly threatened by the presence of English-speakers within Quebec itself.

In 1977, French-speakers in Quebec tried to protect their language by passing a law that, in many ways, restricted the use of English. For example, it required that all signs in public places be in French, and French alone. This became a point of resentment among English-speakers, including small-business owners like Allan Singer. For years, Mr. Singer had run his modest shop beneath a simple hand-painted sign that read, 'Allan Singer Limited—Printers and Stationers'. Under the new law, Mr. Singer's sign became illegal; he would have to replace it with a sign in French.

Well, Mr. Singer refused—and took his case all the way to Canada's Supreme Court. The court's ruling was a compromise of sorts, but it reflected the realities of Canadian society in a way that most Canadians found fair and just. The court decided that Mr. Singer did *not* have the right to keep his sign in English only. But the new law could *not* require him to replace it with a sign in French only, to the exclusion of English—or Spanish, Chinese, or any other language that he might wish to use in addition to French. So business owners *could* be required to use French on their signs, but the law *could not* interfere with their freedom to post bilingual or multilingual signs—signs reflecting the linguistic diversity of Quebec, and of Canada as a whole.

Ultimately, this brouhaha over signs provided an opportunity for Canada to clarify its commitment to protecting the language rights of *all* of its citizens. But the tensions haven't gone away. On two occasions, in 1980 and 1995, Quebec's citizens even went to the polls to vote on whether their province should secede from Canada and become an independent French-speaking nation. It didn't happen—but the 1995 vote was extremely close, with a margin of less than one percent.

In these and other conflicts, much more than language is at stake. Our language is part of who we are. It gives us a powerful sense of belonging with those who speak like us, and an equally powerful sense of difference from those who don't. Little wonder, then, that when someone attacks our language—or even our accent—we feel that *we* are being attacked. And we respond accordingly. Discriminate against a language, and you discriminate against its speakers; disrespect my language, and you disrespect me.

About the author

Paul B. Garrett, Associate Professor of Anthropology at Temple University, is a linguistic anthropologist whose research focuses on the creole languages and cultures of the Caribbean—particularly the island of St. Lucia, where he has done long-term ethnographic fieldwork. His other interests include language contact, ideologies of language, and political economy of language. www.temple.edu/anthro/garrett.

Suggestions for further reading

In this book

The topic of frictions and hostilities in multilingual environments is addressed in Chapters 9 (lingua francas), 10 (pidgins and creoles), 31 (accents), 40 (New World Spanish), 41 (Cajun), 42 (German in the U.S.), 43 (Gullah), and 63 (languages of India).

Elsewhere

Harris, Roxy and Ben Rampton, eds. *The Language, Ethnicity and Race Reader* (Routledge, 2003). This collection of classic and contemporary readings examines the relationships between language and such issues as identity, ethnic diversity, nationalism, colonialism, and migration.

Joseph, Brian D., et al., eds. *When Languages Collide: Perspectives on Language Conflict, Language Competition, and Language Coexistence* (Ohio State University Press, 2003). Fifteen essays examine cases of language contact worldwide (due to trade, migration, etc.), considering factors that give rise to both peaceful and conflictual outcomes.

Schmid, Carol L. *The Politics of Language: Conflict, Identity, and Cultural Pluralism in Comparative Perspective* (Oxford University Press, 2001). Focusing on the many languages spoken within the U.S., this book examines both historical and contemporary conflicts and controversies.

22

What does it mean to be bilingual?

Dora Johnson

Is everybody who knows two languages bilingual?
Can you be bilingual for life?

If you speak just one language, you probably think that you're pretty normal, and that people who speak more than one are an exception, or at least a minority. In fact, it's just the opposite. Three quarters of the people in the world, including many in the U.S. and Britain, are bilingual or multilingual. It's *monolinguals* who are a minority breed.

Bilingualism, of course, can mean different things. And not all bilinguals speak two languages at the same level. For example, after September 11th, 2001, bilinguals responded to U.S. government calls for people who could handle both English and Arabic. But some had skills that weren't good enough to meet the need. Some spoke both languages fluently but couldn't read and write one of them well; others turned out to have full skills in one language but limited ability to translate to or from the other.

So how do you get to be bilingual? Often it happens early in life, in a home where two languages are spoken. Parents sometimes speak both languages to the child; sometimes one parent uses one language and another uses the other. There also exists what linguists call 'additive' bilingualism, where you add a new language to your repertoire later in life. You can obviously do that by learning a language in school. Or maybe your parents move to Armenia when you're little and you learn Armenian while continuing to develop English skills at home.

A bilingual capability may also wither away, for example if you move to a new country and the language of the majority largely *replaces* your original language. We call this 'subtractive' bilingualism, and we see it often in immigrant families. For example, you may overhear a parent speaking to a child in the 'old country' language, with the child responding in English. The child is *subtracting* her first language from her repertoire. This begins quite early. By about age two and a half a bilingual child starts to make choices in language use, and it's usually in favor of the majority language. Think of little Quang who moved to the U.S. from Vietnam. He runs errands for his grandmother when she speaks to him in Vietnamese, and may even answer her in Vietnamese, but not in the presence of his friends! He's decided that English is the language he's going to use most, and his skill in Vietnamese starts to fade. It can be revived, and he'll *re*-learn it more quickly than someone who starts learning Vietnamese from scratch, but it'll take some serious effort on his part.

Parents often worry that their child will become confused if exposed to different languages. They needn't be concerned. There are moments when a child's language development can cause some anxiety for parents and other adults in their lives, but the advantages of using two languages in the home rather than only one far outweigh any disadvantages. Children are amazing in their ability to code-switch, that is, transfer back and forth between two systems. They will sometimes mix them up, but they quickly learn to use each language appropriately.

Immigrant families who want their children to retain their community's *heritage* language, as well as English, have to consciously work at it. Children rarely have the chance to continue learning their heritage language at school, especially if it's not French or Spanish but a less commonly taught language like, let's say, Swedish or Tagalog. So some communities start special language programs after school or on Saturdays to help keep the language alive. Being bilingual as a child doesn't automatically mean being bilingual for life.

Bilingualism is not the same thing as bilingual *education*, an approach to educating children who speak a language other than English. The thrust of bilingual education is to help such students learn school subjects through their native tongue at the same time as they're learning English. For a variety of reasons such programs have been very controversial.

In recent years, *dual* language education has become popular, and seems to show promise. Dual language programs offer monolingual kids the chance to speak and do schoolwork in two languages (one of which is always the majority language), and thus to develop *additive* bilingualism. Both language-minority and language-majority kids can become bilingual in classrooms where they learn together and help each other.

There are, of course, important reasons for new citizens of English-speaking countries, both adults and children, to learn English. But there are also important reasons for them to keep, nurture, and strengthen a language they learned at their mother's knee. In the U.S., and perhaps in other countries as well, new citizens have sometimes been so strongly encouraged to assimilate that they've been *discouraged* from retaining their original language. That's a national loss, whenever and wherever it happens. True bilinguals—and by this I mean people whose skills in both languages are very strong—have an enormous advantage in society. They can function in more than one culture. They can be bridges for communication in their communities and the globalized world. We need to find ways to produce more of them.

About the author

Dora Johnson is an associate at the private nonprofit Center for Applied Linguistics in Washington, D.C. Her work at CAL has centered around the teaching and learning of less commonly taught languages. At present she is working on a project to develop a network of Arabic K-12 language teachers in the U.S.

Suggestions for further reading

In this book
Opportunities and requirements for professional use of language abilities are discussed in Chapters 2 (what linguists do), 39 (America's language crisis), 45 (language-related careers), 46 (dictionaries), 47 (interpreting and translating), 49 (forensic linguistics), 56 (Russian), and 59 (Arabic). Persons with skills in multiple languages are discussed in Chapter 23 (hyperpolyglots).

Elsewhere
Cunningham-Andersson, Una and Staffan Andersson. *Growing Up With Two Languages: A Practical Guide* (Routledge, 1999). The authors of this manual for parents and professionals draw on the experiences of some fifty families from around the world. They provide practical advice on what to expect and how to plan, beginning before the birth of a child!

Baker, Colin. *A Parents' and Teachers' Guide to Bilingualism* (Multilingual Matters, second edition 2000). Poses and answers the most frequently asked questions about raising bilingual children.

King, Kendall and Alison Mackey. *Raising Bilingual Children: Common Parental Concerns and Current Research* (Center for Applied Linguistics, 2006). This two-page digest is designed to provide accurate information to address the concerns that parents, educators, pediatricians, and therapists have about raising bilingual children. Available online at: www.cal.org/resources/digest/raising-bilingual-children.html.

Pearson, Barbara Zurer. *Raising a Bilingual Child* (Random House, 2008). This book provides research-based information for parents about language learning and accounts of real families about their experiences with bilingualism.

The Bilingual Family Newsletter. This quarterly periodical, now discontinued, was published at www.bilingualfamilynewsletter.com, which still maintains an archive of short informative articles written in clear language. In addition to summarizing the latest research and information on language learning, bilingualism, biculturalism, etc., it presents real-life accounts of how families have developed solutions to the problems they encounter in raising bilingual children.

23

How many languages can a person learn?

Richard Hudson

What's the most languages anybody has ever mastered?
Do you have to be abnormal to learn so many?

Most of us are impressed by people who know a lot of languages, but how many is 'a lot'? A typical American or Brit knows precisely one language, maybe with smatterings of one or two others; so we're impressed if someone knows three or four well. But if you lived in some parts of India or the Australian outback you'd probably know six languages as a matter of course; three would be rather a limited repertoire.

What, then, is the human capacity for language-learning? Rather surprisingly, nobody really knows. Linguists and psychologists have done enormous amounts of research on people with linguistic handicaps, but almost nobody has looked at those who are superbly good at languages. We don't even know how many languages such people know, let alone how they do it. Most of what I say below is based on the excellent book by Michael Erard that I cite in my suggested reading.

'Human capacity' is rather vague, so let's be more precise and ask about 'normal capacity' (how many languages could any average one of us learn?) and 'extreme capacity' (what's the world record for language learning?). As we'll see, although we don't have solid answers, we do know enough to guess.

First, then, what language-learning capacity comes with a normal collection of human genes? The gene pool is pretty much the same across the whole world—after all, we know that any human baby, regardless of genetic origin, can learn the language or languages of any community in which they happen to be raised. So to determine what capacity is normal, we should study communities where most or all members are multilingual. Ideally these would be places where a lot of languages meet on fairly equal terms, like India or the Australian outback (but unlike, say, London, where hundreds of immigrant languages meet on very unequal terms with English).

This kind of research has not yet been done systematically, but impressions based on partial studies seem to converge on about five or six as the upper limit for what we can call 'community multilingualism'. The communities concerned have so many languages in circulation that ordinary people grow up naturally speaking five or six, without any formal instruction at school.

A quibble: are the languages of these communities similar enough that it's not so hard to learn five or six of them? In a word, no. We're talking about languages at least as different as (say) English and German, and in some cases as different as English and Chinese. Not surprisingly, perhaps, when a particular combination of languages is shared by a community for a long time—hundreds of years—their grammars tend to converge. They stay resolutely different in vocabulary, though. This is because each language belongs to a different sub-community (such as a tribe or a caste), and may be the most important evidence of membership in that community. So long as the sub-communities keep separate, they need their languages to stay distinct as well.

We could also quibble about how well these people speak their various languages. Are they totally fluent and 'native-like' in every language? Once again, we simply don't know, but we can be sure that they know them well enough to get by in everyday conversation. Maybe they know more words and constructions in some languages than in others (and doubtless there are some concepts, linked to group cultures, that they can talk about more easily in just one of the languages). And almost certainly they won't be able to read and write all of them—indeed, they may not be able to read and write any of them. But their knowledge of all the languages goes well beyond what we'd call a smattering, and also beyond the stumbling and limited ability reached in most of our schools. Maybe the best way to describe their ability is as 'a good working knowledge'. Moreover, so long as interaction is regular and frequent, these languages are all ready for immediate use—they don't get 'rusty'.

So you and I have inherited brains that could, in principle, hold a good working knowledge of at least five or six completely different languages. The only thing that prevented me from achieving this feat is my social history—the fact that the people round me have always spoken only one language, so I never needed to learn more. Your social life may, of course, have been different from mine—and that may be why you're reading this chapter. If so, rejoice! But the main point is that learning five or six languages is completely within the normal range, and requires no skills other than those we use when we learn our first language in childhood. We are all born as potential polyglots.

What about the world champions, the great and exceptional language learners (for whom I've coined the term 'hyperpolyglot')? This is where Erard is the expert. Most famous among the hyperpolyglots of history was Cardinal Giuseppe Mezzofanti (1774–1849), who claimed to speak 50 languages and to understand 20 more, as well as reading 114. Another nineteenth-century figure, Sir John Bowring, was said to have spoken 100 languages and to have read an additional 100. These people were famous in their day, so we have plenty of independent reports from people such as Lord Byron, who visited Mezzofanti and confirmed his ability in some languages; but it is impossible now to check the extraordinary numbers.

There are real hyperpolyglots walking the earth today, and Erard has succeeded in tracking some of them down. Their language numbers may seem modest—the 20-to-30 range is typical—but unlike Mezzofanti's, they have been verified by reasonably objective tests (such as U.S. government scales of language proficiencies). None of these prodigies can speak all their languages equally easily; typically some languages are always available, some need to be brushed up, and others need the help of a dictionary. But even so, some really do deserve the name 'hyperpolyglot'; for example, an Englishman called Derick Herning told Erard that he knows 30 languages, of which 12 are always available. (In 1990, 22 of these languages were independently certified.)

How do hyperpolyglots do it? Certainly not by leaving it to 'natural' language learning. These are scholars who learn from books and follow strict schedules for learning and practising their languages. They just love learning languages. Do they have a special aptitude? Nobody knows for sure, but I leave you with a fascinating fact: they are nearly all men.

About the author
Richard Hudson is Professor Emeritus of Linguistics in the Department of Phonetics and Linguistics at University College, London, where he worked from 1964 through 2004. He has a B.A. in Modern and Medieval Languages from Cambridge and a Ph.D. from the School of Oriental and African Studies, London, with a thesis on the grammar of the Cushitic language of the Beja (or Bedawie) people in the north-east of the Sudan.

Suggestions for further reading

In this book
Multilingual societies are discussed in Chapters 9 (lingua francas), 21 (language conflict), 58 (Hebrew and Yiddish), and 63 (languages of India); the development of multilingual individuals is discussed in Chapters 15 (babies and language), 17 (language and the brain), 22 (bilinguality), 32 (adult language learning), 33 (advanced adult language learning), and 36 (children and second languages).

Elsewhere
Erard, Michael. *Babel No More: The Search for Extraordinary Language Learners* (Free Press, 2012). A highly readable book that surveys the research, or lack of it.

24

What is 'speaking in tongues'?

Walt Wolfram

What happens when religious people 'speak in tongues'?
Is their speech a real language? What is its relationship to
natural language?

The utterances flowed effortlessly from his mouth: 'La horiya la hariya, la hayneekeechee aleekeechi arateeli haya.' It sounded like poetry in a foreign language, but no one else spoke the language or understood it. That didn't make any difference; the speaker who uttered these words in his private prayers considered them a special language for talking to God. Although it seems esoteric and mysterious to those who encounter it for the first time, 'speaking in tongues', or, more technically, 'glossolalia', is not an uncommon linguistic phenomenon. Millions of English speakers around the world have spoken in tongues and speakers of many other languages have experienced a similar form of linguistic expression. It has a long history in Christianity and in other religions as well, perhaps as long as humans have had language. In Christianity, it has been well documented since the Day of Pentecost, with the last century witnessing a significant revival in its use, especially in so-called holiness churches but also in some more liturgical churches such as Catholic and Anglican congregations.

Glossolalia has also been documented in other religions and in some non-religious practices. For example, practitioners of the

Peyote cult among Native American Indians, shamans exercising witchcraft in Haiti, and Tibetan monks uttering various chants may also use a type of glossolalia. What exactly is it? Is it language? If not, what is its relationship to natural language? And how does it function in religious expression and in society?

Linguists have been studying the structure of glossolalia for some time now using the methods applied to the analysis of natural language. Studies include identifying the sounds, the sequencing of sounds into syllables, and the arrangement of segments into larger units similar to words and syntax in natural language. Glossolalic fluency may range from minimally organized, barely formed grunt-like sounds to highly organized streams of consonants and vowels that sound like highly expressive natural language.

The majority of sounds used in glossolalia come from a person's native language, though some speakers are capable of using other sounds as well. When compared with a speaker's native language, however, the inventory of sounds is restricted in ways that make it somewhat comparable to the speech of young children. For example, if a language has forty significant vowel and consonant sounds, only ten to twenty of those sounds might be used in the glossolalia. And syllables also tend to be somewhat simpler than in natural language, so that alternating sequences of a single consonant and single vowel are repeated. For example, notice how *lahoriya* in the sample alternates between a simple consonant and vowel. Glossolalia may, however, also exhibit traits of expressive or poetic language: rhyming and alliteration are found in some speakers' utterances. Notice, for example, the rhyming in phrases like *la horiya la hariya* or *haneekeechi aleekeechi*.

In some worship traditions within Christianity, after one person utters glossolalia in a public meeting, another person will follow with a prophetic 'interpretation' into a natural language such as English or Spanish. Usually these interpretations reinforce religious themes shared by the group. An analysis of utterances and the interpretations using the techniques of translation theory, however, reveals that such interpretations are not literal translations. There are also reports of knowledgeable audience members recognizing the utterances of glossolalists as particular foreign languages ('xenoglossia'), but recorded documentation of such cases has proven to be elusive.

Linguistically, glossolalia is a kind of 'pseudolanguage'—nonsense syllables of a familiar language that are reminiscent of an earlier, prelanguage babbling stage. While most people stop using nonsense syllables in childhood, once they have acquired a natural language, glossolalists return to a stage in which sounds are used for purposes other than the communication of specific thoughts. Of course, not all adult language users completely give up uttering nonsense syllables. The writer J. R. R. Tolkien had a proclivity for speaking nonsense syllables throughout his life, and some modern music genres (think of 'scat' singing in jazz) are also characterized by the use of nonsense syllables. Speaking in tongues may also be an acquired capability, in which regular practice results in more fluently constructed strings of syllables. Tolkien, for example, apparently practiced his production of nonsense syllables regularly in order to refine the expressive effect of his utterances.

Though some psychologists have connected speaking in tongues with hypnotic trance, hysteria, or even schizophrenia, such assessments seem far too severe and judgmental. In fact, normal, well-adjusted people may speak in tongues in socially specified situations such as personal prayer, religious ritual, or public worship. The religious significance of speaking in tongues lies mostly in its demonstration that in such situations a speaker is able to transcend ordinary speech.

About the author
Although Walt Wolfram is most noted for his research on American dialects, his sociolinguistic career started with the study of speaking in tongues. In the mid-1960s, he conducted one of the first linguistic analyses of glossolalia based on an extensive set of tape recordings of its public and private use. Decades later he still thinks that the collection of naturally occurring samples of glossolalia was the most sensitive fieldwork situation he ever encountered.

Suggestions for further reading

In this book

The topic of how social contexts influence the way languages function and interact is addressed in Chapters 10 (pidgins and creoles), 21 (language conflict), 41 (Cajun), 42 (German in the U.S.), and 43 (Gullah).

Elsewhere

Goodman, Felicitas D. *Speaking in Tongues: A Cross-Cultural Study of Glossolalia* (University of Chicago Press, 1972). A comparison of speaking in tongues in different cultures that explains it as a kind of hypnotic trance. Though this psychological explanation does not hold up, the comparison of glossolalia across cultures is useful.

Nickell, Joe. *Looking for a Miracle: Weeping Icons, Relics, Stigmata, Visions, and Healing Cures* (Prometheus, 1993). A historical, forensic discussion of speaking in tongues along with other kinds of paranormal religious behavior. The focus is on explaining the need for the establishment of supernatural events within Christian religious tradition.

Samarin, William J. *Tongues of Men and Angels: The Religious Language of Pentecostalism* (Macmillan, 1972). Though somewhat dated, this still remains the most comprehensive linguistic description of glossolalia, which is presented as a kind of pseudolanguage comparable to prelanguage babbling.

Samarin, William J. 'Variation and variables in religious glossolalia'. *Language in Society* vol. 1 (1972) pp121–30. A concise, technical linguistic description of glossolalia written primarily for linguists and sociolinguists.

25

What happens if you are raised without language?

Susan Curtiss

Are there really such beings as 'wolf children,' raised without human contact? Can a person raised without language catch up? When is it too late? Is it worse to grow up without hearing or without language?

It is almost impossible for most of us to imagine growing up without language—which develops in our minds so effortlessly in early childhood and plays such a central role in defining us as human and allowing us to participate in our culture. Nevertheless, being deprived of language occasionally happens. In recent centuries children have been found living in the wild, said to have been raised by wolves or other animals and deprived of human contact. It is hard to know the real stories behind these cases, but they are all strikingly similar with respect to language. The pattern is that only those rescued early in childhood developed an ability to speak. Those found after they were about nine years old learned only a few words, or failed to learn language at all.

One of the most famous of these cases is that of Victor, the 'wild boy of Aveyron', immortalized in a film by Francois Truffaut called *The Wild Child* (*L'Enfant Sauvage*). Victor was captured in 1800, when he was about ten or eleven. He was studied by a young physician named Jacques Itard, who creatively and painstakingly tried to teach him to speak, read and write. But despite Itard's best efforts (many of which became the foundation of the Montessori Method for teaching), Victor never learned to speak; he learned to read and print only a small set of words.

We also know cases in which children grew up in social or linguistic isolation because of tragic family circumstances. One of the best-known of these is the case of Genie, whose childhood was one of extreme neglect, deprivation and abuse. For over twelve years, her father shut her away in a small bedroom, tied with a harness to an infant potty seat. When her blind mother finally escaped with Genie in the early 1970s and applied for welfare, the police intervened, and Genie was put in the rehabilitation ward of a children's hospital. She was thirteen and a half years old and knew no language.

Genie was studied by linguists for almost a decade. She was of normal intelligence; she rapidly learned words within a few months after her discovery, and soon began to combine them. However, she did not use grammatical elements like tense or agreement markers, articles, pronouns, or question words—the pieces of English that turn a string of words into grammatical speech. Most of her linguistic development consisted of learning more words and stringing them together into longer, semantically coherent utterances. In context, she could make herself understood. Her speech did not stick to standard English subject–verb–object word order, but she performed well on word order comprehension tests: she differentiated sentences like 'The girl is pushing the boy' from 'The boy is pushing the girl', showing that she understood more than she could produce. Even after many years, however, she developed little knowledge of grammar. Interestingly, Genie was a powerful *non-verbal* communicator, providing strong evidence that language is not the same as communication.

Children without hearing are not as handicapped as Genie was. A deaf child can still have language and relate normally to others through signing—as long as language development starts early. There are a number of studies that show that the sooner a deaf child is exposed to a natural sign language, such as American Sign Language, the more proficient a signer he or she will become. As in other cases of linguistic isolation, the ability of deaf people to learn new *words* is not affected by the age at which they are exposed to language. But their ability to learn grammar is dramatically affected. Studies of deaf children first exposed to sign language after the pre-school years show that there is a critical window for grammatical development, which ends, perhaps, in the early school-age years.

Exciting recent evidence that a child brings something unique and necessary to language development comes from the creation of a new sign language in Nicaragua. After the Sandinista movement came to power there in 1979, for the first time deaf teenagers and adults had the opportunity to form a Deaf* community. This first generation created a rudimentary system of gestures for communication. But when young children, under the age of ten, joined this community, they transformed this system into a real language, embodying the structural elements and characteristics that define all human grammars. Over a very few years, that language has become increasingly rich and complex grammatically.

People without hearing are typically normal and grow up in caring social environments that allow them to lead full lives. This is especially true for those who become part of culturally Deaf communities and learn to communicate in sign. Hearing people who are raised without language, on the other hand, typically grow up with no social community, in circumstances that have profound, negative psychosocial effects. Therefore, while growing up without hearing poses many difficulties in life, growing up without *language* is significantly worse. Language is so central to being human that lacking it can mean a lifetime of social deprivation and isolation.

About the author

Susan Curtiss is Professor of Linguistics at UCLA. She is the author of *Genie: A Psycholinguistic Study of a Modern-Day 'Wild Child'*, as well as of close to one hundred journal articles and book chapters. She has

---

* 'Deaf' with a capital D indicates some connection to Deaf culture and idenity; 'deaf' with a small d refers to hearing loss not connected to Deaf identiy.

also authored numerous language tests, including the Curtiss-Yamada Comprehensive Language Evaluation (the CYCLE), used by researchers across the U.S. and overseas. Her research spans the study of language and mind, the 'critical period' for first language acquisition, Specific Language Impairment, mental retardation, adult aphasia, progressive dementia, and the genetics of language. Her current work focuses on language development following hemispherectomy (removal of one hemisphere of the brain) in childhood.

Suggestions for further reading

In this book
Other chapters discussing language acquisition by children include 10 (pidgins and creoles), 15 (babies and language), 17 (language and the brain), 26 (sign languages), and 36 (children and second languages). The importance of grammar as a part of full language capability is discussed in Chapters 13 (grammar in general), 14 (universal grammar), and 16 (animal communication).

Elsewhere
Curtiss, S. *Genie: A Psycholinguistic Study of a Modern-Day 'Wild Child'* (Academic Press, 1977. A fascinating account of Curtiss's experiences and research with Genie and the implications of this work.

Lane, H. *The Wild Boy of Aveyron*. (Harvard University Press, 1976). A rich, very readable description of the case of 'Victor' and the issues his case raises.

Newport, E. L. 'Maturational Constraints on language learning', in *Cognitive Science* vol. 14 (1990). Describes research on the effects of age on the acquisition of the grammar of American Sign Language (ASL) by Deaf individuals who were exposed to ASL at different ages, some not until adulthood.

Senghas, R. J., A. Senghas, and J. E. Pyers. 'The emergence of Nicaraguan Sign Language: Questions of development, acquisition, and evolution', in J. Langer, S. T. Parker, and C. Milbrath, eds., *Biology and Knowledge Revisited: From Neurogenesis to Psychogenesis* (Lawrence Erlbaum Associates, 2006). Describes the emergence of a brand-new sign language in Nicaragua and the special properties young children bring to language learning.

26

Do Deaf people everywhere use the same sign language?

Leila Monaghan

Is sign language really a language? Can you use it no matter what country you go to?

There are two widespread myths about sign languages. One is that they aren't languages at all. The second is that signing is a *universal* language—that any signer can understand all signers anywhere in the world. Both of these beliefs are false.

It's easy to understand why you might doubt sign languages are really languages—they're so different from what we often call 'tongues'. They have to be seen rather than heard. And some signs look like what they represent, making them easy to dismiss as mere gestures. But that view was refuted in 1960 when William Stokoe published the first scientific description of American Sign Language (ASL). Stokoe was an English professor at Gallaudet University (the world's only liberal arts university for Deaf* people) and found the language being used around him as systematic and as grammatical as any other language. He showed that (except for sound) sign languages have all the linguistic features that spoken languages have.

---

* See footnote on page 112.

A word in spoken language, of course, is composed of sounds, made with your mouth and tongue. In ASL, the components of a word can include how you shape your hand, where you place it, and how you move it. For example, the signs for APPLE and CANDY are made at the same place, by the side of the mouth, but their handshapes are different: APPLE is made with a crooked index finger while CANDY is made with a straight index finger. Sign languages have complex grammars, so that words can be strung together into sentences, and sentences into stories. With signs you can discuss any topic, from concrete to abstract, from street slang to physics. And if you have any doubt, think about public events you've seen recently. After watching a signer interpret a political speech or a play, could anyone still believe it's not a language?

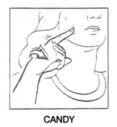 

CANDY   APPLE

As for the second myth, people often don't realize that sign languages vary, just as spoken languages do. Whenever groups of people are separated by time and space, separate languages, or at least separate dialects, develop. This is as true for sign as it is for spoken languages: there are, for example, differing dialects of ASL. Like spoken English, it varies both geographically and across social groups. And the variations in sign language are even more evident internationally. The signs used in Italy aren't readily understood by a signer using ASL, and vice versa. Even languages that you might think are connected may or may not actually be. British Sign Language and American Sign Language, for example, are unrelated to each other, despite the fact that the two countries share English as their spoken language: the histories of the British and American Deaf communities are separate. American Sign

Language is actually related to French Sign Language because Laurent Clerc, a Deaf Frenchman, helped start many of the earliest schools for deaf children in the United States. Although some signs in all sign languages are iconic (they look like the object they are representing), even iconic signs can differ. In ASL, the sign TREE is made by holding up a single hand with fingers spread. The Danish version is done by tracing the outline of a tree with both palms. Both signs are based on the same image, a classic leafy tree, but they look quite different.

American Sign Language   Danish Sign Language

Whenever people can see each other but are somehow prevented from communicating with speech or writing, they turn to signing of some kind. Think about monks who have taken vows of silence but need to cooperate on monastery business, or widows from certain Australian Aboriginal groups, who are expected not to speak during a long period of mourning. In cases like these, the sign languages developed reflect the grammar of the languages the monks or widows knew and could speak if they chose. But those are exceptions. Most sign languages are *not* based on the spoken language in the culture around them.

There are millions of sign language users around the world. For example, there are at least a half-million users of ASL in the U.S., and possibly as many as two million. It's routinely taught in schools across the country, and all 50 states recognize it in some way. At the last count, there were 147 colleges and universities whose language requirement could be satisfied by the study of ASL. In Britain, there are estimated to be around 370,000 sign language users; and on March 18, 2003, the U.K. government officially recognized BSL as an official British Language.

Sign language is remarkable for its ability to express everything spoken language does, using completely different human capabilities. According to Hearing people who have learned it, communicating in sign opens a window to a different culture and can give you a totally different perspective—especially an understanding of how Deaf people perceive the world. So the next time you think about learning a new language, think about learning how to sign.

About the author

Leila Monaghan teaches Anthropology and Disability Studies at the University of Wyoming and the University of Maryland, University College. She received her Ph.D. in linguistic anthropology at the University of California, Los Angeles and her dissertation work was with the New Zealand Deaf community. Her other publications include the co-edited book *Many Ways to be Deaf* (2003), a 2002 *Annual Review of Anthropology* article on Deaf communities with Richard Senghas, and *HIV/AIDS and Deafness* (co-edited with Constanze Schmaling, 2006). She also does research on the history of linguistic anthropology.

Suggestions for further reading

In this book

Languages designed by their users are discussed in Chapters 64 (Esperanto) and 65 (artificial languages in general). Other chapters discussing language acquisition by children include 10 (pidgins and creoles), 15 (babies and language), 17 (language and the brain), 25 (language deprivation), and 36 (children and second languages).

Elsewhere

Klima, Edward and Ursula Bellugi. *Signs of Language* (Harvard University Press, 1979). Classic and very readable introduction to sign language linguistics.

LeMaster, Barbara and Leila Monaghan. 'Sign languages', in A. Duranti, ed., *A Companion to Linguistic Anthropology* (Blackwell, 2004) Introduction to the study of sign languages and Deaf communities in linguistic anthropology and sociolinguistics. Both disciplines look at the interaction between language and culture rather than just at languages themselves.

Mathur, Gaurav and Donna Jo Napoli. *Deaf Around the World* (Oxford University Press, 2011). Latest on issues in sign language linguistics and Deaf civil rights issues from an international group of Deaf and hearing scholars and activists.

Monaghan, Leila, Constanze Schmaling, Karen Nakamura, and Graham H. Turner. eds. *Many Ways to be Deaf* (Gallaudet University Press, 2004). A collection of fifteen articles from fourteen countries on the history, culture and language of local Deaf communities. Includes a brief overview of five hundred years of Deaf history.

Padden, Carol and Tom Humphries. *Inside Deaf Culture* (Harvard University Press, 2005). Two of the United States' foremost experts on Deaf Culture. Interesting and accessible.

In addition, the following interesting websites offer sign language resources:

http://library.gallaudet.edu

www.aslpro.com/cgi-bin/aslpro/aslpro.cgi

www.deaflibrary.org/asl.html

http://bda.org.uk

www.sign-lang.uni-hamburg.de/bibweb

www.signpostbsl.com

27

Why do languages die?

Christopher Moseley

What do we mean when we speak of a language 'dying'?
How does it happen? Can it be predicted? Can it be prevented?

This is not a happy subject. For those of us who love languages, it's terrible to see that they're dying at a very rapid rate. About half the world's languages have fewer than ten thousand speakers—about enough to fill a small-town football stadium—and some are down to only a handful. When those last speakers die, the language dies too. Some experts think that nearly 90 percent of the languages spoken in the world today, including even some that still have millions of speakers, may be lost by the end of this century.

Why do languages disappear? The short answer is that they are no longer passed on to younger speakers, and eventually only the elderly speakers are left to die out. But what would make a community no longer want to pass on its spoken heritage to the younger generation? The circumstances vary from place to place. Let's look at some examples. In the mountains of India we can find—if we hurry—the Sulung people, now down to only a few thousand, who've been driven to a remote area by constant warfare with neighboring tribes. If they're wiped out by their enemies, their language will vanish. Wars destroy more than people.

You might ask, can there be any new languages left to discover? Surprisingly, yes. A few have recently come to light when previously uncontacted peoples were found in isolated places. In 1991, for instance, a previously uncontacted language known as Gongduk was discovered in the Himalayas. For linguists, this was like finding the fabled lost valley of Shangri-La. And in the deep Brazilian interior there are still languages being discovered, some of them apparently unrelated to any other known tongue. But stories like that are rare. The overwhelming trend is in the direction of extinction.

For the most part, geographical barriers—high mountains, steep valleys, lack of infrastructure or roads—afford little protection, not even in the far corners of the earth. Think about the speakers of Rapanui, on Easter Island in the Pacific. After a millennium and a half of separation from the world, in the nineteenth century they were taken from their island as slaves to collect guano from the coast of South America. Very few came back; today there are just a few thousand people who have kept Rapanui alive in the face of Spanish, imported from Chile.

Thirty years ago in Brazil, ranchers and illegal timber cutters drove the Jiahui people out of their traditional lands into the hands of hostile neighbors. The few that were left joined a less hostile group or drifted to the cities. Now the Jiahui have reclaimed some of their lands, but how many of them are left? Just fifty.

Or what about the Rikbatsá people in Brazil's Mato Grosso state? They were great warriors, but they couldn't fight epidemics of influenza and smallpox that were brought by Jesuit missionaries. Diseases imported from Europe decimated them and dozens of other native peoples of the Americas—and with them their native tongues.

And if human invasions aren't bad enough, nature itself can swallow up languages. In 1998 a terrible tsunami struck the north coast of Papua New Guinea, killing nearly all the speakers of the Warapu and Sissano languages. Just a few who weren't home at the time are the only ones left to keep the languages alive.

Finally, so-called 'killer languages'—like English or Spanish— are so dominant that people may *voluntarily* give up their mother tongue—for convenience or economic reasons. Indigenous peoples sometimes abandon their language to overcome discrimination, or fit into a majority culture. As children stop learning them, the languages slowly wither away.

Why should we care? Because with the loss of a language comes the loss of inherited knowledge, an entire thought-world. I've often heard it compared to losing a natural resource or an animal species. Yes, linguists have ways of reconstructing an extinct language from surviving evidence, but what that leaves us with is not much more than words on paper. We can't bring back from the dead a society that spoke the language, or the heritage and culture behind it. Once a language is gone, it's gone forever. The best cure for endangerment is to put self-confidence back into the minds of the speakers—by encouraging education and literacy from an early age.

It's only in the past couple of decades that the urgency of the question of language extermination worldwide has been realized. Organizations have been set up to do what they can to preserve language diversity. There are the U.S.-based Terralingua and the U.K.-based Foundation for Endangered Languages, both dedicated to encouraging and supporting research into threatened languages and their maintenance; there is the UNESCO Endangered Languages Project; and recently a department for endangered languages was set up at the University of London.

About the author

Christopher Moseley (Chrismoseley50@yahoo.com) is a university lecturer, writer, and freelance translator, editor of the *Encyclopedia of the World's Endangered Languages* (2006), and co-editor of the *Atlas of the World's Languages* (1993). In 2009 he edited the third edition of the UNESCO *Atlas of the World's Languages in Danger*. He has a special interest in artificial languages (and has created one himself).

Suggestions for further reading

In this book

The topic of how languages become extinct (or escape extinction) is discussed in Chapters 3 (languages of the world), 28 (language rescue), 44 (U.S. dialect change), and 53 (Latin).

Elsewhere

Nettle, Daniel and Suzanne Romaine. *Vanishing Voices* (Oxford University Press, 2000). A serious and thoughtful study of the problems, causes and effects of language endangerment all over the world, relating the issue to biological diversity.

Crystal, David. *Language Death* (Cambridge University Press, 2000). An impassioned plea on behalf of the world's smaller languages, full of interesting anecdotal information about the treasures we are losing.

Evans, Nicholas. *Dying Words: Endangered Languages and What They Have to Tell Us* (Wiley-Blackwell, 2010). A fascinating tour through some of the world's more obscure language communities, living, dead and half-dead, explaining what exactly is lost from human expression in each language that dies.

Abley, Mark. *Spoken Here: Travels among Threatened Languages* (Heinemann, 2004). A personal travelogue of the author's visits to some of the world's smallest language communities to see how they are faring in the modern globalized community.

Ostler, Nicholas. *Empires of the Word* (HarperCollins, 2005). Takes a sweeping overview of the world's recorded history from the point of view of the big victorious languages—the other end of the telescope—and shows how successive empires have spread their 'international languages' all over the known world. English is just the latest in a long line of conquerors.

28

Can a threatened language be saved?

Akira Y. Yamamoto, Marcellino Berardo,
Tracy Hirata-Edds, Mary S. Linn, Lizette Peter,
Gloria Sly, Tracy Williams, and
Kimiko Y. Yamamoto

*Can threatened or dying languages be revived? What skills
and resources does language revitalization require? Is it worth
the effort?*

Languages, like nations, wax and wane. Some survive by evolving
into forms unrecognizable by earlier speakers, but none last forever
unchanged. When the number of people able to teach a language,
or willing to learn it, gets too small, the language dies. Many of the
world's languages today are like the rare and beautiful whooping
cranes—hanging on for dear life. Saving these languages takes a
great deal of work, but it can be done.

Take Cherokee: in the past four decades, the number of children acquiring it as a first language has declined so sharply that it
could disappear in just another generation. But here is a scene that
provides hope: on a colorful carpet in a preschool classroom in
Tahlequah, Oklahoma, three- and four-year-old children are sitting
with their teachers, reading together from a picture book. It looks
like a typical preschool anywhere—but the book is in Cherokee,
and Cherokee is the only language used in the classroom. The hope

is that by the time they reach sixth grade, these children will be fluent enough in their ancestral tongue to become a new generation of Cherokee speakers. And they are well on their way.

Similar intensive programs—from infant day care through high school classes—are achieving success among the Mohawk people in New York State and Canada, the Blackfoot in Montana, the Arapaho in Wyoming, the Hawaiians, and in other Native American communities. In 2010, organizations in four states joined to form the Consortium of Indigenous Language Organizations, which will train teachers and language advocates in language immersion planning and practices.

Another challenge these programs have to overcome is the 'exposure problem': simply put, you can't learn a language well if you don't hear it, see it, or feel it, and live your life through it. In endangered language communities, learners do not get enough exposure to their ancestral languages to become fluent in them. Successful revitalization programs have found both traditional and innovative solutions to this problem. Gaelic (being revitalized in Ireland), Maori (made an official language of New Zealand in 1987), and Hebrew (used only for religious purposes for centuries before being revived to become the official language of Israel) are examples of such successes.

It has taken the world a long time to realize the value of sustaining languages, but within the past thirty years, language revitalization has become an international movement. The idea has been embraced by the U.S. (through the Native American Languages Acts of 1990 and 1992), UNESCO, and organizations like the Endangered Language Fund, the Foundation for Endangered Languages, and The Hans Rausing Endangered Languages Project of the School of Oriental and African Studies. In Africa, literature on AIDS is being used to teach literacy in local languages. In the Amazon rain forest, the Yanomami people are learning about hygiene through literature printed in their tribal language. Teachers in Siberia are being trained by Russian and Dutch linguists to teach local languages to children.

Where there is any willingness to keep their endangered language alive, language community members, linguists, and educators are working to document, describe, and use it. In communities with only a few elderly speakers left, young language learners are spending time with their elders, doing everyday chores in the language so that they too can become speakers. And in places where the languages have not been spoken for years, language researchers and practitioners of the language communities are using archives and oral histories to revive them, just as spoken Hebrew was revived from scriptures and rituals. In California, Oklahoma, and elsewhere in the U.S., 'Breath of Life' workshops train community language researchers and practitioners to locate, read, hear, and interpret archived documents and recordings, and to use them for language revitalization work. Preservation efforts extend even to cross-cultural forms of speech like Gullah, a creole that combines English and west African linguistic elements and is spoken on the coasts of Georgia and South Carolina. Indigenous languages are being taught in colleges and universities in Arizona, Hawai'i, Kansas, New Mexico, Oklahoma, and Oregon. The language revitalization movement is growing, and it is our best hope to stem the loss of languages.

Linguist Ken Hale has compared the loss of a language to 'dropping a bomb on a museum.' It destroys a culture, intellectual wealth, and works of art. It is a sobering thought that most of the languages alive today may not live to see the next century. This is why we need to care for the ones that are threatened ... as if they were whooping cranes.

About the authors

Akira Y. Yamamoto (Professor Emeritus at Kansas University) has been active in bringing together language communities and professional communities for language and culture revitalization programs. Marcellino Berardo (Applied English Center, KU) has been active in language revitalization programs in the U.S. Midwest; his specialties include language description, social aspects of language learning, and second language pedagogy. Tracy Hirata-Edds (Applied English Center, KU) has been working with the Cherokee Nation's revitalization efforts, along with teaching revitalization workshops through the Oklahoma Native Language Association. Mary S. Linn (Anthropology, University of Oklahoma; Sam Noble Oklahoma Museum of Natural History) works with native language teachers and programs in Oklahoma; as curator of native languages, she is building a language resource collection and revitalization programming in collaboration with Oklahoma tribes. Lizette Peter (Department of Curriculum and Teaching, KU) is an associate professor of second language acquisition and serves as an advisor to the Cherokee Nation on several of their language initiatives. Gloria Sly (Tsalagi Culture Center Director, Cherokee Nation, Oklahoma) has initiated and guided various language programs of the Cherokee Nation. Tracy Williams (Oneida Language Revitalization Program Director, Oneida Nation of Wisconsin and doctoral student, University of Arizona) has been engaged in revitalizing her language, Oneida, and is currently pursuing a doctoral degree in indigenous language education. Kimiko Y. Yamamoto (Professor Emerita, KU) works with Native educators in developing literature.

Suggestions for further reading

In this book
Language extinction and rescue are discussed from various angles in Chapters 3 (languages of the world), 27 (language death), 44 (U.S. dialect change), 53 (Latin), and 58 (the revival of Hebrew). Also of possible interest is Chapter 52 (Native American languages).

Elsewhere
Hale, Ken and Leanne Hinton, eds. *The Green Book of Language Revitalization in Practice* (Academic Press, 2001). An inspiring book full of immediately usable examples of language revitalization programs. This is the starter book for anyone interested in language revitalization.

Hinton, Leanne. *How to Keep Your Language Alive: A Commonsense Approach to One-on-One Language Learning* (Heyday Press, 2002). A delightfully useful handbook about nurturing new speakers of severely endangered languages.

Nettle, Daniel and Suzanne Romaine. *Vanishing Voices: The Extinction of the World's Languages* (Oxford University Press, 2002). Readable and comprehensive, this book covers the causes and effects of language extinction throughout the world.

Here is a selection of potentially useful websites:

http://portal.unesco.org/culture. UNESCO (see 'Intangible Cultural Heritage').

www.endangeredlanguagefund.org. The Endangered Language Fund.

www.ogmios.org. The Foundation for Endangered Languages.

www.hrelp.org. The Hans Rausing Endangered Languages Project of the School of Oriental and African Studies.

29

How are the sounds of language made?

Peter Ladefoged

What kind of sounds make up languages? Do all languages have consonants and vowels? Do they all have the same ones?

Everyone knows that when you talk you use your tongue and lips. You probably also know that speech sounds often involve the action of the vocal cords—nowadays more usually called vocal folds, as they are two thin folds of muscle in the throat that vibrate when air is blown between them. To get the vocal folds to vibrate you have to push air out of your lungs. To talk, we then move parts of the vocal tract and, in various ways, alter its shape to produce consonants and vowels. Here are some examples of how it all works.

The lips are used to make the consonants at the beginning of the English words *pea, bee, me*. In the *p* sound, pressure is built up behind the closed lips. The vocal folds do not vibrate and there is usually a little puff of air (called aspiration) when the lips open and before any following vowel begins. This puff of air is missing when you say *b*, and there may even be some voicing (vocal fold vibration) while the lips are closed. There is always voicing during the lip closure for *m* in which the air comes out through the nose.

The English consonants *t, d, n* and *k, g, ng* are pronounced in ways similar to *p, b, m*, except that for *t, d, n* the air is stopped from flowing out of the mouth by raising the tip of the tongue to form a closure just behind the teeth; and for *k, g, ng* the closure is made by raising the back of the tongue to contact the soft palate, the fleshy part at the back of the roof of the mouth. Other consonant sounds, such as those in the words *fie, thigh, sigh, shy*, don't have a complete closure stopping air from flowing out of the mouth but are produced by forming a narrow gap through which the air hisses and hushes as it escapes. In these sounds the vocal folds are not vibrating. There is, however, another set of fricative sounds in which there *is* voicing, as in the sounds at the ends of the words *move, smooth, ooze, rouge*.

Most forms of English have twenty-two consonant sounds and anywhere from thirteen to twenty-one different vowel sounds. You can hear many of the different vowel sounds between the consonants *b* and *d* in the words *bead, bid, bayed, bed, bad, bawd, booed, bide, bowed, bode, Boyd, bud, bird*. It is very difficult to make accurate descriptions of vowels in terms of their tongue and lip positions, but they can easily be specified in terms of their acoustic overtones.

So how do languages differ with respect to the sounds they use? All spoken languages have consonants and vowels, but the sounds of the world's languages vary so extensively that altogether they may have as many as six hundred different consonant sounds and two hundred different vowels as modified by different pitches and voice qualities.

Sounds like *p, t, k* occur in 98 percent of all the languages in the world. Hawaiian is one of the languages that does not have all three; it lacks *t*. Interestingly, Hawaiian has only eight consonants, *p, k, m, n, w, l, h*, and a glottal stop (a closure of the vocal folds), written with an apostrophe, as in the word *Hawai'i*.

Other languages have consonants that don't occur in English. Spanish and Italian, for example, have trilled *r* sounds. Trills made with the lips occur in a number of small, endangered languages such as Melpa and Kele in Papua New Guinea. Lip trills preceded by a special kind of *t* occur in Oro Win, a language spoken by only half a dozen people living near the border between Brazil and Bolivia. American Indian languages have a wealth of sounds not found in English, sometimes including long strings of complex consonants. In Montana Salish the word for 'wood tick' in an English spelling would be something like *chchtsʼelshchen.*

The only speech sounds that can be made without using air from the lungs are the clicks that occur in languages spoken in central and southern Africa. These sounds are made by sucking air into your mouth, much as you might do when dropping a kiss on your grandmother's cheek. A language called !Xóõ, spoken in the Kalahari Desert, has eighty-three different ways of beginning a word with a click sound. Zulu, a more well-known language, spoken in South Africa, has three basic clicks, each of which has five variants.

Where European languages stand out is in their number of vowels. French has vowels, not found in English, in which the lips are rounded while the tongue is in the position for the English words *tea* and *day,* forming the French words *tu* 'you' and *deux* 'two'. The largest number of vowels occur in Dutch and German dialects.

It falls to phoneticians to be concerned with describing the sounds of the world's languages: what sounds there are, how they fall into patterns, and how they change in different circumstances. Because there are so many languages and dialects, because the vocal apparatus can produce such a wide variety of sounds, and because each of us has a different way of speaking our own language, it is an infinitely challenging task—and one of the most fascinating aspects of the study of language.

About the author
Peter Ladefoged, Professor of Phonetics Emeritus at UCLA, was the world's foremost linguistic phonetician and one of the most important figures in linguistics in the twentieth century. He published 10 books and 130 scholarly articles on various aspects of the theory and practice of phonetics and the phonetic properties of specific languages. The essay above was one of the last pieces he wrote before his death in early 2006.

Suggestions for further reading

In this book

Other chapters that talk about the sounds of language include 30 (U.S. Southern English), 31 (foreign accents), 52 (Native American languages), 56 (Russian), 59 (Arabic), 60 (African languages), and 61 (Chinese).

Elsewhere

Ladefoged, Peter. *A Course in Phonetics* (Harcourt Brace, 1975; fifth edition, Thomson/Wadsworth 2006). The standard textbook in the field, which has been used to train generations of linguists.

Maddieson, Ian. *Patterns of Sounds* (Cambridge University Press, 1984). A useful reference text that describes the distribution of sounds in more than three hundred languages of the world. Readers can look up a sound and find which languages contain it, or they can look up a language and find its particular phonetic inventory.

International Phonetic Association. *Handbook of the International Phonetic Association* (Cambridge University Press, 1999). A comprehensive guide to the phonetic alphabet used by linguists all over the world. The principles of phonetic analysis are described and examples of each phonetic symbol are given.

Some of the sounds of the hundreds of languages Dr. Ladefoged studied can be heard at www.phonetics.ucla.edu.

30

Why do American Southerners talk that way?

Walt Wolfram

Do all Southerners have the same dialect? What are the ingredients of the way they talk? Where did their speech come from?

No dialect in the U.S. is more noticed—and commented on—than Southern English. This is where a person *totes* objects, but *carries* friends to see a *show*. And where else do we *cut on* the lights and *mash the button* on a machine? To quote the title of a recent book on Southern terms, *Y'all is Spoken Here.*

But is the South really united linguistically? Try telling people from the Carolinas or Virginia that they all talk alike. Along the coast, people speak some of the most distinctive English dialects used anywhere. Someone on the Outer Banks of North Carolina or the Eastern Shore of Virginia may say *It's hoi toid on the saned soid.* That's *high tide on the Sound side* for those who don't recognize the vowel sounds of the coast—or *hah tahd on the sound sahd* in the mainland South.

Traditional Charleston, South Carolina speech seems to have a vowel system all its own. The pronunciation of the vowel in *so* and *row* sounds like the /o/ of French or Spanish (which does not glide into an 'oo' ending as the 'o' sounds of most other English dialects do), and *out* and *about* sound like the Canadian *oat* and *aboat.* Travel to the Sea Islands and you find Gullah—a creole language, also known as Geechee, that goes back to the days of rice plantations populated largely by blacks from Africa and the West Indies. The sounds and rhythms of Gullah are popularized in the *B'rer Rabbit* stories and in George Gershwin's opera *Porgy and Bess*. This variety of English is closer to the creoles of the Bahamas and Jamaica than to dialects of the Southern mainland.

Travel to the western parts of Virginia, the Carolinas, and Georgia, and you'll find the imprint of the Scotch Irish and Germans who migrated west and south from Philadelphia and settled in the southern mountains. The topography of those mountains channeled the various European settlement groups in ways that contributed to the diversity of the South. In the Smoky Mountains, you might be greeted with *Hit's nice to see you'uns*. The plural form *you'uns* is, of course equivalent to the infamous, widespread Southern *y'all* . And *hit* for 'it' is a relic of an older English pronunciation. This is where a *boomer* is a red squirrel—not a thundershower as in other parts of the South. In the mountains, something not quite plumb is described as *si-gogglin'* (pronounced *SIGH-guhg-lin*); other Southerners may say *catawampus* or *whopperjawed* instead. And older mountain people may still call a soft drink *dope*, thanks to some of its original ingredients.

Now add the sounds of African Americans in the Piedmont and Coastal Plain to the mix. And don't forget the unique dialects of Native American groups like the Lumbee Indians along the North and South Carolina border. With over fifty-five thousand members, the Lumbees are the largest group of Native Americans east of the Mississippi. While they no longer maintain a Native American Indian language, their dialect is ethnically distinct from those of their neighbors, both white and black. Put all these voices together and you have dialect differences greater than those in just about any other region of the United States.

Why such diversity? First, there's the so-called 'founder effect'. Groups of speakers came from different parts of the world and left their imprints on the speech of the region—the Scotch Irish influence in Appalachia, a Scots flavor in dialects of the Cape Fear valley; speech patterns from Southwestern England in the Outer Banks; and, of course, the African influence on the Sea Islands.

But there's also a cultural aspect. Children of antebellum Southern aristocrats were sent to England for a proper education. There they found and brought home a brand of English in which *r* sounds at the end of syllables (like *four, fear,* or *fair*) had gone silent around the seventeenth century. Meanwhile, African-origin words like *tote* for 'carry', *goober* for 'peanut', and *cooter* for 'turtle' were arriving in Southern English through the Charleston port. The result was an ironic mixture of African slave language and prestigious British pronunciation.

Given all these tendencies toward diversity, is there really one Southern dialect? Well, in fact there are some pronunciation, grammar, and vocabulary features that seem to flourish throughout the American South. Pronunciations like *tahm* for 'time', *pin* for 'pen', and *bewt* for 'boot' are spread throughout the Southern mainland, as are distinctive grammar patterns like double modals (*I might could be there tonight*), the intentional form *fixin'* to (*I'm fixin' to leave in a minute*), and the avertive *liketa* (*I was so scared I liketa died*). Also widespread throughout the region are vocabulary items mentioned above, like *y'all* for the second person plural, *carry* for 'take', *tote* for 'carry', and *cut off/on* for 'turn off/on', as well as *co-cola* for 'carbonated drink', *poke* for 'bag', and intensifying *plumb* (as in *We were plumb tuckered out*).

Surprisingly, researchers are discovering that many of those distinctive features—like the *pin/pen* sound merger, and even the stereotypically Southern *y'all*—are relatively new. They were barely present in the antebellum South; their development since the Civil War parallels the growing cultural, political, and ideological separation of South from North. Over the past hundred and fifty years, this dialect germinated on its own, took root, and spread through the South like a linguistic kudzu.

About the author
Walt Wolfram, William C. Friday Distinguished Professor of English Linguistics at North Carolina State University, describes himself as a

dialect nomad. He has studied dialects ranging from African American varieties in large metropolitan areas to the speech of small, isolated island and mountain communities. He has authored more than twenty books and three hundred articles, in addition to producing a number of TV documentaries. More information on Dr. Wolfram's media productions is available at www.talkingnc.com and www.ncsu.edu/linguistics.

Suggestions for further reading

In this book
Dialects are discussed in Chapters 4 (dialects versus languages), 20 (British, American, and other versions of English), and 44 (U.S. dialect change). Various languages of America are discussed in Chapters 28 (rescuing threatened Native American languages), 38 (U.S. language survey), 39 (America's language crisis), 40 (New World Spanish), 41 (Cajun), 42 (German in the U.S.), 43 (Gullah), and 52 (Native American languages).

Elsewhere
Bernstein, Cynthia, Tom Nunnally, and Robin Sabino, eds. *Language Variety in the South Revisited* (University of Alabama Press, 1997). A collection of articles from a decennial conference dedicated to the study of language in the American South.

Nagle, Steven and Sara Sanders. eds. *Language in the New South* (Cambridge University Press, 2003). An anthology on different dialects of the American South, including regional and ethnic varieties. Important overviews of major Southern dialects are included.

Wolfram, Walt and Ben Ward, eds. *American Voices: How Dialects Differ from Coast to Coast* (Blackwell, 2006). A major section in this collection of brief, popular profiles of dialects in North America and the Caribbean is dedicated to the American South. The sections on sociocultural dialects and island dialects also include some Southern dialects.

31

What causes foreign accents?

Steven H. Weinberger

Where do foreign accents come from? What makes one foreign accent different from another? Can you learn to speak a foreign language without an accent?

Foreign accents have been around for as long as humans have had language. The Hebrew Bible tells a story about how the Gileadites destroyed the infiltrating army of their enemy, the Ephraimites: they set up roadblocks and made each man who approached them say the Gileadite word 'shibboleth'. The Ephraimites couldn't pronounce the 'sh' sound, so when they said the word it came out 'sibboleth'—and the Gileadites killed them on the spot.

The consequences aren't often that dramatic, but we're all experts at detecting things about people from the way they talk. Not only do we often make immediate biased judgments about a person simply based upon their accent, but even on the phone we know a person's sex, approximate age—even whether he or she is smiling. And like the Gileadites, we usually know right away whether the person is a native speaker of our language.

For example, if you heard a recording of someone saying a sentence including the words 'zeeze seengs', you might be able to recognize that the speaker meant 'these things', but you'd certainly know that she was a foreigner. You'd draw a similar conclusion if you heard a different voice say 'deeza tings'.

What is it about the speech of these two people that would let you immediately recognize them as non-native English speakers? And why would their accents be different from each other? While many factors influence foreign accents, much of the answer lies in something linguists call 'language transfer'. When you first learn a new language, you'd like to sound like a native, but you unavoidably carry over, or transfer, some of the characteristics of your own language to it.

The 'zeeze seengs' speaker, for example, wants to say *these things*, but her native language (which happens to be French) doesn't have the 'th' sounds of English, so she uses the closest approximations to them that she can find in her inventory of French sounds: a 'z' for the voiced 'th' of *these* and an 's' for the unvoiced 'th' of *things*. Another English sound missing from the French inventory is the short 'i' vowel of *things*, so native French speakers will tend to replace it with the nearest handy sound, the long 'ee': 'zeeze seengs'.

The 'deeza tings' speaker has similar difficulties, but he's attempting the English phrase under the influence of his own native language (which happens to be Italian). He doesn't have the problem the French speaker has with the short 'i' vowel of English, but he, too, lacks our voiced and unvoiced 'th' sounds; he substitutes a 'd' and a 't' for them instead of the 'z' and 's' the French speaker used. He also seems to avoid ending a word with a consonant—English has lots of final 'p', 't', 'k', 'b', 'd', 'g', 'f', 's', 'v', 'z' sounds, but Italian does not—so he tends to tack a little neutral vowel after some English final consonants: 'deeza tings'.

It's the ability to recognize and reproduce these features of language transfer that enable professional actors to portray foreign speakers of English convincingly, and sometimes for comic effect. Think of Chico Marx portraying an Italian aviator or Peter Sellers transforming himself into the incomparable Inspector Clouseau. Each of them filters his English through a foreign sound inventory, exaggerates a bit, and the results are humorous.

Does this mean that when foreigners speak English—and when we try to speak foreign languages—we're doomed to sound like comic caricatures forever? Of course not. While we may initially start out a little like that, language learners can, with a bit of practice, pronounce a second language well enough to be understood without comic effect.

Can we ever sound just like native speakers? Well, almost. Professional linguists say that people who start learning a new language after what's called the *Critical Period* (early childhood) can never completely get rid of traces of their original tongue—most listeners can spot these characteristics, and certainly sensitive instruments in a linguistics lab can detect them. But even if we are biologically constrained to speak a language with an accent, there's nothing wrong with that so long as we can make ourselves understood. In any case, accents certainly add to the interesting diversity and recognizability of human speech.

About the author
Steven H. Weinberger (weinberg@gmu.edu) is Associate Professor and Director of the Linguistics program at George Mason University in Virginia. He teaches courses in phonetics, phonology, and second language acquisition. His principal research deals with language sound systems and foreign accents. He is co-editor of *Interlanguage Phonology: The Acquisition of a Second Language Sound System* (1987), and he is the founder and administrator of the *Speech Accent Archive* (http://accent. gmu.edu/), a Web database of thousands of different accents in English.

Suggestions for further reading

In this book
Chapters relevant to language learning by adults include 17 (language and the brain), 32 (adult advantages in language learning), 33 (language learning tips), 34 (history of language teaching methods), 35 (study abroad), and 37 (language-teaching technology). Chapters discussing the sounds of language include 30 (U.S. Southern English) and 29 (phonetics). Frictions between language-defined groups are addressed in Chapters 9 (lingua francas), 10 (pidgins and creoles), 21 (language

conflict), 41 (Cajun), 42 (German in the U.S.), 43 (Gullah), and 63 (languages of India).

Elsewhere

Blumenfeld, R. *Accents: A Manual for Actors* (Proscenium, 2000). A guide to producing more than eighty different speech accents for English speakers. It is designed for actors, but it contains insights into speech production and comparative linguistics.

Lippi-Green, R. *English with an Accent* (Routledge, 1997). A thorough analysis of American attitudes towards English accents. It focuses on language variation linked to geography and social identity, and looks at how institutions promote linguistic stereotyping.

Swan, M. and B. Smith. *Learner English* (Cambridge University Press, 2001). A practical reference text that presents and compares relevant linguistic features of English with about twenty-two other languages. It utilizes linguistic transfer to predict learners' errors, and is a valuable resource for ESL teachers.

Weinberger, S. *Speech Accent Archive* (http://accent.gmu.edu, 2010). A Web based phonetic analysis of native and non-native speakers of English who read the same paragraph that is carefully transcribed. The archive is used by people who wish to compare and analyze the accents of different English speakers.

32

Can monolingualism be cured?

Katherine Sprang

Is it possible to learn a new language as an adult? Isn't it a lot harder than it is for children? Are there any tricks to learning?

When was the last time you studied a foreign language? Some of us think about that experience with pleasure; others think of it as one we wouldn't *ever* want to repeat. If you're over sixteen and trying to learn a new language—or thinking about learning one (and I hope you are)—remember that adults and children learn languages in very different ways.

When we ask ourselves why it takes so long to learn a foreign language, it is easy for us, as adult language learners, to envy children. They learn language as part of learning about the world; their minds absorb the words, phrases, and sentences they hear while they are playing or exploring—and with no apparent effort. Language learning is the child's exciting full-time job for the first few years of life: no studying necessary, and no homework!

But don't forget that even with that sponge-like ability to absorb linguistic information, children have to hear and use their mother tongue for thousands of hours in order to master it; it typically takes them over ten years before they're fully capable of non-childish everyday language use. Adults usually don't have that much time to spare, but that doesn't mean that we can't learn languages and learn them very well. In some ways adults have an *advantage* over children. First, some elements of language can be categorized, analyzed, and explained, and these can be learned by adults more rapidly than by children learning their first language. Second, because we already have a language, adults can use what we know of our first language to organize our learning of the sounds, words, and grammar of the new one. We don't start from scratch when we learn another language.

For example, even if a language has some sounds that English doesn't (maybe a trilled r as in 'burro'—or an 'ng' sound at the beginning of a word, like 'nga'), chances are that *most* of its sounds will be familiar. Adults can take advantage of this to prioritize their pronunciation effort where it is most needed.

Or the new language may use word orders like "The boy brave with his rifle the tiger fierce shot.' That sounds unnatural to an English speaker, but foreign grammatical patterns are not so different from English that they can't be figured out and mastered, like a puzzle—again, a skill that improves with age.

Learning foreign vocabulary inescapably requires many exposures to the words in different contexts, but even here adults are well equipped to spot words related to words they already know and use them as stepping-stones into the new language. They can recognize prefixes and suffixes, and understand the roles that those parts of words play in the new language. Adult language students—especially when aided by good teachers, textbooks, and technical aids, have the knowledge, experience, and analytic ability to recognize what's already understandable in a new language and what's different from our first language. By *focusing attention on the differences*, we as adults can jump-start our learning.

By contrast, other elements of language need to be absorbed through continual and repeated exposure. When the mind is relaxed and not seeking explanations or patterns, it's capable of categorizing and sorting information about some elements of language without conscious effort. The aspects of language taken in best through this unconscious process—called implicit learning—tend not to be captured in textbooks, and they're seldom explained well by teachers. In fact, in some ways it can be more effective simply to watch TV or listen to the radio in the language you're trying to learn, rather than poring over rules and patterns and vocabulary lists.

The better we are at combining both approaches—explicit learning and implicit learning—the more effectively and quickly we can build our knowledge of a new language. And it's not enough just to acquire knowledge. To a great extent, speaking, writing, and understanding a foreign language are a matter of developing skills—like learning to play the piano—that you can't master without practice, practice, PRACTICE. Here again, children have it easier, if only because they're uninhibited. Practicing a foreign language means you have to get past the very adult fear of embarrassment, the discomfort of doing something you are not expert at. Are you willing to walk up to strangers from another country—say, a group of tourists—and try to talk with them in their language? To the extent that you are willing to try out your budding language skills, to practice them (even if your performance is not perfect), and to learn from making mistakes, your ability in the foreign language will continue to grow.

Until around the middle of the twentieth century, language learning in school was pretty dull. It was all about memorizing vocabulary, talking about grammar—in English—and translating as many paragraphs as you could stand. We've learned a lot about teaching languages since then. Since the 1970s, the new discipline of Second Language Acquisition, an interdisciplinary field combining cognitive science and applied linguistics, has also emerged. Through it we are gradually discovering which elements of a language are best taught through explicit instruction and which are best absorbed through sustained exposure to the language. As answers to these questions are uncovered through research, language instruction continues to improve, and adults are learning languages better than ever. So if you're a monolingual adult, there's no reason to continue in that sad condition. Monolingualism *can* be cured.

About the author
Katherine Sprang holds a Ph.D. from the German Department at Georgetown University, with primary specialization in Second Language Acquisition (SLA). She is particularly interested in how excellence in teaching can help language students achieve superior foreign language skills. She works currently at the Foreign Service Institute, U.S. Department of State, as Coordinator of FSI Regional Programs and Training.

Suggestions for further reading

In this book
Language learning by adults is also discussed in Chapters 17 (language and the brain), 31 (foreign accents), 33 (language learning tips), 34 (history of language teaching methods), 35 (study abroad), and 37 (language teaching technology).

Elsewhere
Byrnes, Heidi and Hiram Maxim. *Advanced Foreign Language Learning: A Challenge to College Programs* (Heinle, 2003).

Larsen-Freeman, Diane. *Teaching Language: From Grammar to Grammaring* (Heinle, 2003).

33

What does it take to learn a language well?

Nina Garrett

Do you have to be clever to learn a new language? How long does it take to learn one well? Is 'total immersion' the only way to do it?

People often say things like 'I had four semesters of Language X, but I can't speak a word.' That, in fact, may be the typical experience of adult classroom language learners. Why is it so common? The implication seems to be that we're not very smart, or we had poor teachers, or we're just bad at learning languages. But probably none of that is true. Speaking another language fluently isn't a matter of IQ or academic smarts: there are millions of people who have no formal education at all but who speak several languages fluently.

Nor is it a matter of youth: it's too pessimistic to say that only children can learn languages. The Modern Language Association insists 'Never too early, never too late.' Children exposed to a new language with playmates, grandparents, or babysitters are certainly quicker at mastering pronunciation and casual or everyday conversation, but older learners have cognitive advantages when it comes to formal learning of real-world communication skills.

Is it aptitude, flair, a 'feel' for languages? Some people delight in language learning while others find it the grimmest of work, but we don't really know what 'language aptitude' consists of. A good ear helps, as does a good memory, but equally important is the willingness to be open-minded about new ways to understand the world, to listen for levels of meaning beyond the factual, to try out new ways to engage with others in their cultural context, to take the chance of making mistakes.

Is it enough just to live for a month (or even a year) in the country where the language is spoken? If you're starting as an adult, probably not. Imagine a foreigner just starting to learn English, who hears an American acquaintance say 'Wutchagonnado?' There'll come a day when she can recognize that, and understand it, as a colloquially compressed version of the six-word sentence 'What are you going to do?' But as a beginner, she—or any of us meeting a new language—is likely to hear just a single burst of sound. How do you learn to make sense of those bursts? Not through 'total immersion' in a foreign country: the native speakers around you there are simply communicating with each other, freely using their own language's versions of 'Wutchagonnado'. They're not there to analyze them for you—they probably don't even know how. But without some explanation of what's in those bursts of sound, your learning will be random and inefficient. Another thing 'total immersion' won't give you is cultural background—the important things native speakers *don't* explicitly include in their conversations with each other because 'everybody knows that.'

After puberty most of us need classroom work to create a framework for hearing sounds, figuring out how sentences work, and understanding the cultural context. Adults who acquire a language without that framework often end up with a kind of 'abominable fluency'—a lot of words, good speed, maybe even decent pronunciation, but typically mangled grammar and not much cultural sensitivity about how words are used. A language is not just a set of words and phrases that you can memorize to get simple here-and-now meanings across; it's a multidimensional system for interacting with the world and sharing ideas. You don't want to massacre the language, sounding like Inspector Clouseau of the *Pink Panther* films. So don't believe the ads in airline magazines for courses that guarantee 'mastery' of a language in just a few weeks—that's just nonsense. Language learning takes time, and the less similar the language is to English, the more time it takes. Think about this: in a typical four-semester course in college, you'll have fewer than two hundred hours of contact time with the language. In U.S. government schools, where languages are taught for real proficiency, even courses in 'easy' languages like French or Spanish require six hundred hours of full-time study, and getting to proficiency in the languages most difficult for English speakers—Chinese, Japanese, Korean, and Arabic—takes twice as long.

Still, the classroom experience alone isn't enough. If you took a language course and a few years later couldn't remember what you learned, it's probably because you left out the second step— prolonged interaction with people who speak the language. You can achieve that by traveling to their country, of course, but you can also accomplish it in an intensive summer language school or camp, or by dating a near-monolingual speaker of the language, or by 'talking' with native speakers in Internet chat rooms, where you'll find 'spoken' language even in written form. Emerging technologies are increasingly good at simulating the experience of communicating with native speakers—or even providing it for real, through video-assisted telephone or computer conversations. The Internet also offers lots of foreign-language audio and video material you can use to bridge the gap between the classroom and your live-interaction learning: news broadcasts, movies, popular music, and more—much of it with transcripts available. The ideal approach is a well-planned multiple-year sequence of language study that eventually includes experience living abroad. It's sad but true: there are no short cuts.

Learning a language *well* means being able to do much more than just get a meal, a hotel room or a train ticket. These kinds of practical but superficial communication needn't take more than a few weeks of focused effort and good materials. But conversing easily with native speakers about current events or shared professional interests, including expressing opinions or asking questions in culturally appropriate terms, calls for more than memorized words and phrases. Real-world language use rests on language-specific knowledge about topics and issues as well as vocabulary.

Learning a language to this level takes motivation and a serious time commitment, but once you've gotten to the point of real competence and comfort in another language the advantages of your fluency—and the pleasure it brings—will give you all the motivation you need to keep it up.

About the author
Nina Garrett has taught French and German at junior high school, high school, and college levels, and has also taught graduate-level courses on Second Language Acquisition, especially as its theory underlies language pedagogy. Her first language was Dutch, and she has also studied Russian, Latin, and Spanish. She is internationally known in Computer Assisted Language Learning for her work in developing the use of computer technology both for teaching languages and for conducting research on how language is learned. Formerly Director of the Center for Language Study at Yale University (www.cls.yale.edu), she continues to consult and write on issues of adult language learning.

Suggestions for further reading

In this book
Chapters relevant to language learning by adults include 17 (language and the brain), 31 (foreign accents), 32 (adult advantages in language learning), 34 (history of language teaching methods), 35 (study abroad), and 37 (language teaching technology).

Elsewhere
Lightbown, Patsy and Nina Spada. *How Languages are Learned.* (Oxford University Press, third edition 2006).

34

How have our ideas about language learning changed through the years?

June K. Phillips

What's the history of foreign language teaching? Have there been a lot of different methods? How different are they? Are today's methods best?

The first language taught to anyone in America was, of all things, Algonquian. Seventeenth-century arrivals from England learned to communicate in native American languages as a matter of survival. But later settlers, as good Europeans, built schools that taught languages for academic purposes, not for communication with local people. Language study in eighteenth-century America meant learning to read and write—not speak—Ancient Greek or Latin, or both.

When Americans began studying modern languages—only French, Spanish, Italian, and German at first—they learned them the same way they did the classical languages, and for the same reasons, even though these were languages with living speakers. In 1824, a year before his new University of Virginia opened, Thomas Jefferson said that '[the] Latin and Greek languages constitute the basis of good education and are indispensable to fill up the character of a well educated man.' The next year he wrote, 'We generally learn languages for the benefit of reading the books written in them.' So much for language as a way of communicating.

For the next century and beyond, Americans continued to study languages, not to talk with native speakers but to learn to read—and not to read newspapers or pamphlets of the day but to read literature. Language classes were all about reading, translating, and analyzing grammar—not just in Latin and Greek but in modern languages too. So if you studied a language in the first half of the twentieth century, you probably didn't learn to speak it, because no one intended that you should. Speaking wasn't the goal.

And then came World War II. Suddenly the U.S. urgently needed a way of mass-producing *speakers* of foreign languages— soldiers and civilians—who could not just conjugate French verbs or read *Don Quixote*, but actually talk with people in all parts of the world. And what was needed included a dazzling *variety* of languages—everything from Dutch to Burmese.

The linguistic profession was pressed into war service ... and the teaching of languages changed dramatically. This time period was also the heyday of behaviorism as an explanation for learning in all fields. Foreign language teachers were trained to use stimulus and response to imprint language patterns in student minds. Students were to learn by memorizing dialogues and producing rapid-fire responses in all kinds of oral drills, rarely by producing messages of their own.

This 'audiolingual' method worked, to an extent. More people learned more languages faster and more fluently (if you define fluency as rapid repetition and recitation) than could ever have been trained through the reading-oriented grammar-and-translation method. U.S. government needs for foreign language specialists— Russian in particular—remained high as World War II gave way to the Cold War. Ancient Greek fell off the charts. Latin experienced ups and downs in popularity and was successfully promoted as a way of building vocabulary competency in English.

By the early 1960s, the audiolingual method, firmly planted in behavioral psychology and descriptive linguistics, was widely used across America. But its flaws began to show up. There were severe limitations on stimulus–response as a model for learning something as complex as a language. Researchers looked more closely at how language is acquired, and came to see the process as an evolution rather than as something one could accomplish mechanically, through daily exercises. Language teaching changed again to reflect those insights.

In the old paradigm, the objective was linguistic mastery: students practiced and practiced until they could handle building-block materials perfectly. But all too often the building was never raised. What piano student would be content with just doing five-finger drills and never reaching the point of playing a piece or creating a tune?

The new paradigm recognizes that novice learners can and do communicate; they get their message across even if all they can produce is a series of words without grammatical structure. In a tavern, 'Me want beer' gets you one! If you're a more advanced speaker, your request can be more nuanced: 'What do you have on draft?' The U.S. language teaching community has adopted this communication-first paradigm as the cornerstone of the National Standards for Foreign Language Education, a document that lays out strategies for improving language programs in the twenty-first century.

And this comes none too soon, because students today have unprecedented access to resources that enable them to take on real-world tasks and actually use the languages they study. If Jefferson were brought back to see what's happened since 1824, he'd mourn the diminished status of Greek and Latin and literary studies in western European languages. But he'd no doubt be fascinated to visit a typical classroom. He'd see computers and video clips and games in the target language, students working in pairs, moving around the room, chattering in short sentences, using imperfect but understandable grammar, and filling in meanings with gestures when necessary. Above all, communicating. I suspect it looked a lot like that when their ancestors were learning Algonquian.

About the author

June K. Phillips is Professor and Dean of Arts and Humanities Emeritus from Weber State University in Utah. She has taught French (at the junior high school through college levels) and methods of foreign language teaching. She served as President of the American Council on the Teaching of Foreign Languages (ACTFL) in 2001. She was ACTFL's project director for the National Standards for Foreign Language Education and is co-director of a project looking at their influence after a decade or more; she also co-chaired the development of Program Standards for the Preparation of Foreign Language Teachers, jointly promulgated by ACTFL and the National Council for Accreditation of Teacher Education. She served as a consultant to the National Assessment of Educational Progress evaluation of Spanish teaching in the U.S. and to the WGBH/Annenberg Video Library for Foreign Languages, a nonprofit educational resource. She has published and edited extensively on pedagogical topics.

Suggestions for further reading

In this book

Adult language learning is also discussed in Chapters 17 (language and the brain), 31 (foreign accents), 32 (adult advantages in language learning), 33 (language learning tips), 35 (study abroad), and 37 (language teaching technology).

Elsewhere

National Standards in Foreign Language Education Project. *Standards for Foreign Language Learning in the 21st Century* (Allen Press, 2006;1999). This book provides background information on the widely adopted Standards, a broader set of goals than were aimed at in past language learning. They are commonly called the 'Five Cs': Communication, Cultures, Connections, Comparisons, and Communities.

Shrum, Judith L. and Eileen W Glisan. *Teacher's Handbook: Contextualized Language Instruction.* (Heinle, Cengage Learning, fourth edition 2010). Preliminary chapter and Chapters 1–2 provide historical information on language teaching theories.

35

Why study languages abroad?

Sheri Spaine Long

Can you learn a language without going abroad? Isn't it easier to pick up a language by living in a country where it's spoken than by sitting in a classroom in your own country? Are there any pitfalls to 'total immersion' learning?

Are you one of those language learners who love to be plunked into an ongoing stream of talk, soaking it up, mimicking what they hear, unruffled if they don't understand what is being said? Or do you find yourself needing more structure, wanting to know what each word means before trying it out, and being frustrated when waves of incomprehensible speech wash over you?

As a language professor, I often hear people say, 'The only way to learn a language is to go abroad.' That's not strictly true. And it's particularly not true to think that by being in another country you will automatically 'pick up' the language. I dislike that phrase—'pick up a language'—because it implies that language learning somehow happens without effort. Not so.

Learning styles vary, so a good way to think about learning a language abroad is from the point of view of readiness. For most people, to parachute into a foreign culture with no previous study of the language, no preparation at all, is not only disorienting but inefficient. With no framework to help make sense of what you're hearing, progress is slow. Readiness differs from one person to the next, but for most of us, it's best to have some formal study of a language before you pull the ripcord. And once you're on the ground, it's best to enroll in a structured learning experience, a language class of some kind. You take the class to get knowledge about the language, then use the street, pubs and clubs of the community as your lab to practice speaking and hearing it.

The great advantage of studying and living abroad is that you can experience the language in its cultural context. Words and phrases that you hear in a sometimes 'sterile' classroom come alive, even change meaning, when you hear them from a native speaker over drinks in a café. Or when you join the crowds in a soccer game. Or deal with the local bureaucracy.

But being confronted with a foreign language is fatiguing at first. It takes constant effort to listen, concentrate, and try to make sense of what you hear; it's easier than you think to spend a long time abroad and still come home monolingual. If your goal is to learn a foreign language, try to use as little English as possible while abroad. Even a little before you think you're ready, make a vow to yourself to communicate only in the target language, and do it as much as you can—around the clock. Don't hang around with your fellow expatriates; emergencies aside, don't stay in touch with home by letters, international phone, e-mail, texting, social media, or whatever. Also, be careful to avoid the 'dreaded anglophile', the local who takes advantage of your homesickness to practice English with you. He or she gains—you lose.

When a friend of mine was a junior in college—after a couple of semesters of Spanish—she signed up for a program in Spain, her first experience with language study abroad. After orientation on the first day, the instructor shifted to Spanish and told fifteen nervous Americans to take a 'no English' pledge. From then on my friend was immersed in a dialect of Spanish that she slowly adopted as her own. She spoke almost no English for five months. She didn't socialize with English speakers. She watched Spanish TV and movies (with no subtitles), and spent as much time as she could with locals. At first she spoke broken Spanish; but by the end of the semester, she was using the language comfortably, expressing herself at an advanced level. That was a successful total immersion in the language and culture. She spent all her waking hours, seven days a week, speaking or thinking exclusively in the target language.

Study abroad accelerates the learning process, provides authentic cultural context, and encourages good life-long language learning practices. Most people return from their time abroad enthusiastic about linguistic gains and new cross-cultural skills; they're likely to bring back a fresh perspective on their home culture, as well. There are a great many study-abroad programs, offered by a wide variety of providers who serve the business, health, and educational communities. But before selecting a program, make sure that its goals are in line with yours and that the time abroad is focused on language learning. Ask questions such as: does the provider offer structured academic classes and immersion activities? Does the provider offer lodging and dining situations that enhance language and cultural immersion? Does the program offer university or secondary school credit, proficiency credentials or diplomas?

If study abroad isn't feasible, then domestic immersion is a strong second choice. The best domestic programs mirror the study-abroad experience both in spirit and practice, and can provide good language-learning opportunities at a fraction of the cost of going overseas. While domestic experience can rarely offer the same depth of cultural learning as study abroad, programs in places like Concordia Language Villages and Middlebury Language Schools can be very effective. In all such schools you'll take a pledge to work, study, eat, and socialize only in the foreign language for the duration of the program. If you conscientiously keep the pledge—just as you would in an overseas environment— the combination of a structured class and total immersion in the language really works.

About the author
Sheri Spaine Long is Professor of Spanish in the Department of Foreign Languages and Literatures at the University of Alabama at Birmingham.

Currently she is serving as a Distinguished Visiting Professor at the United States Air Force Academy. Dr. Long, who earned her Ph.D. at the University of California, Los Angeles, has directed study-abroad programs to Spain and Latin America. She received special commendation for international education from the Universidad de Jaén (2007). Her publications include eight co-authored college Spanish textbooks as well as over forty scholarly articles, notes and reviews on contemporary Spanish literature and culture, language pedagogy and policy. She currently serves the American Association of Teachers of Spanish and Portuguese as the Editor of *Hispania*, a journal devoted to the teaching of Spanish and Portuguese, and is the former Editor-in-Chief of *Foreign Language Annals*.

Suggestions for further reading

In this book
For other discussions of adult language learning see Chapters 17 (language and the brain), 31 (foreign accents), 32 (adult advantages in language learning), 33 (language learning tips), 34 (history of language teaching methods), and 37 (language teaching technology).

Elsewhere
www.studyabroad.com offers a comprehensive way to search for study-abroad providers and compare options.

www.ciee.org (Council on International Educational Exchange) special-izes in options for academic international exchange.

www.nafsa.org (National Association of Foreign Student Advisors; also known as the Association of International Educators) contains a variety of useful publications about study abroad.

These two journals contain research results on individual study-abroad programs:

- *Frontiers: The Interdisciplinary Journal of Study Abroad*, www.frontiersjournal.com.
- *Journal of Studies in International Education*, http://jsi.sagepub.com.

These two organizations provide domestic immersion experiences:

- Concordia Language Villages, www.concordialanguagevillages.org/newsite.
- Middlebury Language Schools, www.middlebury.edu/ls.

36

Is elementary school too early to teach foreign languages?

Gladys C. Lipton

Is there any advantage to teaching languages in primary school? Is there a risk of overloading children's brains? Aren't other subjects more important at that age?

I recently got a note from a mother whose daughter's school had a program teaching Chinese and Spanish to elementary students. 'Will it result in linguistic confusion?' she asked. It's a good question, but it's not a worry. Children under the age of ten are absolutely hardwired to learn languages. In many countries they learn three or four, often at the same time—with no ill effects. In America, multilingual though it is, the tradition has been not to start language study until high school or middle school—and American children are poorer for it. Now, though, Americans are recognizing what a joyous thing language learning is for children, and more and more schools offer it. The most widely used terms for such programs are 'FLES' (Foreign Language in the Elementary School) and 'early language programs'.

The theoretical underpinning for FLES comes from studies of the brain. Researchers report that it's most receptive to language learning before the age of ten, but then begins to lose this plasticity. (Readers fortunate enough to have started learning a foreign language in childhood probably speak it without an accent.) Does this mean that you can't learn a foreign language well if you don't start until secondary school? Not at all—you just have to work harder at it.

In addition to this *neurological* advantage, children exposed to the sounds and rhythms of other tongues are *culturally* flexible. Part of learning languages is getting past the notion that English is the 'right' or only way to talk and other languages are 'funny'. Children who take FLES outgrow such attitudes rapidly, and don't have the inhibitions teenagers often feel when they start a language. Researchers have found that children under ten not only love to imitate new sounds, they're highly receptive to other people's customs, traditions, and different ways of doing things. FLES can open children's minds to other cultures, especially in the earliest grades, where songs, learning games, the arts, science and social studies are included in language study.

What results can you expect from a FLES program? Above all, greater proficiency: students who start a language early and stick with it achieve higher scores on Advanced Placement tests than those who start the language in their teens. What explains this? A great deal of research has shown that success in language learning depends on three things: time on task, motivation, and frequency or intensity of learning sessions. All three flow from starting a foreign language early. Children who start early automatically get more exposure time; the *fun* of language learning motivates them; and they're likely to want to get more of it. Most FLES students are successful language learners.

But, some may ask, isn't the grade school day already full? How can we squeeze in another subject, even if it's worthwhile?

Part of the answer is that, according to emerging research, time spent on languages is *not* subtracted from the rest of the curriculum. The interdisciplinary approach used by FLES teachers reinforces what students learn in other classes. When a FLES teacher works on days of the week, weather, maps, shopping, and other real-life topics in the language class, she or he is reviewing what other classes are teaching about numbers, dates, geography, temperature, colors, and money.

For all these reasons, many parents are very interested in internationalizing the schools their children attend. They can be daunted, though, by the perceived cost of establishing a FLES program. There is certainly no magical answer to this problem, but there are many creative options. Where regular classroom teachers are fluent in a foreign language and have been trained in language teaching methods, they can form the nucleus of a program. Sometimes it makes most sense for one or more language teachers to travel between several classes or several schools. In some cases, video conferencing can help limited language-teaching staff cover more schools.

Even when budgets are very limited, it is highly recommended that parents, teachers, administrators, counselors and other community members work together to formulate age-appropriate, realistic program goals.

To return to that mother's question, should we teach foreign languages in the elementary school? The answer is unequivocally 'Yes!'

About the author

Gladys Lipton is the Director of America's National FLES* (pronounced 'flestar') Institute, and serves as a consultant to schools, school districts and other agencies. She has directed national teacher development at the University of Maryland. Her past leadership positions include Program Coordinator in Foreign Languages and ESOL for the Anne Arundel County Public Schools in Maryland, and Director of Foreign Languages for the New York City Public Schools. Dr. Lipton has served as Editor of the newsletter of the Northeast Conference on the Teaching of Foreign Languages. She has chaired the national FLES committees of both the American Association of Teachers of Spanish (AATS) and the American Association of Teachers of French (AATF). She has also served as an Associate Editor of the AATS journal *Hispania,* and as national president of AATF. She has received many awards for her work in the profession, including ACTFL's Steiner Leadership Award and, in 2010, *Commandeur in the Order of Academic Palmes* from the French government.

Suggestions for further reading

In this book
Other chapters discussing language acquisition by children include 10 (pidgins and creoles), 15 (babies and language), 17 (language and the brain), 25 (language deprivation), and 26 (sign languages).

Elsewhere

Boyer, E. *The Basic School.* (The Carnegie Foundation for the Advancement of Teaching, 1995). Boyer's description of an ideal school (pp71–74) includes early language learning.

Curtain, H. and C. Dahlberg. *Languages and Children* (Pearson/Prentice-Hall,fourth edition 2010). Information about FLES research, methods, and curriculum.

Lipton, G. *Practical Handbook to Elementary Foreign Language Programs (FLES*)* (National FLES* Institute, fifth edition 2010). Offers detailed assistance in planning and supporting effective FLES* programs.

Lipton, G. 'FLES* Advocacy and Promotion' in the *AATF French Advocacy Kit* (Advocacy Online Resource Wiki—Advice from Colleagues, online at www.frenchteachers.org, 2009). Presents FLES* benefits for children, the FLES* Scale for program evaluation, and suggestions for effective advocacy and promotion of FLES*.

Lipton, G. 'A Retrospective on FLES* Programs' (*Hispania* 83(4), 1998, pp76–87). Traces early attempts to implement foreign language programs in U.S. elementary schools.

Marcos, K. *Why, How, and When Should My Child Learn a Second Language?* (Center for Applied Linguistics, 2003). Suggestions for parents who wish to help with early language programs.

Thompson, P., J. Giedd, et al. 'Growth Patterns in the Developing Brain Detected by Using Continuum Mechanical Tensor Maps' (*Nature* 404, September 3rd, 2000). Validates early language learning concept with vital research on brain activity at various ages.

Portman, C. 'English Is Not Enough' (*The Chronicle*, April 18th, 2010). Provides a strong statement encouraging elementary school foreign language programs.

Reese, S. 'How to Teach Our Youngest Language Learners' (*The Language Educator,* April 2009, pp22–29). An overview of the rationale and research for early language programs; describes several different successful program models.

Saxon, H., E. and K. Kurk Huelbig, eds. *FLES* Works.* (American Association of Teachers of French, 2009). This report from AATF's National FLES* Commission provides anecdotal testimonies of successful FLES* practices.

37

Can computers teach languages faster and better?

Sue E. K. Otto

Can you converse with a machine? What technology exists to help people learn languages?

Imagine asking a high school French student 'What did you do in class today?' and, instead of getting the usual 'Oh, nothing,' hearing an enthusiastic account of several hours spent in France, thanks to the school's advanced virtual world simulator: 'I ate a croissant and sipped an espresso at an outdoor café (the croissant was delicious and the waiter was *very* impressed with my French!), I wandered through Monet's gardens in Giverny (the smell of roses was lovely!), and Claude Monet himself talked with me about impressionism and critiqued the picture I was painting. It was awesome!'

Could such a simulation, involving multilingual androids and convincingly detailed computer-generated virtual realities, be available to twenty-first century French students—even *late* in the twenty-first century? Well, disappointing though it may be to those of us whose high expectations have been fed by movie special effects, the answer is almost certainly 'No.' What, then, can technology realistically do for language teaching and learning?

In the 1960s, as computers started to gain traction in our society, educators predicted that they would revolutionize education, serving as teacher surrogates that would deliver scientifically designed programmed instruction, realistic simulations, and effective, efficient skill-building practice of all kinds. In the field of language learning, the vaunted 'revolution' materialized in the form of rudimentary computerized flashcard programs for vocabulary practice and electronic workbook programs for grammar instruction and practice. The computer was touted as a patient tutor and drillmaster, able to provide individualized feedback instantly for errors and keep records of performance, thus sparing the teacher the drudgery of mechanical tasks. However, computers had virtually no capacity to understand and respond intelligently to naturally spoken or written language, or to engage in sophisticated activities with media; so they were viewed skeptically by many language teachers and remained essentially at the margins of the language curriculum.

Nowadays, computers and digital technologies are ubiquitous—present in nearly every schoolroom, home, and business, in every backpack, purse and pocket. Increasingly, students split their lives between the real world and online virtual spaces. Not surprisingly, the same technologies these students use in everyday life have also become an integral part of their language learning experience.

As computing and digital technology evolved, a wide variety of compelling computer-based activities for language teaching and learning were developed: reading texts enhanced with glosses and informational notes available on demand to help students read and comprehend both the linguistic and cultural content; interactive video programs that allowed control over playing and replaying segments, providing help (subtitles or glosses) and notes to facilitate listening comprehension and promote cultural observation; massive searchable databases of authentic written and spoken language to illustrate language forms and functions; pronunciation tutors with animations demonstrating production of sounds and voice recorders to allow students to record and compare their pronunciation with a model speaker; simulated conversation activities based on voice recognition technology where the computer 'understands' what students say within the narrow context of the conversation and responds in a logical way (akin to the exchanges you have when you call an airline to get flight information); adventure games and video-based simulations in which students become actors in a story; and writing environments with built-in dictionaries, grammar help, spelling and grammar checkers.

Multimedia enhancements—video, audio, animations, still images—take center stage in these kinds of instructional applications, allowing students to engage with the language and culture in self-paced, multifaceted interactions that were not possible with static printed texts and linear media. The best multimedia programs encourage students to grapple with authentic (native-speaker) language, culture and content, teaching them strategies to cope with the complexities and difficulties of language produced by its native speakers in real life situations.

Computer programs that present multimedia language activities to students working alone to master language fundamentals remain a standard fixture of virtually all beginning- and intermediate-level language programs available from publishers. Students must have opportunities to practice in order to become proficient in a language and the computer can effectively provide such practice in a private, non-threatening manner. Yet working in isolation on a computer without intelligent interlocutors is not, in the final analysis, completely satisfying for language learners.

A technological sea change occurred with the emergence of the World Wide Web. Early on, the Web grew to be a vast, readily accessible repository of information. Language teachers and learners gained access to a wealth of authentic linguistic and cultural resources from all over the world. Perhaps more importantly for language learning, the Web quickly expanded to accommodate a number of highly participatory services that connected people virtually, promoting social networking and information creation and sharing, including text and video chats, blogs, wikis, podcasts, fan forums, Facebook, Flickr, YouTube, Twitter, and many others. This new social Web makes it possible (and commonplace) for learners to communicate and collaborate readily with others, including native speakers of their language of study. However, success in exploring the Web's resources and engaging foreign cultures online still requires human intervention in the form of careful planning and expert guidance from teachers with combined skills in language, culture, and technology.

Can you converse with a machine in a meaningful way? No. Nevertheless, current technologies can and do help people learn languages, by presenting individualized instruction and practice to build language skills, and by enabling meaningful communication and cultural exchange in the online global community.

About the author

Sue E. K. Otto is Director of the University of Iowa Language Media Center and Adjunct Associate Professor of Spanish and Portuguese and International Programs. She holds a Ph.D. in Spanish from the University of Iowa. She is Past Chair of the Executive Board of the Computer Assisted Language Instruction Consortium (CALICO) and Past President and Past Executive Director of the International Association for Language Learning Technology (IALLT). She has devoted her research and development efforts for the past three decades to foreign language authoring tools, authentic video resources, and multimedia software. She is a faculty member of the FLARE Ph.D. program in Second Language Acquisition (SLA) and she teaches courses on multimedia and SLA. http://clas.uiowa.edu/dwllc/spanish-portuguese/people/sue-otto.

Suggestions for further reading

In this book

For other discussions of adult language learning see Chapters 17 (language and the brain), 31 (foreign accents), 32 (adult advantages in language learning), 33 (language learning tips), 34 (history of language teaching methods), and 35 (study abroad). Other linguistic/technological topics appear in Chapters 38 (interactive map of U.S. language communities),

48 (machine translation), 49 (forensic linguistics), 50 (the Museum of Languages), 53 (Latin), and 64 (Esperanto).

Elsewhere

http://en.wikipedia.org/wiki/Computer-assisted_language_learning is a general introduction to the field of computer-assisted language learning.

Language Learning and Technology (http://llt.msu.edu). Online journal for second and foreign language scholars and educators.

CALICO Journal (http://calico.org). Journal of CALICO (Computer Assisted Language Instruction Consortium).

ReCALL (www.eurocall-languages.org/index). Journal of EUROCALL (European Computer-Assisted Language Instruction Consortium).

www.ict4lt.org/en/index.htm: collection of training modules in Information and Communications Technology (ICT) for language teachers. Produced by a project funded by the EU, the site reflects a generally European perspective.

Computer Assisted Language Learning (www.tandf.co.uk/journals/titles/09588221.asp). The online journal for the professional organization devoted to computer-assisted language learning (CALL).

38

What's the language of the United States?

David Goldberg

Isn't the U.S. monolingual? What languages other than
English are spoken around the country? How do you find
out who speaks what languages where?

It always seems peculiar to hear people say that the U.S. is an
English-speaking country, and that Americans 'aren't good at other
languages.' Actually, tens of millions of people in the U.S. speak
languages other than English—a lot of other languages. The 2000
US Census found that more than forty-seven million people speak
languages other than English at home (although about 93 percent
of them also spoke English). By 2009 the number had risen to
almost fifty-five million, according to the American Community
Survey, which now tracks these data for the Census. Did you
know that people in Idaho speak over seventy languages, including almost a thousand who speak Shoshoni? That over eighty-six
thousand people speak Polish in Chicago? Or that almost half of
New York City's residents don't speak English at home? In fact, the
only exclusively English-speaking parts of the country are rural
and less populated areas like Appalachia, the deep South, and
parts of the Midwest. In most of the country, especially the larger
cities, multilingualism is the rule.

The language abilities of people in the U.S. are a valuable
national resource in many ways, and the nation is not using this

resource as well as it might to meet its language-related needs. Support for language programs already in place in schools and colleges would go far toward meeting language shortfalls in government, commerce, and international relations. Also important are heritage language schools, where people with limited knowledge of their family language can strengthen their language skills.

How do we know about how many Americans speak which languages and where? By referring to an online Language Map created by the Modern Language Association of America. Using data from the 2000 Census, the MLA has created interactive maps and tables that show the linguistic composition of the entire U.S., state by state, county by county, city by city—down to the neighborhoods defined by postal delivery codes—at the touch of a button. The MLA Language Map also shows where each of these languages is taught in colleges or universities, and how many students are studying in each mapped program.

You can see how languages are distributed across the country, and zoom in on places that have speakers of a language you're interested in. You can see maps showing the prevalent language other than English in each of the U.S.'s 3,141 counties. Using the Language Map's Data Center, you can call up tables that rank the fifty states according to numbers of speakers for each language. You can find, for instance, that California, Texas, and Washington are the three states where Vietnamese is most spoken.

If you look at Minnesota, which you may think of as settled by Scandinavians, you'll find that the most spoken languages after English are Spanish, German, and the southeast Asian language Hmong—there are three times as many speakers of Hmong as there are speakers of Swedish, Norwegian and Danish combined. You could look up Androscoggin County in Maine and find that it has 13,951 speakers of French and 271 speakers of German—not to mention well over thirty other languages. The map also separates speakers into age groups: seventeen and under, eighteen to sixty-four, and sixty-five and over. In Brooklyn, for instance, there are more than twenty-four thousand Yiddish speakers under eighteen; in Miami, there are none. You might look up the ages of the thirty thousand speakers of Navajo in New Mexico's McKinley County. Data like these may provide clues to a language community's future. One set of tables and graphs combines state-level data from both 2000 and 2005, allowing you to compare which languages are spoken in a growing number of U.S. homes and which are diminishing.

There are dozens of ways planners, teachers and students, corporate researchers, librarians, or ordinary citizens can use the information presented in the electronic MLA Language Map. Marketers who want to reach speakers of Urdu or Korean can find the postal codes where a mass mailing might be most effective. Government agencies can use it for providing effective social services, or for disaster preparedness. The map can tell Justice Department officials which languages they need to use to inform new citizens of their rights and responsibilities; it can tell officials in the Office of Trade and Information how it might help a company with interests in China find Americans who know the language. And the map can help language learners find places in the U.S. where they can practice the languages they're studying without spending money to go abroad.

The U.S. Census Bureau's archives, and their website, the American FactFinder, contain a wealth of information about American speakers of languages other than English; the MLA's work has made it easier to find and easy to use.

The U.S. has long been described as a cultural melting pot into which languages other than English disappear. The MLA Language Map reveals that this is far from being the case. You can investigate for yourself by going to www.mla.org and clicking on the Language Map, or click on Data Center and type in the name of a town or a U.S. postal code (ZIP code). You may get a surprise.

About the author

David Goldberg is Associate Director of the Office of Foreign Language Programs and the Association of Departments of Foreign Languages at the Modern Language Association. He is responsible for the continuing development of the MLA Language Map. Goldberg holds a Ph.D. in Yiddish literature and has taught Yiddish language and literature in heritage language schools and at Columbia University and the University of Pennsylvania. He is the author of an intermediate Yiddish textbook published by Yale University Press.

Suggestions for further reading

In this book
The language landscape of the U.S. is discussed in Chapters 28 (rescuing threatened Native American languages), 30 (U.S. Southern English), 39 (America's language crisis), 40 (New World Spanish), 41 (Cajun), 42 (German in the U.S.), 43 (Gullah), and 52 (Native American languages). Other linguistic uses of technology are the subjects of Chapters 37 (language teaching technology), 48 (machine translation), 49 (forensic linguistics), 50 (the Museum of Languages), 53 (Latin), and 64 (Esperanto).

Elsewhere
www.mla.org

McKay, Sandra Lee and Sau-ling Cynthia Wong, eds. *New Immigrants in the United States: Background for Second Language Educators* (Cambridge University Press, 2000). Discusses language issues from the perspective of the year 2000 in communities of Americans from Mexico, Puerto Rico, Cuba, Vietnam, Southeast Asia, China, Korea, the Philippines, Russia, and India. Includes studies on language and law, as well as on language and education.

McKay, Sandra Lee and Sau-ling Cynthia Wong, eds. *Language Diversity: Problem or Resource?* (Newbury House, 1988). Discusses language issues from the perspective of the year 1988 in communities of Americans from Mexico, Puerto Rico, Cuba, Vietnam, China, Korea, and the Philippines. Includes studies on language and law, language and education, and data from the 1980 Census.

Ferguson, Charles A. and Shirley Brice Heath. *Language in the USA* (Cambridge University Press, 1981). Discusses language issues from the perspective of the year 1981 in communities of Native Americans, African Americans, Filipino Americans, and American speakers of European languages, including Spanish, Italian, French, German, Yiddish, Russian, and Polish. Includes studies on language and law, language and education, and data from the 1970 Census.

39

Is there a language crisis in the United States?

Catherine Ingold

What kind of foreign language capabilities does America need? What gaps are there? What can be done?

Well, if it's not a crisis, it's certainly a serious problem. The U.S. needs professional-level competence in well over a hundred different languages. While some skills are available, there are huge gaps, including some in jobs of tremendous national importance.

Shortages in defense and intelligence have received the most attention, but they aren't the only needs: the globalization of business has radically increased demand for people who can move information from one language to another. You wouldn't be happy with German-only instructions for your car radio, or a computer whose help wizard understood only Japanese: the *localization* industry (preparing products for use in another language and culture) is a multibillion dollar business. In addition, many U.S. residents need language assistance for essential public services until they learn English; U.S. civil rights law requires in many cases that such assistance be made available—in as many as two hundred languages.

You might ask how there can be a problem when thousands of kids are studying languages in high school and college every year. Well, first of all, America's schools and colleges rarely teach some of the world's most important tongues. Many school districts have added Chinese, but other 'critical' languages such as

Arabic are growing much more slowly, to say nothing of Hindi or Urdu, which give access to a wide array of related south Asian languages.

Beyond that, the *effectiveness* of world language teaching in the U.S. is an issue. In terms of personally and professionally useful skills as measured by accepted standards, the output of America's education system is modest at best. A real handicap for learners is the scant time allotted to language learning. In many countries, children start a foreign language in the fourth or fifth year of primary school (or even earlier) and continue it through high school, adding a second foreign language along the way. Few U.S. schools have such programs. That's a real pity, since learning a language to a professional level takes a lot of time. And we also need to provide opportunities to develop career-specific language skills. Think about the special language needs of the court interpreter, the social worker, or various medical professionals.

Professional-level skill *can* come from living and studying in a country where the foreign language is spoken, but relatively few Americans study abroad, and they often choose English-speaking countries. (Learning to say, 'G'day, mate' doesn't do much toward filling the gaps in U.S. language capabilities.) Of course there are exceptions: people who love languages and other cultures gravitate to the Peace Corps or diplomatic service. In general, professionally useful skill in a language requires a long sequence of education, at least some time spent in a country where it is spoken, and extensive, meaningful use of the language in real-world communication tasks. Several states and local jurisdictions have established early-start, long-sequence language programs that fit that pattern, but these are available only to a very small percentage of American students. We language educators have started to refer to a 'ZIP code disparity' in language learning opportunities.

Well, don't immigrants bring language skills to the U.S.? Aren't they filling the gap? Not so much. In the 2000 census (the latest to provide language data), forty-seven million people reported speaking a language other than English at home at least part of the time. That count includes two million speakers of Chinese, over

600,000 speakers each of Arabic and Korean, and 300,000 speakers of Hindi—four critically needed languages. But here's the catch: most language-related U.S. jobs demand professional-level skills in both a foreign language and English, and many newly-arrived immigrants don't speak *English* well enough to fill them. Their children may speak the family language at home, but once they're in school they quickly switch to English; and by the third generation the family language is gone.

So despite being a nation of immigrants, the U.S. can't produce the capable, well-educated, bilingual professionals it needs without serious investment in training. The excellent Urdu, Chinese, or Persian of the first generation often needs to be complemented by advanced English—well beyond typical school and college offerings in English as a Second Language (ESL). For the second generation, high-quality ESL programs, paralleled by training to develop competence in their family language, can achieve the goal.

In order to fill critical roles in government, business, and community service, we need to provide wider and deeper education in far more languages—not only to introduce new languages to monolingual Americans, but also to bolster the skills of people who speak another language at home. We are wasting huge linguistic resources in the U.S. by failing to do so.

In 1957, the Soviet Union surprised the West by putting the Sputnik satellite into space. The U.S. Congress responded by creating a generation of scientists, engineers, and linguists who helped win the Cold War. September 11th, 2001 was another Sputnik moment for America. Congress responded by supporting expanded programs in critical languages, but much of the expansion has (understandably) focused on training adults to basic functional levels in languages the defense and intelligence communities need right now. In contrast, the most cost-effective way to develop the language capacities we need—and the only way to have 'surge' capacity when bad things happen—is to build early-start, long-sequence language programs into school systems around the U.S. This work lies ahead of us. If we want to remain a leading nation in this century and beyond, we must attend to development of our intellectual capital—and language capabilities are an increasingly important component of that capital.

About the author
Catherine Ingold is Director of the National Foreign Language Center (NFLC, an action-oriented language policy institute at the University of Maryland). She is currently principal investigator of the STARTALK project, which provides summer programs for students and teachers of ten critical languages in almost every state in the U.S. In addition, she is principal investigator of a large-scale language materials project to develop online language learning materials at advanced levels in more than sixty critical languages. Dr. Ingold holds an M.A. in Romance Linguistics and a Ph.D. in French from the University of Virginia. At Gallaudet University, she chaired the foreign language department and served as Dean of Arts and Sciences and then Provost, learning American Sign Language. As President of the American University of Paris, she presided over a faculty with thirty-five native languages and a student body from seventy-six countries. She joined NFLC in 1996.

Suggestions for further reading

In this book
Opportunities and requirements for professional use of language abilities are discussed in Chapters 2 (what linguists do), 22 (bilingualism), 45 (language-related careers), 46 (dictionaries), 47 (interpreting and translating), 49 (forensic linguistics), 56 (Russian), and 59 (Arabic). Another view of U.S. language capabilities is presented in Chapter 38 (U.S. language survey).

Elsewhere
Garcia, Ofelia and Joshua A. Fishman, eds. *The Multilingual Apple: Languages in New York City* (Mouton de Gruyter, second edition 2002). A wealth of information, accessible to the general reader, on immigrant language communities in New York City.

Brecht, Richard and William Rivers. *Language and National Security in the Twenty-First Century: The Federal Role in Supporting National Language*

Capacity (National Foreign Language Center, 2000). A strategic analysis that has greatly influenced public policy in the wake of September 11.

Ingold, C. W. and S. C. Wang. *The Teachers We Need: Transforming World Language Education in the United States* (National Foreign Language Center, 2010). A 35-page white paper offering guidance to local, state, and federal authorities.

40

What's the future of Spanish in the United States?

Maria Carreira

Is Spanish in the U.S. to stay? Will it remain the same as Spanish in other countries?

> Apply yourself to the study of the Spanish language with all of the assiduity you can. It and the English covering nearly the whole of America, they should be well known to every inhabitant, who means to look beyond the limits of his farm.
> (Thomas Jefferson, Letter to Peter Carr, 1788)

More than two centuries since Jefferson wrote them, these words have proven remarkably prophetic. Today, the U.S. is home to the fifth largest and third wealthiest Spanish-speaking population in the world. New York has as many Puerto Ricans as San Juan, the capital of Puerto Rico. Miami is the second-largest Cuban city, Los Angeles the second largest Mexican city.

But what about the future? During more than three centuries of immigration, dozens of languages have landed on American shores, only to fade away in a generation or two. Think of Italian, Dutch, or Polish. Judging purely from history, Spanish could be expected to follow the same path, gradually losing speakers and eventually disappearing. But will Spanish go the way of other immigrant languages—or will it find a way to survive?

As a general rule, immigrants to the U.S. strongly prefer their native language over English. This certainly applies to the millions of foreign-born Latinos here. However, with each successive generation of Latinos, Spanish use declines sharply. By the third generation, few remain proficient in the language of their parents and grandparents. Young Latinos abandon Spanish to fit in, or to attain the social status that comes with English. And practically speaking, some worry that Spanish will interfere with their ability to speak English and their ability to make a good living. So it's only a matter of time before Spanish fades away. Or is it?

So far, the generational loss of speakers has been offset by a steady flow of new immigrants from Latin America—up to a million a year. But even if immigration declines as some experts predict, the sheer number of speakers in the country gives Spanish the advantage of critical mass—far larger than any other immigration in history—which will give it staying power. As of 2009, there were over forty-eight million Hispanics in the U.S., constituting 16 percent of the nation's total population. Most Hispanics are bilingual: nearly 80 percent speak Spanish at home and over half report speaking English very well.

There are parts of the country—like Texas, Florida, California, and New Mexico—where Spanish has a history dating back many decades, if not hundreds of years, as Jefferson's words attest. More recently, Spanish has made its presence felt in places as far away from the nation's southern contours as Washington State, Oregon, and Minnesota, as new waves of immigrants travel further into the country in search of a livelihood.

From the newly arrived to the native born, Latinos in the U.S. are avid consumers of all things in Spanish. In Los Angeles and Miami, Spanish-language television and radio have a larger audience than their English-language counterparts. Everywhere Latinos live, Spanish can be heard and seen in churches, businesses, schools, and government offices.

And let's not forget non-Latinos who, for many reasons, choose to become fluent in the language. From kindergarten to postgraduate programs, Spanish is the most widely studied language in the U.S. At the secondary level, it is the language of choice of an astounding 70 percent of learners. But Spanish is not just for those in school. Professionals from all walks of life—including some of America's most powerful politicians—seek to tap into the power of this language.

However, the future of U.S. Spanish doesn't depend just on external factors like social pressures, economic incentives, and demographics; it may also be affected by linguistic developments. Impressive as the numbers of speakers are, what's perhaps even more impressive is the variety of accents, usage and dialects, as Spanish-speaking immigrants arrive from places ranging from Buenos Aires to Tijuana. Mexicans are by far the largest national group, but there are sizable immigrant populations from all the other Spanish-speaking countries, particularly from the Caribbean and Central America. There's been nothing like this in the history of the Spanish-speaking world.

In this new linguistic environment, sometimes dubbed the 'United Hispanic States of America', Spanish is being reinvented day by day, partly through dialect mixing and partly through incorporating elements of English. A U.S. mixture of Spanish and English is evolving, often referred to as 'Spanglish'. Think of 'Livin' la Vida Loca,' or 'Hasta la vista, Baby.' Spanglish is popular and contagious among the young, and is even spreading to other Spanish-speaking countries. Bilingual puns and wordplay can be found in the works of many U.S. Latino writers such as Oscar Hijuelos, Sandra Cisneros and Junot Díaz. But many language purists object to this type of mixing. Octavio Paz, the Mexican Nobel Prize winner for literature, has harshly described Spanglish as 'abominable', 'illegitimate' and a 'bastard language'.

Spanglish is only one sign that Spanish in the U.S. is mutating, adapting to its linguistic environment, and therefore becoming more likely to thrive. Three generations from now U.S. Spanish will likely be a new blend, still understandable by people in Spanish-speaking countries, but further enriched by the variety of Hispanic and English influences it will continue to absorb.

Whatever new shape Spanish takes, we should recognize that it is no longer a *foreign* language in the United States. The state of New Mexico has acknowledged that by proclaiming itself officially bilingual in Spanish and English. The rest of the country, while not taking that official step, is rapidly adapting to the fact that Spanish now functions as a U.S. language second only to English.

About the author

Maria Carreira is professor of Spanish linguistics at California State University, Long Beach and Co-Director of the National Heritage Language Research Center at UCLA. Her publications focus on Spanish in the United States and Spanish as a world language. She has co-authored three college-level Spanish textbooks: *Nexos* (2005), *Sí se puede* (2008), and *Alianzas* (2010). Dr. Carreira received her Ph.D. in linguistics from the University of Illinois at Urbana Champaign.

Suggestions for further reading

In this book

Various languages of America are discussed in Chapters 28 (rescuing threatened Native American languages), 38 (languages of the U.S.), 39 (America's language crisis), 41 (Cajun), 42 (German in the U.S.), 43 (Gullah), and 52 (Native American languages), and 55 (languages of Spain and Portugal). The dynamics of life in multilingual communities are touched on in Chapter 21 (language conflict).

Elsewhere

Dávila, Arlene. *Latinos Inc.: The Marketing and Making of a People* (University of California Press, 2001). Documents the growing influence of Latino culture in the U.S. and explores Latino identity through the prism of the Hispanic marketing industry.

Carreira, Maria. 'Mass Media, Marketing, Critical Mass and Other Mechanisms of Linguistic Maintenance', in *Southwest Journal of Linguistics* (Vol. 21, No. 4, December 2002). Discusses the role that the Spanish-language media, Latino demographics, and commercial factors are playing in maintaining and promoting Spanish in the U.S.

Krashen, Stephen. 'Bilingual Education, the Acquisition of English, and the Retention and Loss of Spanish', in Roca, Ana, ed. *Research on Spanish in the United States: Linguistic Issues and Challenges* (Cascadilla Press, 2000). One of America's foremost authorities on foreign language education argues that American society, and business in particular, stands to benefit from stemming the generational loss of immigrant languages in the U.S.

41

What is Cajun and where did it come from?

Robyn Holman

Where did Cajun come from? Is it really French?
How important is it today and what is its future?

Did you know that French was once the language of everyday life in Louisiana? Claimed by France as a colony in 1682, Louisiana remained French territory until President Thomas Jefferson bought it from Napoleon in 1803—along with a great swath of land that has since been divided among fourteen other states—and it is still the place in the U.S. where French is spoken most. According to the 2000 U.S. census (the latest to include language data), over a million Louisiana residents claim French ancestry, with around two hundred thousand saying they speak some type of French at home. The specific size of the Cajun-speaking population is not known, though, and estimates of it vary greatly.

So how did all those French speakers get there? Some have ancestors who came from France as early colonists or as refugees from the French Revolution, speaking 'official' French. The ancestors of others came from Africa, often by way of the Caribbean, and the French they brought with them was a creole like that of Haiti. But the most widely spoken variety of French in Louisiana, and the one we hear the most about—probably because of the food and music that made it famous—is Cajun. Oddly enough, it came from Canada.

Here's how it happened: around 1600, emigrants from France settled along the coast of present-day Nova Scotia, in a colony they called *Acadia*. After struggles between France and England, the territory finally came under British control. But the Acadians refused to swear allegiance to the king of England, and during the '*grand dérangement*' of 1755 they were deported. Forcibly loaded onto boats and driven out, many Acadians died at sea. Some, with the help of Indians, took refuge in the forests of New Brunswick, while others found their way to settlements farther south, traveling by sea as far as Louisiana. This tragic episode attracted little attention until Longfellow's poem *Evangeline* appeared, a century or so later, telling the story of an Acadian girl who was separated from her fiancé during the deportation and spent the rest of her life trying to find him.

The refugees from Nova Scotia who settled in Louisiana called themselves 'Acadiens', and came to be known locally as 'Cajuns'. Their language—still spoken by their descendants—is French. But is it 'real' French? Actually, yes. The Cajuns may not always speak according to Parisian rules, but Cajun French doesn't differ from 'standard' French any more than other varieties do—like the French of Morocco, Quebec, or the West Indies. Cajun adds its own spice to the rich stew we call the French language.

Acadian French was somewhat different from the French spoken by the people who came to Louisiana directly from France, because the strains developed separately for up to 150 years. However, the two have blended over time. Most linguists no longer distinguish between Colonial and Acadian French, but use the term 'Louisiana Regional French (commonly called Cajun)' to refer to the variety of French spoken in southern Louisiana today. Although generally homogeneous, Cajun varies slightly throughout Acadiana, with certain areas having distinctive pronunciations and idioms.

The majority of words and structures in Cajun are certainly recognizable to French speakers from other countries. The differences can be compared with those between British and American English. Cajun has kept some words that have become obsolete in European French, and produced new words to describe new situations. This includes borrowing words from other languages. For instance, *chaoui* from Choctaw names an animal that didn't exist in Europe, the raccoon. African languages also made contributions, such as the Bantu word *gombo* ('okra'), which Cajun borrowed to name a spicy regional stew. Cajuns call shrimp *chevrette*, a word that sounds odd in France, where the Norman dialect word *crevette* replaced it.

Today, like other non-English languages in the U.S., Cajun faces an uncertain future. Members of the younger generation do not hear and use French as much as their parents and grandparents did, and many Cajuns speak little or no French. Although groups like CODOFIL (Conseil pour le développement du français en Louisiane), Action Cadienne, and Les Amis de l'Immersion have been working to preserve the Cajun language and culture, primarily by emphasizing bilingual education programs in the schools, many consider Cajun French to be an endangered idiom.

Natural and man-made disasters since 2005 have undermined the Cajun way of life, potentially increasing the rate of French language loss. Three major Gulf Coast hurricanes between 2005 and 2008 (Katrina, Rita, and Gustav), followed in 2010 by a massive crude oil spill (from the offshore drilling rig Deepwater Horizon), caused severe damage to life, property, and animal breeding grounds in the Acadiana region.

These calamities have cast doubt on the survivability of a culture dependent upon the bayous that open onto the Gulf of Mexico; some have even suggested that a second 'grand dérangement' may lie ahead. Others, though, point out that Cajuns are hard to defeat; recent setbacks, they say, may only serve to strengthen their age-old family-based self-reliance, and their determination to persevere in a harsh environment.

About the author

Robyn Holman is an Associate Professor of French at the College of Charleston, South Carolina, where she also directs the graduate program for language teachers. She received her Ph.D. in French linguistics from the University of Colorado, and most often publishes in the field of medieval French language and culture.

Suggestions for further reading

In this book
Other languages of America are discussed in Chapters 28 (rescuing threatened Native American languages), 38 (languages of the U.S.), 39 (America's language crisis), 40 (New World Spanish), 42 (German in the U.S.), 43 (Gullah), and 52 (Native American languages). Other sociolinguistic topics are talked about in Chapters 10 (pidgins and creoles) and 21 (language conflict).

Elsewhere
Ancelet, Barry Jean. *Cajun and Creole Folktales: the French Oral Tradition of South Louisiana* (Garland Publishing, 1994). Includes three categories of Cajun French folktales: animal and magic tales, jokes and tall tales, and legends and historical tales. Each story comes with an English translation and biographical information on the storytellers.

Brasseaux, Carl A. *Acadian to Cajun: Transformation of a People* (UP of Mississippi, 1992; second printing 1999). Examines Acadian community life in the nineteenth century, including cultural evolution, demographic growth, and political involvement. Also available in electronic book format (Netlibrary, 2000).

Cajun French at LSU. http://appl003.lsu.edu/artsci/frenchweb.nsf/ $content/Cajun+French+Definition?OpenDocument. Defines Cajun, presents information on the evolution and variability of the Cajun dialect, and addresses its preservation and perpetuation.

Kein, Sybil, ed. *The History and Legacy of Louisiana's Free People of Color* (LSU Press, 2000). A collection of articles dealing with cultural and linguistic topics such as the origin of Louisiana Creole, the use of Creole in Southern literature, race and gender issues, Afro-Caribbean connections, and creole music and food.

Valdman, Albert, project director. *Discovering Cajun French through the Spoken Word* (Indiana University Creole Institute, 2003). Authentic samples of Cajun speech recorded on CD-ROM.

42

Did German almost become the language of the United States?

Nancy P. Nenno

What part did German immigrants play in eighteenth-century America? Did they come close to making the young United States a German-speaking country? What's 'Liberty Cabbage', and how did it get its name?

The official language of the United States of America was almost—German? It's not true, but the so-called Mühlenberg legend is one that never seems to die. As the story goes, the U.S. would have become a German-speaking country in 1795 had it not been for a single vote in the House of Representatives—ironically, a vote putatively cast by a bilingual Representative from Pennsylvania, Frederick Augustus Conrad Mühlenberg. What's the real story? Well, it's true that German was widely spoken in Philadelphia when the Congress met there. And it's true that a group of Virginia farmers petitioned in 1794 for a German translation of some American laws. But the cliffhanger vote that saved English? It never happened.

So where does the notion that German came close to supersed-ing English as America's language come from? It's not completely far-fetched. Germans began immigrating to the U.S. as early as

1683, and from then until the First World War, German was the most prevalent language in Pennsylvania after English. Not everybody was happy about this conspicuous German presence. 'Why,' asked one senior statesman from the Revolutionary period, 'should *Pennsylvania*, founded by the English, become a Colony of *Aliens*, who will shortly be so numerous as to Germanize us instead of our Anglifying them, and [who] will never adopt our Language or Customs, any more than they can acquire our Complexion?'

It might surprise you to learn that this diatribe flowed from the pen of none other than Benjamin Franklin, whose hostility seems to have been aroused by the success of German-speaking business competitors.

Anti-foreign sentiments persisted through the nineteenth century, but German continued to thrive in the U.S. German-Americans celebrated their heritage in social organizations all over the country, and German-language publications flourished. That all ended with the First World War. Most states actually eliminated German from their schools; some eighteen thousand people in the Midwest were charged during the war years with violating English-only statutes; and sauerkraut makers demonstrated patriotism by relabeling their product 'Liberty Cabbage'.

Attitudes towards German-Americans and German culture during the Second World War weren't nearly so harsh—perhaps because, like the first German immigrants to America, many of the German speakers who came to the U.S. before and during the war were fleeing religious and political persecution. Eminent scholars like Theodore Adorno, writers like Thomas Mann, and scientists like Albert Einstein have enriched the intellectual climate of the U.S.; and film actors and directors like Conrad Veidt and Otto Preminger have been highly visible in American popular culture. Ironically, these refugees and exiles from Hitler's Europe became part of a Hollywood that for decades has used German accents as a kind of aural shorthand for evil. Ever since the 1940s, in scores of films from *Casablanca* onward, the bad guys are always the ones who pronounce their W's like V's. There are, of course, a lot of exceptions to that stereotype. Marlene Dietrich's songs derived much of their sexy appeal from her German accent. And Arnold Schwarzenegger's Austrian cadences have become intimately intertwined with the U.S. cultural—and political—landscape.

During the Cold War, demand for German—as a language of both the East German enemy and the West German ally—was high. Today, it is unified Germany's leading position as economic and political powerhouse of the European Union that attracts new students to the study of German and makes it the third most studied language on college campuses.

It's really astonishing how many people of German heritage there are in America. The best known, probably, are the so-called Pennsylvania Dutch. (Their ancestors, by the way, came to the U.S. not from the Netherlands but from Germany. They called themselves 'Deutsch'—the German word for 'German'—but their English-speaking neighbors modified that to a more familiar-sounding word.) Beyond Pennsylvania, there are so many people of German ancestry in the U.S. heartland that the states from Ohio to Missouri and from Michigan to Nebraska are sometimes known as 'the German belt.' There are even pockets of German speakers in the Shenandoah Valley, where they are referred to as the 'Valley Dutch.' And in 1990, the so-called 'Texas Deutsch' emerged as the third largest ethnic group in that state. In fact, according to a 2008 American Community Survey, 50.3 million Americans claimed German descent—that's over 16 percent of the population, more than those with Irish, English or Italian ancestry.

On top of everything else, German has enriched English with marvelous vocabulary—from Autobahns to Zeppelins, from Frankfurters to Fahrenheit, from Wienerschnitzel to Weltschmerz. And even though German never seriously challenged English as the primary language of the U.S., the ties between the two languages are long and deep.

About the author

Nancy P. Nenno is Associate Professor of German and Chair of the Department of German and Slavic Studies at the College of Charleston,

South Carolina. She earned her degrees at Brown University in Rhode Island and the University of California at Berkeley, and has studied at the University of Tübingen and the Free University of Berlin. Her research and publications focus on twentieth-century culture, literature and film. Her ongoing project examines German representations of African Americans between the world wars, and she has recently published on Victor Trivas's 1931 film *Niemandsland*.

Suggestions for further reading

In this book
Other languages of America are discussed in Chapters 28 (rescuing threatened Native American languages), 38 (languages of the U.S.), 39 (America's language crisis), 40 (New World Spanish), 41 (Cajun), 43 (Gullah), and 52 (Native American languages). Other sociolinguistic topics are talked about in Chapters 10 (pidgins and creoles) and 21 (language conflict).

Elsewhere
Adams, Willi Paul. *The German-Americans: An Ethnic Experience* (German Information Center, 1993). Part of the *Peoples of North America* series, this booklet offers an historical and cultural overview of German immigration and assimilation in the U.S. Includes an excellent chronology of Germans in America. Also available online through the Max Kade German-American Center: www.ulib.iupui.edu/kade/adams/cover. html.

Arndt, Karl J. R., 'German as the Official Language of the United States of America?' in *Monatshefte*, vol. 68, no. 2 (summer 1976) pp129–50. Highly readable and detailed overview of the German-language press in colonial America and the Revolutionary War. Arndt attributes the Mühlenberg legend to misreading of a suggestion by J. H. C. Helmuth, a Lutheran pastor in eighteenth-century Philadelphia, that in communities where German was the lingua franca, legal matters might *also* be handled in German.

Bussman, H., et al. 'Pennsylvania Dutch', in *Routledge Dictionary of Language and Linguistics* (Routledge, 1996) p353. A concise history of the characteristics and continued existence of this dialect in the Eastern United States.

Crystal, David. 'A planning myth', in *The Cambridge Encyclopedia of Language* (Cambridge University Press, second edition 1997), p367. A concise description of the famous vote-that-never-was.

Gilbert, Glenn G., ed. *The German Language in America. A Symposium* (University of Texas Press, 1971). A collection of papers from a scholarly conference.

Barron, Dennis. 'Urban legend: German almost became the official language of the U.S', www.watzmann.net/scg/german-by-one-vote.html. Barron demolishes the Mühlenberg myth and reveals that German-speakers were even blamed for the severe winters in Pennsylvania.

www.census.gov/compendia/statab/2011/tables/11s0052.pdf

43

What's Gullah?

Elizabeth Martinez-Gibson

Where did Gullah come from? Does anyone speak it today?

Unless you're a linguist specializing in creoles and pidgins or in American dialects and languages—or you've lived or visited along the southeast coast of the U.S.—you may never have heard of the *Gullah* or *Geechee* language. Even some who have heard of it think it's a Native American language, or some variation of African American English. Actually, it's a creole blend of African languages with English, developed in the slave communities of the coastal South Atlantic in the seventeenth and eighteenth centuries. Even before the U.S. existed as a country, Gullah was spoken along the North American coast from North Carolina to northern Florida. Remarkably, the language has survived for over three hundred years and continues to be an important part of identity for the Gullah community.

There's no exact count of how many people speak Gullah, but a good estimate is that it's the primary language of at least three hundred thousand and the only language of at least seven thousand. Most of them are older people who live in quiet isolation on a cluster of small islands off the South Carolina and Georgia coasts. There's also a substantial population who live on the coastal mainland and speak English as their primary tongue, but switch to Gullah when they're among friends and family. If you hear them, you may think they're speaking Jamaican or another English-based creole of the Caribbean, like Bahamian or Trinidadian.

You may understand some of what you hear—because it contains many English words—but the longer you listen, the more you'll realize that Gullah is not a dialect of English but in fact another language.

There have been many theories about the origins of Gullah. Some thought it was a 'corrupted' form of Elizabethan English. Some considered it 'broken English' or a 'baby-talk' used by whites to communicate with their slaves. Others thought it was a language deliberately created by slaves so their owners would not understand them. Not until 1949, when Lorenzo Dow Turner published his research on *Africanisms in the Gullah Dialect*, did Gullah's origin in African languages become clear.

Some recent studies have shown great similarities between Gullah and the creole language Krio spoken in Sierra Leone. They share some vocabulary, such as *bigyai* (greedy), *pantap* (on top of), *alltwo* (both) and *swit* (delicious); and many Gullah personal names come from languages spoken in Sierra Leone. This connection was demonstrated during a 1988 visit by the President of Sierra Leone to South Carolina. He at one point spoke to a Gullah audience in Krio, and they understood with no need for translation.

Although some connections exist, Gullah is not the same as Krio or any specific African language; nor is it the same as African American Vernacular English. Although much of its vocabulary is English, it also draws vocabulary, and major elements of its grammar and pronunciation, from several west African languages. It's a kind of pan-African mix, created by slaves who came from different tribes and different countries with no common language. Their need to communicate with each other led to the formation of a pidgin language, which ultimately became a creole. Some theorists believe that the word *Gullah* may have come from *N'gola*, the name of a region of Africa (Angola) and also of tribal groups brought to South Carolina as slaves in the early eighteenth century. Gullah's African connections are most evident in its sounds, especially those it substitutes for certain consonants in words borrowed from English: 'th' becomes 'd' in *dey* ('they'), for example, and 'v' becomes 'w' in *willage* ('village') or sometimes 'b', as in *Debil* ('Devil').

While it is mainly a spoken language, Gullah also exists in written form: for example, the 1925 novel *Porgy*, the basis for Gershwin's musical *Porgy and Bess*, features characters speaking in Gullah. It's also the language of Uncle Remus in Joel Chandler Harris's *Bre'r Rabbit* tales. And in 2005, a Gullah translation of *De Nyew Testament* appeared in U.S. bookstores.

So how has the language survived so long, surrounded by an English-speaking majority? Some linguists believe this was due to isolation. First, a large part of the Gullah community, living on the Sea Islands, was physically separated from the U.S. mainland. There was not even a bridge to the mainland until the 1950s. Second, a fear of tropical diseases—against which the Africans had some resistance—led whites to live away from the low-lying areas along the coast, leaving their slaves in isolation for much of the year. This is not a unanimous view, but in any case, the numerical strength of the black community—and the Gullah people's powerful sense of community life—helped them preserve their language, unique identity, and cultural traditions.

Those traditions are still alive and strong; and the Gullah take pride in their melodic language, seeing it as an important link to their African past. But speakers of Gullah are increasingly harder to find as new generations give way to the American mainstream. Linguists and historians are working with a determined community to assure that the culture will be preserved, and that Gullah will be a living language for years to come. Some of the richest resources on the language and culture can be found at two South Carolina sites: the Avery Research Center at the College of Charleston and the Penn Center on St. Helena Island.

About the author
Elizabeth Martínez-Gibson is a Ph.D. and Professor of Spanish and Linguistics. She has been at the College of Charleston, in the heart of the Gullah region, for nineteen years. She has also taught at the University

of Florida. Dr. Martínez-Gibson has taught courses in Spanish Phonetics and Phonology, Spanish Morphology and Syntax, History of the Spanish Language, General Linguistics, and Language Variation of Spanish and American dialects. In 2009, she also taught a class on Charleston dialects and Gullah for the Honors College Series 'Interdisciplinary Creative Exchange'. She created and directs the Interdisciplinary Linguistics Minor Program at the College of Charleston.

Suggestions for further reading

In this book

Other languages of America are discussed in Chapters 28 (rescuing threatened Native American languages), 38 (languages of the U.S.), 39 (America's language crisis), 40 (New World Spanish), 41 (Cajun), 42 (German in the U.S.), and 52 (Native American languages). Other socio-linguistic topics are talked about in Chapters 10 (pidgins and creoles) and 21 (language conflict).

Elsewhere

Turner, Lorenzo D. *Africanisms in the Gullah Dialect*. (University of South Carolina Press, 1949; reprinted 2002). Turner was the first researcher of the Gullah language and culture in the United States. This pioneering book provides a historical as well as a linguistic perspective on the Gullah language and people.

Opala, Joseph. *The Gullah: Rice, Slavery and the Sierra Leone-American Connection* (U.S. Park Service, 2000). A concise account of the links between Sierra Leone and the Gullah culture.

Holloway, Joseph E. *Africanisms in American Culture* (Indiana University Press, 1990).

Holloway, Joseph E. and Winifred K. Vass. *The African Heritage of American English* (Indiana University Press, 1993). Research on African American language and culture—including Gullah—and their roots in Africa.

www.beaufortcountylibrary.org/htdocs-sirsi/gullah.htm. General information about Gullah, including language samples, recipes, and a bibliography of sources for further research.

www.africanheritage.com/Sierra_Leone_and_America.asp. This website from the University of South Florida provides an informative summary of Joseph Opala's *The Gullah* (listed above), plus much more.

www.seaislandcreole.org. Information about the recent Gullah translation of the New Testament.

44

Are dialects dying?

Walt Wolfram

Is shared popular culture wiping out dialects, in America and elsewhere? Can new dialects appear in today's world? Do you speak a dialect?

How do you say the word 'bought'? In the United States alone there are at least four distinct regional pronunciations of the vowel, from 'awe' to 'ah' to a rural southern version that sounds almost like 'ow' to the 'wo' used by comedians to lampoon dyed-in-the-wool New Yorkers (as in 'cwoffee twok').

Is the carbonated beverage you drink *pop, soda, tonic, co-cola*—or maybe even the older Appalachian mountain term *dope*? When you take the highway circling a city, do you drive on a *beltline*, a *beltway*, a *loop*, or a *perimeter*? And do you get cash at a *bank machine*, an *automated teller*, a *cash machine*, or an *ATM*?

Everyone notices dialects—we can't help it. But most of the time, we notice them in *other* people. 'We don't speak a dialect where we live, we speak normal English.' Speakers from Boston to Birmingham (Alabama and England) and from Medicine Hat to Melbourne (Florida and Australia) all echo the same sentiment. Of course, they do this while pronouncing the vowel in words like *bought* and *caught* in quite different ways. Or while using different names for the same sandwich—a *sub*, a *grinder*, a *hoagie*, or a *hero.*

Dialects are everywhere, not just in those regions—like Appalachia, Liverpool, or the Outback—that seem to get the most dialect press. The fact of the matter is that it's impossible to speak the English language without speaking a dialect, some dialect. Everyone has an accent. When you pronounce the vowel in *bought* or *caught* (or was that *baht* and *caht*?) you've made a dialect commitment—you can't help it. We are all players in the dialect game, whether we like it or not.

But isn't this a different world? A global community where people move fluidly, travel frequently, and speak to each other by cell phone? Aren't dialects dying out, thanks to mobility and the media? Think again! Dialectologists counter the popular myth that dialects are dying by showing that major U.S. dialect areas like the North, Midland, and South remain very much alive—as they have been for a couple of centuries. But the dialect news is even more startling: research shows that Northern and Southern speech in the U.S. are actually diverging—not becoming more similar. Blame those shifty vowels, which in large Northern cities like Buffalo and Chicago are acquiring sounds different from those we hear in other regions. So *coffee* becomes *cahffee*, *lock* sounds almost like *lack*, and *bat* sounds more like *bet*. Have you noticed? Don't worry if you haven't. The change is pretty subtle, and a lot of it flies under the impressionistic radar. But it's very real—and it's gradually making the speech of Northern U.S. cities quite different from that of the South and West.

How can this be? In today's compressed world it seems illogical that dialects could continue developing and diverging the way they did when language communities were more isolated. But language is always changing, and sometimes behaves as though it has a mind of its own. Yes, we all watch the same TV programs; but most of us don't model our accents on TV newscasters—that's way too impersonal. We follow the lead of those we interact with in our daily lives—*they're* the ones who judge how well we fit in with the community.

And there remain plenty of regions where encroaching global culture is held at bay by a strong sense of community that includes local dialect. So working class Pittsburghers are proud to root for the Pittsburgh *Stillers*—instead of the *Steelers*; go *dahntahn*—instead of *downtown*, and put a *gum band* around their papers—

instead of what other Americans would call a *rubber band* and Britons would call an *elastic band*. Part of being a Pittsburgher is speaking Pittsburghese.

But aren't *some* dialects dying, like the ones once spoken in isolated mountain and island communities now flooded by tourists? Some may be, but there are also rural communities that (like Pittsburgh on a smaller scale) keep their dialects alive as a way of fighting back, and ensuring that they won't be confused with what they call 'furriners'.

Perhaps the most surprising news of all is that some areas of increasing prosperity and cultural influence—like Seattle and northern California—are starting to express their new regional identity by developing dialect traits that didn't exist before.

So some traditional dialects may be disappearing, but they're being replaced by new dialects, in a process that can seem like the carnival game 'whack-a-mole'. The famous words of Mark Twain apply well to English dialects in America and elsewhere: rumors of their death are greatly exaggerated. Dialects remain alive and well—and an important part of the regional and sociocultural landscape.

About the author

Walt Wolfram, William C. Friday Distinguished Professor of English Linguistics at North Carolina State University, describes himself as a dialect nomad. He has studied dialects ranging from African American varieties in large metropolitan areas to the speech of small, isolated island and mountain communities. He has authored more than 20 books and 250 articles, in addition to producing a number of TV documentaries. More information on Dr. Wolfram's media productions is available at www.talkingnc.com and www.ncsu.edu/linguistics.

Suggestions for further reading

In this book

Dialects are discussed in Chapters 4 (dialects versus languages), 20 (English in Britain, America, and elsewhere), and 30 (U.S. Southern

English). Language extinction is discussed in Chapters 3 (languages of the world), 27 (language death), 28 (language rescue), and 53 (Latin). Chapters talking more generally about how languages evolve include 8 (language change), 10 (pidgins and creoles), 13 (grammar), 51 (origins of English), and 54 (Italian).

Elsewhere

Labov, William, Sharon Ash and Charles Boberg. *The Atlas of North American English: Phonetics, Phonology and Sound Change* (Mouton/ de Gruyter, 2006). A major new work on the dialects of North America, based on the pronunciation of various vowel sounds. It is mostly intended for the dedicated scholar. A more accessible overview of some of the results from this project can be found at the TELSUR (telephone survey) website: www.ling.upenn.edu/phonoatlas.

Wolfram, Walt and Ben Ward, eds. *American Voices: How Dialects Differ from Coast to Coast* (Blackwell, 2006). This collection contains brief, popular profiles of major and minor dialects in North America. Both dying dialects and new dialect traditions of American English are included in the presentations by major researchers, as well as descriptions of sociocultural varieties of English.

45

Can you make a living loving languages?

Frederick H. Jackson

What kinds of careers are there for people who like foreign languages? What should you do to prepare for them?

Perhaps something like this has happened to you. Let's say you really enjoy languages. At some time in your life—in school, on military assignment, in the Peace Corps, or while traveling abroad—you found that learning how a language works—and using it—was really *fun*. But just as you were thinking that you might want to study the language in depth, or maybe even learn another one, someone looked at you with concern (or pity) and said: 'Foreign languages? Hah!! How are you going to make a living with that?' You may even have been asked whether you were planning to take a vow of poverty.

Well, the answer is that there are *lots* of ways knowing languages can help you make a living—and a fairly good one, too.

It's helpful to divide those ways of making a living into two broad categories. On the one hand are professions centered around and dependent on language skill. Let's call them 'Careers in Language'. On the other hand are many more types of jobs where language ability is an important tool that enables you to do something else entirely; these we will call 'Language in Careers'.

Careers in Language are directly based upon outstanding ability in one or more languages. One such career that comes quickly to mind is teaching a language, and there are certainly a lot of positions for language teachers in schools and colleges and other training institutions. Some states in the U.S. are importing teachers from other countries because they are in short supply locally. If you like languages and cultures, you should certainly think about teaching them. It can be a very rewarding career.

And then, of course, there are translating and interpreting. Both careers require extremely strong language skills, deep understanding of the cultures involved, and subject matter expertise, plus special training. Both offer a wide variety of different jobs.

Translators may be called on to translate any kind of document—a scientific article, for example, or a legal contract, a work of literature, a suspicious e-mail, even an advertisement for peanut butter. (Translating advertising copy into another language is often just as demanding as translating more 'official' material, because of the need to address a large audience in a way that doesn't run afoul of subtle cultural differences.)

Interpreters can help a monolingual patient describe symptoms to a doctor who doesn't speak the patient's language; or help executives or diplomats negotiate with foreign counterparts; or maybe serve on the 'language line', a telephone system that connects interpreters with people who need them; or facilitate international meetings or conferences, such as at the United Nations or the European Union, making sure all participants can understand each other. Really good translators and interpreters are not easy to find, so there are a great number of positions in national and regional government agencies, as well as in international firms and other non-governmental organizations.

None of those 'Careers in Language' jobs can be done without truly advanced language skills. But most people with strong language skills work at jobs of a different kind—what we are calling 'Language in Careers'. The list of such jobs is long: business people, social workers, law enforcement officers, actors, medical personnel, marketers, journalists, historians, and many more—a very wide variety of professions in which subject matter expertise is the core, but language is a tool that gives you leverage, making you a better performer. The business person with a second language has an advantage in the global economy, so it's common for new hires with language skills to come in at higher pay; scientists can read the work of foreign researchers who may not write in English; librarians can work with books from other countries; environmentalists can fight more effectively to preserve the rain forest; doctors and nurses can understand the needs of their patients.

And there is government. Diplomats in all countries need strong proficiency in at least one language to advance in their careers—more commonly two or three languages—and the U.S. military has established a similar requirement for its officers. Intelligence and law enforcement agencies, courts, homeland security, and even purely administrative organizations like census bureaus are likely to have hundreds of positions that require language skill. A 1999 survey identified more than eighty federal agencies that needed people with professional skills in more than a hundred languages. Those needs are certainly even greater now, and include not only jobs *centered* on language, like teaching and translating, but also jobs in which language skills *enhance* the effectiveness of employees and the agencies they work for.

One other field that attracts people interested in language is linguistics. Several chapters of this book describe some of the specialties within this field. Professional linguists use their knowledge in many important kinds of work, from writing grammars and dictionaries to doing research on electronic communication, machine translation, or artificial intelligence, to training new linguists in colleges. Linguists investigate and give expert advice on effective political discourse, public relations, doctor–patient communication, and cultural differences in use of language in a courtroom. One linguist you may know is Professor Deborah Tannen, who has written several insightful books on how people may miscommunicate on the job, at home, or within the family. Another area of rapidly increasing interest to linguists and other social scientists is language documentation, the effort to record and describe endangered languages—perhaps as many as half of the nearly 7,000 spoken today—before they are lost forever, along with whatever they may have to tell us about human history, development and cognition.

So if you start learning a language, and you find that you love it, follow your heart. Give it the time needed to learn it well. One way or another your ability will pay off.

About the author
Frederick H. Jackson is Senior Research Scientist at the National Foreign Language Center of the University of Maryland. Previously, he was at the School of Language Studies of the Foreign Service Institute (FSI), the training arm of the State Department, where he also served as Coordinator of the U.S. government's Interagency Language Roundtable (ILR, www.govtilr.org). He has an M.A. in English as a Second Language and a Ph.D. in Linguistics, both from the University of Hawai'i. He has published research in language teacher education and in the languages of Micronesia and Mainland Southeast Asia, and has made numerous professional presentations at national and international conferences.

Suggestions for further reading

In this book
Other chapters discussing professional opportunities for people with language skills include 2 (what linguists do), 22 (bilingualism), 39 (America's language crisis), 46 (dictionaries), 47 (interpreting and translating), 49 (forensic linguistics), 56 (Russian), and 59 (Arabic).

Elsewhere
Crump, T. C. *Translating and Interpreting in the Federal Government* (American Translators Association, www.atanet.org, 1999). Prepared by a professional translator at the National Institutes of Health, this book describes more than one hundred jobs and careers in eighty federal agencies.

Journal of Language Documentation and Conservation. University of Hawai'i. Access at http://nflrc.hawaii.edu/ldc. A free online journal that reports on many of the most cutting-edge efforts in the new field of Language Documentation.

Rifkin, B. 'Studying a Foreign Language at the Postsecondary Level' in *The Language Educator*, vol. 1.2 (2006). Provides advice to college students about why to study foreign languages, how to do it successfully, and what you do with a language after graduation.

Tannen, D. *You Just Don't Understand: Women and Men in Conversation* (Ballantine, 1990). One of the first of Professor Tannen's important books on how communication often goes astray. Written for the lay reader.

Camenson, B. *Careers in Foreign Languages* (McGraw-Hill, 2001). This short book and the two that follow provide detailed information on jobs and careers that involve significant skill in foreign languages. There are more such jobs than you can imagine!

Seelye, H. N. and J. L. Day. *Careers for Foreign Language Aficionados and Other Multilingual Types* (McGraw-Hill, 2001).

Rivers, W. *Opportunities in Foreign Language Careers* (VGM Career Horizons, 1998).

'Careers in Foreign Languages', http://flc.osu.edu/resources/careers/default.cfm. Site maintained by the Ohio State University Language Resource Center. Numerous links for interested language students to explore.

'Ten Jobs You Didn't Know You Could Do with a Foreign Language', www.responsesource.com/releases/rel_display.php?relid=37442&hilite=.

Interagency Language Roundtable, www.govtilr.org/ILR_career.htm.

46

How are dictionaries made?

Erin McKean

What's a lexicographer? How many of them does it take to make a dictionary? How do they decide what to put in and what to leave out? Why don't dictionaries tell us what's right and what's wrong?

Think of our language as an immense glacier, a giant shining mass made of words instead of ice. Like a glacier, language usually changes very, very slowly, with occasional huge surges forward. The English language is moving—changing—very slowly, most of the time. Sure, there are sometimes surprising surges of new words, but most of the changes happen so slowly and gradually that they're almost imperceptible. A slightly different meaning here, a new ending on a word there—who notices? Well, lexicographers notice. Lexicographers keep track of language change and record it in the dictionaries they make—but they're always a step behind.

As recently as a few centuries ago it was possible for one very learned person to create a dictionary single-handedly. But these days virtually all dictionaries are built by whole teams of talented people. For each new dictionary, and each new edition of an existing dictionary, they collect huge amounts of written and spoken language—from newspapers, magazines, books, plays, movies, speeches, TV and radio shows, interviews and the Internet—and sift them for evidence of how language is being used: what words haven't been seen before? What words are changing their meanings? What words are used only in particular ways? What are their histories, pronunciations, grammatical quirks and foibles?

If you think this makes lexicographers sound like scientists, you're exactly right. Most of them see their primary job as data collecting. They try to capture as accurate a picture as possible of how people actually use a language at a given point in time.

But a lot of people in the dictionary-buying public are uncomfortable with scientific neutrality when it comes to language. They don't want their dictionaries to describe how people actually write and speak. They believe that some language is right and some is wrong, period. And they think the lexicographer's job is to tell us which is which. They want prescriptive dictionaries that omit vulgar language and condemn other words they disapprove of, like 'irregardless' or 'muchly'.

If you're one of those people, you'll be disappointed to learn that most modern dictionaries are basically descriptive. They don't prescribe what we ought to say or write; they tell us what people actually do. Like umpires, lexicographers don't make rules—they just call 'em the way they see 'em.

That doesn't mean that prescriptive views are completely left out. People's attitudes toward words are also a legitimate part of a dictionary. For example, the *New Oxford American Dictionary* doesn't forbid its readers to use the unlovely word 'irregardless', but it clearly notes that the word is 'avoided by careful users of English.' Because people no longer use words like 'fletcherize' (meaning to chew each bite at least thirty-two times before you swallow), and because you don't talk the way people did in eight-eenth-century Williamsburg, you know that language is always in flux. So if research finds a lot of good and careful writers using 'irregardless', or creating sentences like 'Anybody could look it up if they wanted to'—using 'they' where you might expect 'he or she'—the dictionary can say with authority that it's becoming standard English—even if prescriptivists disapprove.

There's also a whole new category of dictionary—the online dictionary—where you can see word evidence as quickly as the lexicographers can, without waiting for it to make it through the editorial process. At Wordnik.com (a site I founded), automated processes sift through billions of words to select sentences based on how well they represent the word you're interested in. The site allows users to leave comments, record pronunciations, tag words, and even see images from the online photo site Flickr.com. Purely crowdsourced sites such as UrbanDictionary.com and Wiktionary. org let users put in their two cents, as well. The upside of all these sites is that they can show you much more information than a traditional dictionary, much faster (and Wordnik and Wiktionary also incorporate traditional dictionary information like parts of speech and synonyms). However, you need to use your own knowledge and employ your critical thinking skills to filter the information shown. For instance, if a word's usage is illustrated by plenty of sentences, but they're all from personal blogs, the word is likely considered more informal than one where all the sentences shown are from the *Wall Street Journal*.

So don't think of dictionaries as rulebooks. They're much more like maps. They show where things are in relation to each other and point out where the terrain is rough. And, like maps, dictionaries (especially online dictionaries) are constantly updated to show the changing topography of a language—not just with shiny new words (like 'locavore' or 'staycation' or 'crowdsourced') but new uses for old words (like 'burn' meaning 'record data on a compact disk') and even new parts of words (the suffix -age as in 'signage' or 'mopeage'—which is really just a funnier way of saying 'moping'). Dictionary-makers put as good a map as possible into your hands, but devising a route is up to you.

About the author

Erin McKean is the founder of the new online dictionary Wordnik. Previously she was the Editor in Chief of U.S. Dictionaries for Oxford University Press and the Editor of *VERBATIM: The Language Quarterly*. She is also the author of *Weird and Wonderful Words, More Weird and Wonderful Words, Totally Weird and Wonderful Words*, and *That's Amore* (also about words). Her first novel, *The Secret Lives of Dresses*, was published in 2011. She has a B.A. and M.A. in Linguistics from the University of Chicago, where she wrote her M.A. thesis on the treatment of phrasal verbs (verbs like 'act up', 'act out', and, of course, 'look up') in children's dictionaries. She lives in California. Please send her evidence of new words you've found, by e-mail, to feedback@wordnik.com.

Suggestions for further reading

In this book
How languages evolve over time is discussed in Chapters 8 (language change), 10 (pidgins and creoles), 13 (grammar), 44 (U.S. dialect change), 51 (origins of English), 53 (Latin), and 54 (Italian). The concept of language rules is covered further in Chapters 19 (prescriptivism) and 20 (British and American English). Other professional opportunities for people interested in language are discussed in Chapters 22 (bilingualism), 39 (America's language crisis), 45 (language-related careers), 47 (interpreting and translating), and 49 (forensic linguistics).

Elsewhere
Winchester, Simon. *The Professor and the Madman: A Tale of Murder, Insanity, and the Making of the Oxford English Dictionary* (Harper Perennial, 1999; published in the UK as *The Surgeon of Crowthorne*).
Winchester, Simon. *The Meaning of Everything: The Story of the Oxford English Dictionary* (Oxford University Press, 2003).
The two Simon Winchester books are both wonderful introductions to the greatest dictionary of the English language, the *Oxford English Dictionary*. *Professor* recounts, with novelistic flair, the true story of some of the personalities involved in making the OED; *Meaning of Everything* has more detail and covers the entire scope of the project, which is ongoing.

Murray, K. M. Elisabeth. *Caught in the Web of Words: James Murray and the Oxford English Dictionary* (Yale University Press, 2001). People who are still intrigued can read this biography of James Murray, the original editor of the OED, written by his granddaughter.

Landau, Sidney I. *Dictionaries: The Art and Science of Lexicography* (Cambridge University Press, second edition 2001). This book is the best starting point for people interested in the nuts and bolts of how dictionaries are made.

47

Why do we need translators if we have dictionaries?

Kevin Hendzel

*What does it take to be an interpreter? With a good
dictionary, isn't translating something anybody can do?*

I'm always impressed when I see someone standing behind a president or prime minister, interpreting a foreign visitor's comments
into his ear. What *talent* it takes to translate one language into
another—listening and speaking at the same time! You can't pick
up a dictionary. And you can't just spit out words like a robot. The
interpreter's job is to convey *meaning*. And since a lot of meaning
is expressed by tone of voice or the nuance of words and phrases,
his or her job is far more than translating word for word.

   And what responsibility! Imagine a court case in which the
defendant doesn't speak the language of the judge and the jury.
If an interpreter gets it wrong, how can justice be done? Not everyone can move easily between two languages, but there needs to
be somebody who knows how. That 'somebody' is a professional
interpreter.

   There's the same need for professional translators, who deal
with the *written* word as interpreters deal with *spoken* language.
Think about how important the choice of words or phrases is in,
let's say, a business contract. Or on the famous 'hotline' between
the White House and the Kremlin, which does not—contrary to
what many people think—connect a bright red telephone on the

U.S. President's desk to a similar one on the desk of the Russian leader. Instead, it's an encrypted high-speed data link that transmits written, rather than spoken, messages—and it requires a translator, rather than an interpreter.

So what does it take to be a professional translator or interpreter? And let me emphasize the word 'professional'. Because simply knowing two languages isn't enough—it's just a starting point.

Beyond skill in speaking a second language, an interpreter needs to know the two *cultures* involved, the use of slang or dialects of the languages, and the subject matter to be interpreted. To be really good at it, he or she has to have an exceptional memory—and a lot of training in the art of interpreting.

A *translator* needs somewhat different skills. But again, strong knowledge of two languages is just the beginning, because translating can get very complicated. Think of the technical terminology translators are called on to handle. Lawyers file *writs of mandamus*. Physicians treat *hypertrophic cardiomyopathy*. Terms like these can be pretty daunting, and for translation it's not enough just to look up their dictionary equivalents in another language—you need to understand what they mean. This is why many professional translators and interpreters have advanced degrees in specific technical fields—many are trained engineers, architects, physicians and attorneys. When a translator works from one language into another, that process involves first understanding the concept in one language, and then 'interpreting' or 'describing' that concept in another language. In a nutshell, translation isn't about words. It's about what the words are about.

So how do you get into one of these professions? Well, it's best if you've already had training in a substantive field—like engineering, medicine or finance—that you'll specialize in. It also probably helps to be born somewhere like Belgium, where virtually everyone grows up with two or more languages. But even if you're not bilingual from childhood, with hard work you can get close to it; after that, becoming professionally qualified is mostly a matter of training and practice. You'll need a minimum of a master's degree, which in the U.S. requires two years of study; in Europe, three years or more. And you'll have on-the-job internships before you're turned loose on society. The final step is certification by an organization like the American Translators Association.

Yes, it takes some time. But translation and interpreting are exciting and often lucrative careers. The language services industry is valued at $13.5 billion in the U.S. alone, and was one of the very few professions to actually grow every year during the 'Great Recession' of 2007–2009. And the flourishing of the European Union, with easy movement of people, products and ideas across borders, generates huge demand for certified interpreters in Europe. Training programs for translators and interpreters are on the rise all over the world—and that's a good thing, because there are severe shortages of qualified interpreters and translators in every field.

If you would like to learn more about the translation and interpreting professions, to investigate training programs, or to seek out professional translators or interpreters for your business or institution, one source is the website of the American Translators Association, www.atanet.org. In addition to comprehensive information on the field and a directory of bloggers who write about it (www.atanet.org/careers/blog_trekker.php), this site provides a searchable online database of translators and interpreters, plus contact information for experts on many topics relating to translation and interpreting.

There have been interpreters for as long as people have spoken different tongues; and translators for as long as there has been writing. Contrary to the myth that everyone speaks English, as the world grows smaller we need translators and interpreters more than ever before.

About the author

Kevin Hendzel is a graduate of Georgetown University's School of Foreign Service and was formerly head linguist on the technical translation staff of the Presidential Hotline between the White House and the Kremlin. He is currently the national media spokesman for the American Translators Association. As such he is a well-known commentator on translation and interpreting issues on national and international media, including National Public Radio. His translations from Russian into English include thirty-four books and twenty-two hundred articles published in the areas of physics, technology, and law. He continues to work as a translator, currently specializing in national security areas. These range from nuclear weapons dismantlement and disposition programs in the former Soviet Union to U.S.-sponsored programs aimed at preventing the proliferation of nuclear, biological, and chemical weapons worldwide.

Suggestions for further reading

In this book
Other discussions of opportunities and requirements for professional use of language abilities are discussed in Chapters 2 (what linguists do), 22 (bilingualism), 39 (America's language crisis), 46 (dictionaries), 49 (forensic linguistics), 56 (Russian), and 59 (Arabic).

Elsewhere
McKay, Corinne. *How to Succeed as a Freelance Translator* (Lulu Press, 2006). Designed as an introduction to professional freelance translation, this work by one of the leading bloggers on translation and interpreting (http://thoughtsontranslation.com) provides excellent practical advice on paths to success in commercial translation for both novices and experienced translators.

Durbin, Chris. *The Prosperous Translator* (FA&WB Press, 2010). A collection of the best insight, no-nonsense advice, and witty commentary on working at the very top of the translation field, collected over twelve years from Chris Durbin and Eugene Seidel's online advice column 'Fire Ant and Worker Bee'.

Jenner, Julie and Dagmar Jenner. *The Entrepreneurial Linguist* (EL Press, 2010). This book by longtime translating twins Judy and Dagmar Jenner applies the lessons of business school to the translation and interpreting professions. It is designed for both beginning and established translators and interpreters around the world.

48

How good is machine translation?

David Savignac

*How far in the future are computers like HAL in the movie
2001? Why aren't computers already replacing humans in
tasks like translating foreign languages?*

When the computer was invented, around the middle of the
twentieth century, one of the first things people thought about
was how it might be used to translate foreign languages. But early
efforts at machine translation (MT) can most charitably be said
to have fizzled. In the late 1960s and early 1970s the effort was
almost completely abandoned. You've probably heard the funny
mistranslation stories: the computer that rendered 'The spirit is
willing but the flesh is weak' as 'The whisky is strong but the meat
is rotten'; or the computer that transformed a pumping device
known as a 'hydraulic ram' into a 'water goat'. Machines can
indeed translate texts from one language to another, but the Holy
Grail for humans who use them—'fully automated high-quality
machine translation'—is still elusive. What's causing the problem
here?

Well, the culprit is the complexity of language in general.
This complexity begins at the word level. Take the word 'bark':
a computer doesn't know that a dog isn't covered with wood, or
that a tree doesn't make loud noises when someone approaches,
so it's handicapped in deciding which possible translation of 'bark'

it should choose in a given sentence. Or how about the Spanish verb *comer*? Depending on the sentence it appears in, it can mean 'eat', 'capture', 'overlook', 'corrode', 'fade', 'itch', 'skip', 'slur', 'swallow', or 'take'; picking the correct translation from such an array of possibilities puts significant demands on a computer's calculating abilities.

At the sentence level the complexity gets even worse. Take this sentence: 'John saw the woman in the park with a telescope.' It could mean any of half a dozen things. For starters, who do you think has the telescope, John or the woman in the park? Or is it John who's in the park? Or are there two parks, one with a telescope and one without? A human encountering such a sentence knows enough to look in nearby sentences for clues to the intended meaning, but a computer's mind may well boggle.

Underlying challenges to machine translation is the fact that each language carves up pieces of knowledge in different ways, and there is no one-to-one mapping between them. The less two languages resemble each other, the harder the problems of translation between them are. Where English has three third-person singular pronouns, 'he', 'she', and 'it', Turkish has just one: *on*. Lacking any gender-related cues, how do you translate *on* into English? There are some languages that simply do not distinguish between green and blue, but Russian has two words for 'blue' where English has only one—so if you want to translate 'She's wearing a blue dress' into Russian, you have a fifty percent chance of choosing the right word, unless perhaps you can see the dress. There are many cases in which you just can't make an exact translation between languages.

But now for the good news. Despite its limitations, there are situations in which the machine does a very good job, particularly if the topic of translation is narrow. The Canadian Meteorological Centre, for example, uses machine translation for bilingual weather reporting. In the commercial world, technical writers have learned to write manuals and parts catalogs so that computer-based translations—let's say from Japanese to English—need only a little correction. Even on the Internet, the click of a mouse can translate entire Web pages with fairly good quality, at least for some languages.

And let's remember that machine translation doesn't always have to be perfect. It can be very useful even if it has some garbles. For instance, where human translators are scarce and the volume of material to be translated is great—as is frequently the case in the post-9/11 world—machines are widely used to 'triage' material before it reaches the desk of an overworked human. The National Security Agency's 'CyberTrans' software, created for the Department of Defense and the Intelligence Community, does precisely that: it identifies a language, corrects misspelled words, and translates some sixty-five languages into English, with quality that's usually good enough for scanning.

And the future looks good. Sparked by the events of 9/11 and energized by subsequent government funding, machine translation experts in academia, the commercial sector, and government are implementing new approaches to machine translation and the results to date have been very encouraging. The quality of Arabic-to-English translation, for example, has improved dramatically in the past five years. Machines are making multilingual chat rooms possible on the Web and helping multinational military forces talk to one another. Yes, a human translator is better, but even though the goal of 'fully automated high-quality machine translation' is still not in sight, we've come a long way. Steady progress is being made in quality, and the use of machine translation is increasing by leaps and bounds. The machine is here to stay.

About the author

David Savignac, currently Senior Director of Lexicography at Language Weaver/SDL International, is a former Director of the Center for Applied Machine Translation at the National Security Agency at Fort George G. Meade, Maryland. A multilinguist by training and a bit of a medievalist in his spare time, he holds a Ph.D. in Slavic linguistics from the Slavic Department at Stanford University and worked for the Department of Defense for over three decades.

Suggestions for further reading

In this book
For other discussions of linguistic/technological topics see Chapters 37 (language teaching technologies), 38 (interactive map of U.S. language communities), 49 (forensic linguistics), and 50 (the Museum of Languages). More on the subject of translation appears in Chapter 47 (interpreting and translating).

Elsewhere
The publications cited here are suggested by the author and do not represent the official opinions/endorsement of the National Security Agency/Central Security Service.

Nirenburg, Sergei, Harold L. Somers, and Yorick A. Wilks, eds. *Readings in Machine Translation* (MIT Press, 2003). An outstanding collection of some landmark papers from the last fifty years by people who have thought a lot about machine translation, its potential and its limitations.

Somers, Harold, ed. *Computers and Translation: A Translator's Guide* (Johns Benjamins, 2003). Most books dwell on the technology, theory, taxonomy, evaluation, and other analytic issues involved in machine translation. This book is much more nuts-and-bolts about how to make productive use of it.

Arnold, Doug, et al. *Machine Translation: An Introductory Guide*, (Blackwells-NCC, 1994). Also available, in pdf or html, at www.essex.ac.uk/linguistics/external/clmt/MTbook. The book is slightly dated, with limited coverage of current data-driven methods. But it's easy to browse, and freely accessible!

Hutchins, John. Publications on machine translation, computer-based translation technologies, linguistics and other topics, available at www.hutchinsweb.me.uk. John Hutchins has been the lead historian and documenter of the field of MT for twenty years. His website now has an encyclopedic collection of resources—papers and books by him and many others—all available as freely downloadable pdfs. The site is nicely organized, so it's easy to get general information or drill down to the level of one's interest.

Styx, Gary. 'The Elusive Goal of Machine Translation' in *Scientific American*, March 2006. Written for a broad audience, this article focuses on the 'statistical approach', thought by many to hold great promise for significant improvements in machine translation.

49

Can you use language to solve crimes?

Robert Rodman

What's a voiceprint? Can language usage be analyzed to identify the author of an anonymous letter or a Shakespeare play? to catch a criminal? to exonerate a suspect of a crime?

People who work with languages do a lot of things you probably never thought of. Think about this scenario: It's a dark and stormy night some time in the near future. You're leaving a party. After you slip behind the wheel and turn on the ignition, your car says, 'Count to five.' It won't start unless you do, so you count aloud: one, two, three, four, five. 'Sorry,' says your car, 'you've had too much to drink.' And it shuts off, because by analyzing your voice, the car's computer knows you're intoxicated.

Your voice can tell a lot about you: where you grew up, your emotional state, whether you're lying—even who you are. Voice analysis is one of the things that linguists do; it's part of a field known as Forensic Linguistics. It's the application of linguistic science to matters concerning the law, crime, and the courts.

In computer voice analysis, speech is broken down electronically and then examined for clues about the speaker. You've probably heard this kind of computer product called a 'voiceprint'. Because your voice may change over time, or with illness, voiceprints aren't as accurate as fingerprints or DNA analysis—which are unchanging from birth to death—but they're a very useful tool in solving crimes.

A recording of the supposed voice of the late notorious al-Qaeda leader Osama bin Laden was subjected to speaker authentication by computer analysis a year after the 9/11 atrocity. It was compared with fourteen voiceprints known to be bin Laden and sixteen voiceprints of Arabic male speakers known not to be bin Laden. And guess what? The unknown voice was a better match for the non-bin Laden group. This is just one example of how computer speech analysis has proved useful in authenticating or denying the identity of anonymous voices.

A similar situation occurred when a North Carolina state trooper was demoted in rank for allegedly leaving a racial slur in the voicemail of a fellow officer. The accused trooper requested a judicial hearing. An analysis by the author of this chapter convinced the presiding judge that the accused trooper's voice was not the one heard saying the racial slur. The trooper was reinstated with back pay.

And then there's analysis of writing. Consider The Case of the Dog Club Letters. No, this isn't a Sherlock Holmes mystery. It's an actual case where the committee members of a dog club received threatening anonymous letters. Personal details in each letter hinted that the writer was actually a committee member, but which one? A forensic linguist compared the letters with writing samples from each member. Analysis of their writing styles, including punctuation, capitalization, and spelling, revealed that the letter writer was the committee treasurer. He was drummed out of the club.

Ranging from doggy letters to the text of stage plays that may or may not have been written by Shakespeare, *authorship* can be determined by comparing patterns such as word groupings, sentence length, grammatical usages, and much more. Computers capable of analyzing thousands of such patterns provide powerful evidence as to authorship. This, by the way, is how forensic linguists established beyond doubt the authorship of some of the Federalist Papers, which had been in dispute for two hundred years.

Plagiarism is a bane of academia—often committed by students who take other people's writings from the Internet. Forensic Linguistics to the rescue! The same techniques used on the Federalist Papers can be used to detect whether material is plagiarized. Computer software reads a student's or scholar's paper, then scans millions of written works for duplication of specific words, phrases, sentences—even ideas.

Finally, a major concern of Forensic Linguistics is to clarify legal talk, so that people can understand the meaning of a law that may be couched in gobbledygook. For example, on the subject of expert witnesses one law reads: 'Expert evidence presented to the court should be, and should be seen to be, the independent product of the expert uninfluenced as to form or content by the exigencies of litigation.' The forensic linguist simplifies this to say, 'Expert witnesses should be free from prejudice.' Today, linguists are designing computer programs that automatically translate legalese into ordinary English.

So there's a lot going on in this field. If you want to learn more, use an Internet search engine on the words 'forensic' and 'linguistics'. And the next time you think of crime-fighting superheroes, forget the cape and bulging muscles—and picture a laptop-toting linguist.

About the author
Robert Rodman is a UCLA-trained linguist who is currently a Professor in the Department of Computer Science at North Carolina State University. He is author of *Computer Speech Technology* (1999). Dr. Rodman is also a forensic linguist and consults with the judiciary in matters involving language and the legal system.

Suggestions for further reading

In this book
Opportunities and requirements for professional use of language abilities are discussed in Chapters 22 (bilingualism), 39 (America's language

crisis), 45 (language-related careers), 46 (dictionaries), 47 (interpreting and translating), 56 (Russian), and 59 (Arabic). Other linguistic/technical topics appear in Chapters 37 (language teaching technology), 38 (interactive map of U.S. language communities), 48 (machine translation), and 50 (the Museum of Languages), 53 (Latin), and 64 (Esperanto).

Elsewhere

Coulthard, Malcolm and Alison Johnson (eds). *The Routledge Handbook of Forensic Linguistics* (Routledge, 2010). A unique work of reference to the leading ideas, debates, topics, approaches and methodologies in Forensic Linguistics.

Olsson, John. *Forensic Linguistics* (Continuum, second edition 2008). This is a core text for a rigorous introduction to the field of forensic linguistics. It is a carefully organized, clearly written book by one of Britain's most prominent forensic linguists.

Schane, Sanford. *Language and the Law* (Continuum, 2006). An introduction to the commonalities of language and the law by a pre-eminent American linguist.

Shuy, Roger. *Creating Language Crimes: How Law Enforcement Uses (and Misuses) Language* (Oxford University Press, 2005). A fascinating account with numerous illustrations of the centrality of language in all aspects of law enforcement, from arrest to arraignment to trial to sentencing. The author is a prominent American forensic linguist.

Solan, Lawrence and Peter Tiersma. *Speaking of Crime* (University of Chicago Press, 2005). This little book is another fascinating examination of the complex role of language within our criminal justice system. The authors have compiled numerous cases, ranging from the Lindbergh kidnapping to the impeachment trial of Bill Clinton to the Jon Benét Ramsey case, that provide real-life examples of how language functions in arrests, investigations, interrogations, confessions, and trials.

50
How can you keep languages in a museum?

Amelia C. Murdoch

What would there be to see and learn in a museum of language? Is there such a place?

As a matter of fact, such a place does exist. It's called the National Museum of Language, located in College Park, Maryland, a Washington, D.C. suburb, and it opened its doors to the public in May 2008. What a unique institution! Everyone is familiar with museums where you see (and sometimes touch) physical objects like airplanes, paintings, bleached bones and antique coins. But language, you might think, is mainly sounds and words and books. Don't libraries already exist to store and display them? What'll you do in a language museum? And why?

Language is a subject most of us want to know more about: how it developed, how languages differ, how the body works as a language machine. The Museum's purpose is to answer such questions. It will make clear why language is important; it'll demonstrate what we know about language and how we know it; and it'll give you a chance to explore linguistic knowledge—enjoyably.

The Museum's Allen Walker Read Library is the nucleus of what is intended to become America's most comprehensive collection of information about language. Some of that information will be in the form of printed books and journals, but much of it will be online—accessible wherever you are on the planet. Especially noteworthy will be the library's collection of speech samples—recordings of hundreds of languages and many dialects. This collection—aimed eventually at having a sample of every language in the world—will be an extraordinary resource for language research.

The Museum will also feature interactive multimedia displays of language-related objects and information. You'll see and hear how the science of speech analysis evolved from rudimentary techniques, which used gas flames, to today's digital voiceprint technology. You'll be able to take home an image of your own speech from a sound spectrogram. Or learn how speech synthesizers work—from those annoying telephone voices to important devices that allow physically challenged people like Stephen Hawking to speak. You'll be able to talk with a computer and see how well it does in understanding and creating speech.

There'll be an interactive wall-sized map showing where each of the world's languages is spoken. You'll see how languages develop and change. How they differ. How they spread over space and time. And how they die.

Complementing the world map, there'll be an interactive display using sound bites and video clips to demonstrate the linguistic heritage and diversity of America—including not only the dialects of American English but also the aboriginal tongues and the languages of centuries of immigrants. English-speaking visitors will even get a chance to see where their own dialect fits into the big picture.

There'll be an animated model of the human speech apparatus, showing how the lungs, vocal cords, lips, teeth, and tongue work together to create the infinite variety of sounds in thousands of languages and dialects.

And you'll see what we know about how language is acquired—the way babies learn their first language, and the considerably different ways children and adults learn additional languages later in life.

Fascinating displays will trace the development of the Roman alphabet and other writing systems, with texts in each system and the tools used to produce them.

Other exhibits will explore the role of language in society, reaching back to the beginnings of civilization. One topic will be the many ways in which language study and the law are intertwined, such as forensics and questions of access to justice in multilingual societies. Others will be the importance of language in commerce, government, and technology—all demonstrated with historic documents, radio and television programs, and exhibits explaining things like how linguistic analysis can solve codes and ciphers. Language and religion have interacted with each other for many centuries, as will be shown in exhibits illustrating the role played by missionaries in the study of languages and linguistics.

You'll hear and see the story of dictionaries, from the earliest glossaries to the monumental *Oxford English Dictionary*. Paired with descriptions of the books themselves will be accounts of the lives of their makers—from learned scholars like Dr. Samuel Johnson (that 'harmless drudge') to the numberless, often anonymous men and women whose work makes modern dictionaries possible. The Museum will trace the history of translation and interpretation and will demonstrate how translators and interpreters practice their profession in the worlds of business, diplomacy and intelligence.

Yet another important subject is the preservation of *endangered* languages. Universities and other institutions in the U.S. and other countries—as well as the U.N.—devote considerable effort to collecting information on such languages. But there needs to be a coordinating point where all this information is brought together. The Museum's organizers see it as a candidate for fulfilling this role—as a central repository for preserving ethnic cultures through preservation of their languages.

In 2011 the Museum launched two long-term exhibits: 'Writing Language: Passing It On', and 'Emerging American Language in 1812'. There will be much, much more. Even in its current limited space, the Museum has welcomed enthusiastic visitors from around the world, and negotiations are in progress for a larger facility to expand into.

This is only a peek at what the Museum eventually will become. As it grows, the National Museum of Language welcomes the ideas and participation of everybody to whom language is important— and that includes *you*. Why don't you help it grow by becoming a member?

About the author

Amelia C. Murdoch, Ph.D., founder and President Emerita of America's National Museum of Language, is a retired U.S. government linguist. She began her professional career as a specialist in Medieval French; after joining the federal government, she ventured into the Semitic languages. Over her long career she became convinced that the field of language had to be expanded from the academic and educational worlds into the cultural mainstream. Her experiences in guiding the creation of a seminal exhibit on language provided insights that persuaded her that a museum of language was an ideal means to lead that expansion.

Suggestions for further reading

In this book

The Museum of Language covers a range of subjects similar to that of this book. A sampling of chapters that may be of special interest to eventual Museum goers includes 3 (world language survey), 38 (languages of the U.S.), 27 (language death), 28 (language rescue), 37 (language teaching technology), 47 (interpreting and translating), and 49 (forensic linguistics), as well as Chapters 52–65 on individual languages.

Elsewhere

Comrie, Bernard, ed. *The World's Major Languages* (Oxford University Press, 1990). An authoritative presentation of the most interesting facts of the major languages of the world.

Crystal, David. *The Cambridge Encyclopedia of Language* (Cambridge University Press, second edition 1997). An invaluable comprehensive, indeed essential, reference treating all aspects of language.

McWhorter, John. *The Story of Human Language* (The Teaching Company, 2005). An outstanding series of 36 lectures (30 minutes each, available on DVD, videotape, or audio CD) on the history and development of language.

Wade, Nicholas, ed. *The Science Times Book of Language and Linguistics* (The Lyons Press, 2000). A collection of very readable essays. The topics, organization and style correspond to the approach of the National Museum of Language.

51
Where did English come from?

John Algeo

Was English originally a German dialect? If so, how did it get to be English? How did the Vikings and the French get involved? What can dictionaries tell us about the history of English?

English did come from the same ancestor as German, but there's a lot more to the story. In the fifth century, Celts lived in the British Isles. But warfare among them got so fierce that one local king asked for help from Germanic tribes living in southern Denmark and northern Germany. He got more than he bargained for: the tribes came as allies, but they liked the island so much they decided to take it over.

Two of the main tribes in this group came from regions called Angeln and Saxony, which is why we call the language they brought to Britain 'Anglo-Saxon'. The speech of the tribes who stayed on the European Continent eventually became modern German, Dutch, and Scandinavian languages; and Anglo-Saxon, also known as 'Old English', grew into the English we speak today.

On their new turf, these Germanic Anglo-Saxons started to talk in new ways. The tribes they drove to the fringes of Britain left them some Celtic place names. But more important, the newcomers were converted to Christianity, so a good deal of Latin crept into their language. Another influence showed up in the ninth and tenth centuries, when Britain—which by then was called Angle-land, or England—was invaded again, this time by Scandinavian cousins of the Anglo-Saxons: Viking raiders, who ruled all of England for a couple of decades. Their contact with the Anglo-Saxons was so close that they've given us some of our everyday words—like *sister, sky, law, take, window*, and the pronouns *they, them*, and *their*.

The greatest additions to English resulted from another invasion we all know about: '1066 and all that.' In that year, England was conquered by descendants of a different group of Vikings—the 'Normans', men of the North, who had settled in the tenth century along the coast of France and there learned French. The region of France they ruled still bears their name—Normandy. When they took over England, they made French the government language. So England became a trilingual country: officials used Norman French, the church used Latin, and the common people spoke a version of English we call 'Middle English'.

The common people were by far the majority, and by the late fourteenth century their English reasserted itself over French as the language of Britain. But it was a different English from the Anglo-Saxon spoken before the Conquest. Over the years it had absorbed an enormous number of French words for legal, governmental, military, and cultural matters—words like *judge, royal, soldier*, and a host of food terms like *fruit* and *beef*. And its grammar had changed dramatically, losing many of its inflectional endings.

At the end of the fifteenth century, printing was introduced in England, which helped standardize the language. And in the sixteenth century, Englishmen began to explore the globe. They encountered new things that needed to be talked about with new words. They settled in North America, the Caribbean, Africa, South Asia, Australia, and the South Seas.

As it became a global language, English influenced other languages—and was influenced by them. Most of our core vocabulary comes directly from Old English: words like *mother, earth, love, hate, cow, man*, and *glad*. But we have borrowed words from many other languages: Greek (*pathos*), Welsh (*penguin*), Irish

Gaelic (*galore*), Scots Gaelic (*slogan*), Icelandic (*geyser*), Swedish (*ombudsman*), Norwegian (*ski*), Danish (*skoal*), Spanish (*ranch*), Portuguese (*molasses*), Italian (*balcony*), Dutch (*boss*), German (*semester*), Yiddish (*bagel*), Arabic (*harem*), Hebrew (*shibboleth*), Persian (*bazaar*), Sanskrit (*yoga*), Hindi (*shampoo*), Romany or Gypsy (*pal*), Tamil (*curry*), Chinese (*gung-ho*), Japanese (*karaoke*), Malay (*gingham*), Tahitian (*tattoo*), Tongan (*taboo*), Hawaiian (*ukulele*), Australian Dharuk (*boomerang*), Australian Guugu Yimidhirr (*kangaroo*), Bantu (*goober*), Wolof (*jigger* or *chigger*), Russian (*mammoth*), Hungarian (*paprika*), Turkish (*jackal*), Algonquian (*possum*), Dakota (*tepee*), and Navajo (*hogan*). Most of the words in a large dictionary—perhaps as many as 85 or 90 percent—either are loanwords from other languages or have been invented in English using elements borrowed from other languages.

By now the language has expanded far beyond its tribal beginnings. It's a first language in countries settled by the English. It's a second language in countries like India and the Philippines, which were part of the British Empire or under American influence. And it's a foreign language used around the globe for business, science, technology, and commerce. A Scandinavian pilot landing his plane in Greece talks with the air controller in English. It's also the main language of the worldwide Internet.

So did English come from German? No—it's closely related to German, but what began as the tongue of a small Germanic tribe in northwestern Europe morphed over time into something very different—a blend of dozens of languages that came to be spoken in virtually every country in the world.

About the author

John Algeo is Professor Emeritus at the University of Georgia. He is the author of *British or American English? A Handbook of Word and Grammar Patterns* (2006) and of *The Origins and Development of the English Language* (sixth edition 2010), and editor of *The Cambridge History of the English Language: Volume 6, English in North America* (2002) and of *Fifty Years Among the New Words* (1993). He is past president of the Dictionary Society of North America, the American Dialect Society, and the American Name Society. He and his wife, Adele, wrote 'Among the New Words' in the journal *American Speech* for ten years, and he is now gathering material for a *Dictionary of Briticisms*.

Suggestions for further reading

In this book
Other chapters on the origins and history of languages include 5 (earliest languages), 6 (language relationships), 10 (pidgins and creoles), and 57 (Icelandic); chapters that discuss various aspects of how languages evolve include 8 (language change), 13 (grammar), 44 (U.S. dialect change), 53 (Latin), and 54 (Italian).

Elsewhere
Algeo, John. *British or American English? A Handbook of Word and Grammar Patterns* (Cambridge University Press, 2006). A guide to the many grammatical differences, often unnoticed, between the two principal national varieties of the language.

Algeo, John. *The Origins and Development of the English Language* (Wadsworth, sixth edition 2010). A detailed history of the English language from prehistoric Indo-European to present-day developments in vocabulary and usage.

Hogg, Richard M., ed. *The Cambridge History of the English Language* (Cambridge University Press, 1992–2001). A six-volume history of English written by some of the leading scholars in the subject, dealing with all aspects of the subject and including extensive bibliographies.

Leech, Geoffrey and Jan Svartvik. *English—One Tongue, Many Voices* (Palgrave Macmillan, 2006). A masterful and up-to-date survey of the English language: its global spread, international and local varieties, history from obscurity to primacy, usage and uses, standards and creoles, style and change in progress, politics and controversy.

52
How many Native American languages are there?

Marianne Mithun

Do the Native American languages have any connection with languages in Europe or Asia or Africa? Are they all related to each other? Are they dying out? Is there any point in trying to save them?

A surprising number of people think there's just one language native to the U.S.: 'Indian'. Nothing could be further from the truth.

In fact, we know of nearly three hundred languages that were spoken north of Mexico before the arrival of Europeans. Many have disappeared, but around half are still known. They constitute between fifty and sixty different language families.

Some of the families are quite large. The Athabaskan-Eyak-Tlingit family, for example, contains thirty-nine different languages, spoken in communities scattered over an enormous area stretching from Alaska to the southwestern U.S. This family includes Navajo, the most widely used indigenous language on the continent, with over a hundred thousand speakers.

Another family, called Algic, is best known for its largest branch, Algonquian, spoken along the Atlantic seaboard from Labrador to Virginia. It was Algonquian speakers who met the Pilgrims and Sir Walter Raleigh, and gave American English such words as *caribou, skunk, moccasin, hominy,* and *raccoon.*

Algonquian languages like Shawnee, Fox, Potawatomi, Cree, Cheyenne, and Blackfoot are also spoken across most of Canada and down into the U.S. Great Plains.

A third well-known group is the Siouan-Catawban family. At the time of first contacts with European languages, most speakers of these languages inhabited the prairies, from modern Alberta and Saskatchewan south as far as Arkansas and Mississippi. The name *Minnesota* is a Siouan word (literally 'clear water'). Another familiar Siouan word is *teepee* (literally 'dwell-thing').

The Iroquoian family is somewhat smaller, with eight modern languages, including Mohawk—which is still spoken in Quebec, Ontario, and New York State—and Cherokee, which in the seventeenth century was spoken over a wide area in the southern Appalachians. Like several other indigenous peoples, most Cherokee were forced to march westward in 1838–39 along what is called the 'Trail of Tears', so the largest Cherokee community is now in Oklahoma. Iroquoian languages gave us place names like *Schenectady*, *Ontario*, *Ohio*, and *Kentucky*, as well as *Canada*.

North America even has language isolates, languages with no identifiable relatives at all. Zuni, spoken in what is now New Mexico, is an isolate.

Native American languages generally show no relation to languages anywhere else in the world. Very recently however, an exciting hypothesis has emerged: a possible link between the Athabaskan-Eyak-Tlingit family and the Yeniseian family of Siberia.

The languages indigenous to North America differ tremendously among themselves, but none are like the 'primitive' speech presented in some old Westerns. Many use sounds unfamiliar to English speakers, like 'ejective' consonants (made with an extra popping sound) and distinctive tone (the same syllable spoken with different pitches can mean entirely different things). The grammars of these languages can be very complex, too, sometimes resulting in single words that carry as much meaning as a complete sentence in English.

The Mohawk word *wa'tkenikahrá:ra'ne'*, for example, means 'they saw it.' This word consists of several parts. First comes the prefix *wa'-*, which indicates the speaker's assessment that this event actually happened. There follows the prefix *t-*, which indicates a change of position. A third prefix, *keni-*, is like our pronoun 'they', but more specific: it means 'those two females'. Next comes a noun -*kahr-* ('eye'), followed by the verb root -*r-* ('be on') and two more suffixes: -*a'n-*, ('come to' or 'become') and -*e'*, which tells us that the event happened all at once. The word thus means literally 'the girls came to be visually on it,' that is, 'their eyes fell upon it,' or 'they saw it.'

If you saw the 2002 film *Windtalkers*, you know that the U.S. Marine Corps in World War II had speakers of Navajo use their language as a secret code to baffle the Japanese.

Each of the languages indigenous to the Americas shows us a unique way of looking at the world, of packaging experience into words, of expressing subtle and fundamental distinctions. If you want to say 'that caribou' in an Eskimoan language, for example, you'll find no single word equivalent to the English 'that'. You have to select from many 'that' options: is the caribou standing or moving? If moving, is it approaching or receding? If stationary, is it visible or out of sight? If you can see it, is it near you, near the person you're talking to, or far away? Above you or below you? Is it the same caribou you were talking about earlier? All of these choices get packaged into a single word—translated simply 'that' in English.

Unfortunately, the world is losing the melodies and unique perspectives of these aboriginal tongues. Some have already disappeared because their speakers perished in warfare or epidemics; others, because their speakers chose to use other languages instead. Our heritage as humans has been enriched by these languages, but it is likely that no more than a dozen of them will survive this century. And like an environmental disaster, this will be a great loss.

About the author

Marianne Mithun is Professor of Linguistics at the University of California, Santa Barbara. Her work covers such areas as morphology (word structure), relations between grammar and discourse, language typology, language contact, and language change, particularly the mechanisms by which grammatical structures evolve. She has worked with speakers of a number of North American languages, including Mohawk, Tuscarora, Seneca, Lakhota, Central Alaskan Yup'ik, and Navajo, as well as several Austronesian languages. She has also worked with a number of communities on projects aimed at documenting their traditional languages and training speakers to teach them to younger generations.

Suggestions for further reading

In this book

Chapters on how groups of language are related include 6 (language families), 51 (origins of English), 60 (languages of Africa), and 63 (languages of India). Languages of the U.S. are discussed in Chapters 28 (rescuing threatened Native American languages), 39 (America's language crisis), 40 (New World Spanish), 41 (Cajun), 42 (German in the U.S.), and 43 (Gullah).

Elsewhere

Grenoble, Lenore A. and Lindsay J. Whaley, eds. *Endangered Languages: Language Loss and Community Response* (Cambridge University Press, 1998). A collection of articles on various aspects of language loss around the world, including discussions of how languages disappear, what is lost when they do, and how communities respond to the loss of heritage languages.

Kari, James and Ben Potter, eds. *The Dene-Yeneiseian Connection.* (Anthropological Papers of the University of Alaska New Series, vol 5, no. 1–2, 2010). A collection of articles by linguists, archaeologists, physical anthropologists, and ethnologists examining the hypothesis of a genealogical connection between the Athabaskan-Eyak-Tlingit languages, centered in Alaska, and the Yeneiseian languages of Siberia.

Mithun, Marianne, *The Languages of Native North America* (Cambridge University Press, 1999/2001). An encyclopedic compendium describing the languages and language families indigenous to North America, along with the special structures and areas of complexity and elaboration found in these languages.

Silver, Shirley and Wick R. Miller. *American Indian Languages: Cultural and Social Contexts* (University of Arizona, 1997). An introductory textbook on the languages of the Americas with special emphasis on cultural and social aspects.

53

Is Latin really dead?

Frank Morris

Didn't people stop speaking Latin after the barbarians sacked Rome? Why should anybody but a scholar care about a language that's dead?

Dead? Well, surely we can agree that Latin is vital for specialized historians and philologists and archeologists, but doesn't that prove all the more that for the rest of us Latin is really dead and gone? Surely not! In fact, it is very much at work in today's world. We who love Latin have a long and varied list of evidence to show how alive it is.

To begin, Latin *vocabulary* has never fallen out of use. About 80 percent of the words in Italian, Spanish, French, and Portuguese are inherited from Latin, their parent language. Even in languages a little less directly related to Latin there can be an amazingly high percentage. For example, roughly 60 percent of all English words—and 90 percent of our multisyllabic words—are borrowed or derived from Latin. Words like 'labor', 'animal', 'deficit', 'insomnia', 'stimulus', and 'vigil', to name a very few.

Nor has spoken Latin ever ceased being used to communicate ideas among human beings in the real world. Not so long ago the world witnessed the Latin funeral mass for John Paul II; heard the announcement, *Habemus Papam* ('we have a Pope'), to mark the election of his successor; and listened to the Latin speech the newly elevated Benedict XVI delivered to the College of Cardinals.

All this on live international TV from Rome! Beyond the Vatican, spoken Latin plays both symbolic and substantive roles in ceremonial occasions, such as Harvard University graduations, which for over 350 years have featured a Latin oration by a member of the graduating class.

And if our interest in Latin is less lofty, we can tune in to weekly radio broadcasts in Latin from Finland and elsewhere. Or we can visit enthusiasts around the world who for centuries have been coming together for personal conversation in Latin. Now increasingly we can join them as they turn to the Internet to enjoy daily Latin conversation among themselves.

Actually, Latin is ubiquitous. We find it at work in the courtroom: *habeas corpus* ('you should have a body'); *nolo contendere* ('I do not want to contest'); *subpoena* ('under penalty' to compel compliance); *alibi* ('somewhere else'). Every day we abbreviate our way with Latin: e.g., *exempli gratia* ('for the sake of an example'); i.e., *id est* ('that is'); etc., *et cetera* ('and others'); n.b., *nota bene* ('note well'). We choose Latin mottos to inspire and guide us: *semper fidelis* ('always faithful') for the Marines; *e pluribus unum* ('out of many, one') for all Americans. We turn to Latin for branding and advertising: *Lava* (Latin for 'wash') soap ; *Magnavox* ('great voice') radio. We understand Latin words in medicine: *bacterium, coma, nausea, rigor mortis*; in biology: *phylum, species, larva, nucleus*; in anatomy: *biceps, cranium, sinus*; in astronomy: *Mars, Ursa Major, nova*; in mathematics: *calculus, parabola, isosceles, minus*; in schools: *campus, curriculum, alumnus*; in sports: *gymnasium, stadium, discus*; and in everyday speech: *ad hoc, alma mater, de facto, ex officio, ex libris, non sequitur, per capita, quid pro quo, status quo, vice versa*.

Latin, furthermore, has always had its place in popular culture. In the Harry Potter books, for example, we delight in the Latin phrases for curses, charms and spells: *avis* ('bird') creates a flock of birds; *impedimenta* ('hindrances, things on the foot') creates an obstacle; *obscuro* ('I conceal, I cover') hides something. A gruff Latin grammar lesson from a Roman centurion enables the title character of the Monty Python film *Life of Brian* to correct his faulty graffiti grammar and write *Romani ite domum* ('Romans go home') 100 times on the town wall.

Finally, headlines in various media tell a happy story: 'Latin Makes a Comeback' (*Education World*), 'Schools Reviving a Dead Language' (CNN.com/education) and 'Latin: A Language Alive and Well' (*The Washington Post*). Indeed, in U.S. schools at all levels enrollments in both Latin and Ancient Greek have been increasing sharply. According to a recent survey by the Modern Language Association, undergraduate college enrollments in Latin increased 13 percent from 1995 to 2002. In secondary schools, enrollments in Latin grew 8 percent from 1990 to 2000, and in middle schools, they have doubled since 1985. A recent survey by the Center for Applied Linguistics showed that while overall enrollment in foreign language declined in schools between 1997 and 2008, enrollments in Latin at the elementary school level doubled from 3 percent to 6 percent of all elementary school programs.

What explains this remarkable resurgence of interest in Latin and Greek? One driving force has been the so-called 'Back to Basics' movement. Administrators, teachers, and parents believe that studying Latin disciplines the mind, provides insight into Western civilization and its values, expands English vocabulary, gives an understanding of grammar that results in better use of English, and provides a basis for the study of other languages. They cite research that links the study of Latin with higher scores on standardized tests. On the 2005 Scholastic Aptitude Test, for example, secondary school students with two or more years of Latin had a median score 173 points above the median for all other students. An analysis of Graduate Record Exam scores from 1996–1999 shows that undergraduates in classics ranked first in verbal scores among the 270 fields in which students take the test.

There is more to the resurgence of Latin than just returning to the basics and increasing scores on achievement tests. New audiences and wider curricular applications have been developed. Innovative materials and teaching methodologies are making

Latin and Classics accessible to all students, not just to a traditional elite. Teachers can capitalize on the vast cultural legacy of Greece and Rome to make interdisciplinary connections between Latin and subjects such as language arts, mathematics, science, social studies, literature, art, music, and mythology. But the ultimate reason for Latin's comeback is that, with new, more interactive ways to teach it, students are finding the study of Latin and the Romans to be fun. There are even reports of grade school children who beg teachers to skip recess ... so they don't have to stop their Latin lesson.

So is Latin really dead? Not by a long shot. There were decades, not so long ago, when it was less frequently taught in schools— when school administrators and others may have thought of it as out of fashion or near death. But those days are obviously over. Latin is making a comeback—and it's coming on strong.

About the author
Frank Morris earned a Ph.D. in Classics from the University of Cincinnati and taught Latin and Greek at the College of Charleston in Charleston, SC from 1978 until his retirement in 2010. Prior to joining the faculty at the College of Charleston he taught Latin and Greek at Orange Park High School in Florida. He continues to serve as Director of Charleston Latin Program, and has been training teachers to teach Latin in elementary schools since the mid-1980s.

Suggestions for further reading

In this book
Latin is a vivid case study in the endangered-language issues that are the subjects of Chapters 3 (languages of the world), 27 (language death), and 28 (language rescue), and 38 (languages of the U.S.). Its long history, which continues on into Chapter 54 (Italian), exemplifies the ways of language evolution discussed in Chapters 8 (language change), 10 (pidgins and creoles), 13 (grammar), 44 (U.S. dialect change), and 51 (origins of English).

Elsewhere

LaFleur, Richard A., ed. *Latin for the Twenty-First Century: From Concept to Classroom* (Foresman, 1998). A survey of trends in the teaching of Latin.

Pearcy, Lee T. *The Grammar of Our Civility* (Baylor University Press, 2005). A history of the teaching of Classics in the U.S.

http://yle.fi/radio1/tiede/nuntii_latini. A source for radio broadcasts in Latin.

www.promotelatin.org offers many informative links, such as for conversational Latin: www.promotelatin.org/index.php?option= com_content&view=article&id=61&Itemid=68.

54

Who speaks Italian?

Dennis Looney

When did Latin turn into modern Italian? Do all Italians speak the same language? How many dialects are there in Italy?

Fragmentation defines the linguistic history of the Italian peninsula more than you can imagine. Shortly after the modern state of Italy was founded in 1861, a politician famously reflected, 'With Italy made, we must now make the Italians.' Making Italians meant first and foremost giving citizens of the new country—who spoke hundreds of dialects—one voice, an official national language. This project took another century to complete.

The earliest example of written Italian appears in a legal document from 960 AD. The document, about a debate over property boundaries, is mostly in church Latin, but embedded in the judicial commentary is the statement of a plaintiff in his own vernacular: 'I know that those lands ... [have been held by the Benedictine monks].' A monastic scribe dutifully recorded the speech phonetically, beginning '*Sao ko kelle terre ...*'—four words strikingly similar to the standard language of today: *so che quelle terre*. Somewhere around the end of the first millennium, Latin was changing into what we now think of as Italian.

But, of course, the two languages co-existed for many, many years. This posed a problem for writers, especially educated ones. Should they write in Latin, the revered and long-established language of scholars and the church? Or in the vernacular? This later became known as 'the question of the language', and it was not completely resolved until modern times.

In the early fourteenth century, Dante Alighieri considered writing *The Divine Comedy* in Latin but ultimately chose to use the language of the people, specifically the dialect of his town, Florence, and the region around it, Tuscany. Dante's *Comedy* became the touchstone and starting place for most of the subsequent debates about the language. For scholarly Renaissance humanists, as for Dante, the first choice was between Latin and the vernacular. If one chose the vernacular (as most writers did), there was a second decision: which regional version of it? The dialect of Florence, or that of Venice or Rome or Milan, or some other city or region?

The prestige and political clout of Florentine culture heavily influenced such linguistic decisions. The powerful precedent set by Dante and other Tuscan authors, including Petrarch and Boccaccio, influenced writers from many other parts of Italy. In 1525, Pietro Bembo, a Venetian, proposed a standard Italian vocabulary, grammar, and syntax modeled after Tuscan. Tuscan's dominance over other dialects was reflected in a common saying: 'the Florentine tongue [should be] in a Roman mouth.'

The debate over linguistic models raged into the nineteenth century, when the influential writer Alessandro Manzoni chose the dialect of contemporary Florence for his great historical novel *The Betrothed*. This required Manzoni, whose native dialect was that of Milan, to 'rinse his clothes'—as he colorfully put it—'in [Tuscany's] Arno River.' In the 1860s Manzoni lobbied successfully for educational policies that established the dialect of Tuscany as the standard to be used in schools. By the middle of the twentieth century most Italians spoke a form of the language updated from Dante's medieval Florentine.

In the 1920s and 1930s, Italy's Fascist government undertook, with no great success, a campaign to rid Italian of all foreign influences. The word *sandwich*, for example, was to be ousted by a new made-up word, *tramezzino*, meaning 'the small thing in between'. Legislation in 1938 banished the respectful pronoun *lei* ('you'), requiring instead the 'more Italian' pronoun *voi*. But *lei* and *sandwich* survived, and Italian continued to absorb words from other languages, especially English—or more precisely Anglo-American—throughout the second half of the twentieth century and into the twenty-first. For example, the new English word 'to google'—with an Italian verb ending attached—has recently joined the vocabulary of Italy's computer literate: *googleare*. Italians are not as squeamish about foreign influences on their language as their neighbors in France, and many languages other than Italian are used in Italy; fifteen of them (including German, French, Provençal, Slovenian, Albanian, and Greek) were granted official status as linguistic minorities in 1999.

So, with regional dialects and the infusion of words from other languages, is there now a 'real' Italian, universally understood throughout Italy? Yes, there is: approximately 57 million of the country's 60 million inhabitants communicate in the standard language, as do millions of Italian speakers in other countries. People in Argentina speak a version of standard Italian, making Buenos Aires the second largest Italian city in the world. Standard Italian is also an official language of the European Union, Switzerland, and Vatican City. The rise of mass media has spread the standard language into the country's furthest corners, threatening to extinguish the approximately one hundred dialects that still give the peninsula linguistic richness. Between 1955 and 1995 the percentage of speakers who used only dialect dropped from 66 percent to 6.9 percent. The fragmentation of the language is all but over.

Like all languages, Italian has changed a great deal as its national standard emerged, enriched by its many dialects and by foreign borrowings—and it will continue to change. But at bottom its origins are in Tuscany, and Dante would probably have little trouble understanding it even today.

About the author

Dennis Looney (Ph.D., 1987, Comparative Literature, University of North Carolina at Chapel Hill) is a professor of Italian at the University of Pittsburgh, with a secondary appointment in Classics. He has published

Freedom Readers: The African American Reception of Dante Alighieri and the 'Divine Comedy' (2011). *Compromising the Classics: Romance Epic Narrative in the Italian Renaissance* (1996) won Honorable Mention for the MLA's Prize for Italian Literary Studies, 1996–1997. He is co-editor of *Phaethon's Children: The Este Court and Its Culture in Early Modern Ferrara* (2005), and editor and translator of *'My Muse will have a Story to Paint': the Selected Prose of Ludovico Ariosto* (2010).

Suggestions for further reading

In this book
The history of Italian, which grew out of Latin as described in Chapter 53, demonstrates many of the same kinds of issues covered in Chapters 8 (language change), 13 (grammar), 44 (U.S. dialect change), and 51 (origins of English). Other chapters on individual languages include 52–53 and 55–65.

Elsewhere
Lepschy, Anna Laura and Giulio Lepschy. *The Italian Language Today* (Routledge, second edition 1994). Provides a brief outline of the history of the language with a focus on the evolution of the modern standard language. Includes reference grammar of contemporary Italian.

Maiden, Martin. *A Linguistic History of Italian* (Longman, 1995). A study of the historical development of the elements of Italian. Assumes some knowledge of the language.

Migliorini, Bruno; abridged, recast and revised by T. Gwynfor Griffith. *The Italian Language* (Faber, 1984). Comprehensive work on the history of the language from its origins to the twentieth century.

www.accademiadellacrusca.it. Website of the active linguistic academy founded in the late sixteenth century to create a dictionary of standard Italian based on the rules of Pietro Bembo. English portal.

55

How different are Spanish and Portuguese?

Ana Maria Carvalho

Are Spanish and Portuguese dialects of the same language?
What differences are there between them? How did they
come about?

Well, if Portuguese and Spanish aren't varieties of the same language, they're surely sister languages, and very close sisters at that. If we define dialects as speech varieties that are mutually understood, we can say they are, in fact, dialects of the same language. It's not uncommon to find a speaker of say, Brazilian Portuguese, talking to an Argentinean at an airport: each speaking his own language, both understanding each other, with just occasional need to stop now and then to clarify the meaning of a word. They communicate very well most of the time, as long as they avoid using slang or talking too fast.

Communication works because Spanish and Portuguese share around 80 percent of their vocabulary, and most of the same grammatical structures, things like word order and verb tenses. Where communication breaks down, it's often because of differences in pronunciation. Look at these two sentences, the first in Spanish and the second in Portuguese:

Mis hermanos cantan bien.
Meus irmãos cantam bem.

It's pretty obvious that these are differently spelled and pronounced versions of the same five words (meaning 'My brothers sing well'). Usually the difference that jumps out right away when one hears someone speaking Portuguese—whether from Portugal or from Brazil—is the nasal vowels that Portuguese often uses in words like *irmãos* and *cantam* as opposed to less nasal Spanish pronunciation.

There are also some differences in sentence structure and word forms, as well as some words that sound the same in both languages but have different meanings. The verb 'pegar' in Portuguese, for example, means 'pick up'; in Spanish it means 'hit'. Put that in the context of a babysitter getting instructions for taking care of an infant ... and you can imagine some confusion.

In reading—where, of course, pronunciation isn't a factor—the great amount of overlap in words and grammar means that a speaker of Spanish can read Portuguese with little difficulty. A recent study found that educated native speakers of Spanish with no previous exposure to Portuguese could understand as much as 95 percent of an academic text written solely in Portuguese.

But there are other criteria for distinguishing dialects from languages. As the saying goes, a language has an army behind it, but a dialect doesn't—and Portuguese has had its own army since the founding of Portugal in the twelfth century. It's had an official grammar book, giving it the status of a separate language in the eyes of the Portuguese, since 1536. Like Spanish, Portuguese came from the colloquial Latin spoken by the Romans occupying the Iberian Peninsula, but it emerged on the western side of the peninsula, largely separated by mountains from Spain. With separation came differences between the two languages.

We shouldn't forget that those are not the only languages of the Iberian Peninsula. Catalan, another Latin descendant, spoken by some eight million people along the eastern coast of Spain, has a long-established literary heritage and is widely agreed to be a language separate from both Spanish and Portuguese. Just above Portugal in the northwest corner of Spain is Galicia, a mountain region of around three million people. They speak what some call a dialect of Portuguese, but there are those who consider it a language in its own right. I'd describe Galician as basically Portuguese but heavily influenced by Spanish. And of course there are the Basques, who occupied the peninsula before the Romans came and have outlasted the Empire. They speak Euskera, a language not genetically related to any other European language.

You may be surprised to hear that, including its homeland in Europe, Portuguese is used on five continents and is at least a candidate for the position of fifth most widely spoken language in the world. It's the language of Brazil, an emerging economic powerhouse and one of the few countries in South America where Spanish is not spoken. In Africa, you'll find Portuguese in Mozambique, Angola, Guinea-Bissau, and Cape Verde. You can hear it in Asia too: the islands of East Timor, Macao in southern China, and Goa on the west coast of India. Portuguese is also the eleventh most commonly spoken non-English language in the United States. If you already speak Spanish, Portuguese is so similar that it won't be hard to add it to your repertoire—and then you'll be able to talk to even more people around the world!

About the author
Ana Maria Carvalho is an Associate Professor of Portuguese and Spanish linguistics at the University of Arizona, where she also directs the Portuguese Language Program. She studies the sociolinguistics of languages in contact, especially the contact between Spanish and Portuguese in the bilingual communities of northern Uruguay. In addition to her work on sociolinguistics, she has published on the acquisition of Portuguese by Spanish speakers. Dr. Carvalho received her Ph.D. from the University of California, Berkeley.

Suggestions for further reading

In this book
Other chapters on individual languages include 52–54 and 56–65. Also of particular interest may be Chapter 40 (New World Spanish).

Elsewhere

Carvalho, A. M., J. L. Freire, and A. J. B. Silva. *Portuguese for Spanish Speakers* (http://portspan.cercll.arizona.edu, 2010). This website provides free activities for Spanish speakers interested in learning or improving their Portuguese skills. Sponsored by the Center for Educational Resources in Culture, Language and Literacy, the site provides users with authentic readings, grammatical explanations and exercises on structural aspects of the Portuguese language.

Kelm, Orlando. *Portuguese Reading Workshop for Speakers of Spanish* (www.laits.utexas.edu/orkelm/port/reading/readintro.html, 1997). A great online source covering spelling differences between Spanish and Portuguese, grammatical similarities and differences, and practice sentences and readings.

Simões, Antonio. *Pois Não: Brazilian Portuguese Course for Spanish Speakers, with Basic Reference Grammar* (University of Texas Press, 2008). This book contrasts Portuguese and Spanish, teaching the equivalent of one year of college Portuguese. It also includes a CD containing recordings by native Brazilian speakers.

Thogmartin, C. and J. Courteau. *A Checklist of Phonological, Grammatical and Lexical Contrasts between Spanish and Portuguese* (U.S. Department of Education, 1985). This work provides a short, accessible, and practical list of the most important contrasts between Spanish and Portuguese. It should be highly useful for anyone trying to understand the main differences between the two languages.

Ulsh, J.L. *From Spanish to Portuguese* (Foreign Service Institute, 1971). Ulsh's seminal work will be beneficial for anyone who already has achieved some competence in Spanish and wishes to build on that in order to develop familiarity with Portuguese.

56

Should we be studying Russian?

Benjamin Rifkin

Is Russian less beautiful than other languages? Now that the Cold War is over, is there any reason for non-Russians to learn it?

A colleague of mine who's a professor of Russian tells me that whenever he's on an airplane he likes to read Russian mystery novels. Typically, the person sitting next to him sees that he's reading something with unusual letters, and says something like: 'You teach Russian? But that's so hard!' Or maybe: 'But Russia is so bleak!' Or: 'It's kind of an ugly language, isn't it?' Or: 'What can your students can do with it?' Or even: 'Russian? Don't they spend most of their time drinking vodka?'

Let me say a few things about those myths.

First, Russian isn't as hard as you might think. It does have a different alphabet, but if you've been in a fraternity or sorority, or if you studied mathematics in college, you might be surprised at how many of the letters you already know. They're borrowed from Greek. There are thirty-three letters, and they take only about ten hours to learn. And remember that Russian is a cousin of English in the Indo-European language family, so there are many connections. For instance, the root of the verb 'to see' in Russian is *vid*, related to the English words *video*, *vision*, and *visual*. And of course Russian words have crept into English, like *sputnik*, *babushka*, and *intelligentsia*. Students of Russian are also helped by the language's very logical system of roots, prefixes and suffixes. Once you learn that the word 'to write' is *pisat'*, for example, a whole series of verbs becomes predictable, created by combining the root of this verb with various prefixes. Adding prefix *vy-* ('out') makes *vypisat'* ('to write out'); adding *pro-* ('through') makes *propisat'* ('to prescribe'); adding *pod-* ('under') makes *podpisat'* ('to sign'); adding *pri-* ('adhering to') makes *pripisat'* ('to attribute'); adding *s-* ('from') makes *spisat'* ('to copy'); and adding *do-* ('up to' or 'until') makes *dopisat'* ('to finish writing').

As to the second myth, Russia is in no sense a bleak country. Yes, it has long winters, but the winters are beautiful: most of Russia is not only snowy in the winter, but also sunny. Imagine Russia's many churches, with their golden cupolas, laced in snow, gleaming in the winter sun. Russian villages are beautiful, often nestled on rivers near deep forests. Moscow and St. Petersburg are world-class, cosmopolitan cities. And consider these names as representatives of Russian culture: Dostoevsky, Tolstoy, Chekhov, Pasternak, Akhmatova, Rublev, Repin, Chagall, Malevich, Kandinsky, Popova, Tchaikovsky, Mussorgsky, Stravinsky, Prokofiev, Shostakovich, Eisenstein, and Tarkovsky, to name just a few. If you're not sure of Russia's role in the arts, check out the Bolshoi Theater in Moscow and the Hermitage Museum in St. Petersburg. Even the subway systems in Moscow and St. Petersburg are dazzling.

As for the third myth, about the sound of Russian—well, beauty is in the ear of the listener, but I find it hard to imagine anyone hearing, for example, Alexander Pushkin's poem 'I loved you once' as read at www.russianpoetry.net without agreeing with me that the Russian language is exceptionally beautiful. In fact, that's a great site to explore the beauty of Russian poetry, with the Russian original, an English translation, and many recordings of recitations of the poems in Russian.

Some of the beauty of Russian results from the fact that it's spoken by people who are passionate about friendship. People who take the time to learn Russian and travel to the country are always struck by how intense Russian friendships can be. It's a national characteristic: the weather may be cold, but the people are very warm and hospitable.

The fourth myth suggests that foreigners who study Russian can't use it professionally now that the Cold War is over. The truth is that demand for speakers of Russian is growing and will continue to grow. The Russian economy is booming, and foreign companies are investing like never before. Russia is a top producer of oil and natural gas, with reserves second only to Saudi Arabia's. The energy sector will be of increasing importance to the Russian economy as new pipelines are built to Nakhodka, on Russia's Pacific coast, and Murmansk, on the North Atlantic. The Russian middle class is growing exponentially, thanks in part to energy-sector revenues and investment from countries including the U.S., Germany, Japan, and the U.K. Unfortunately, Russia borders some unstable regions in the Caucasus and Central Asia. It remains geopolitically and strategically important to the U.S. government, which continues to hire people with expertise in Russian language and culture.

Russia is huge: it spreads across one-sixth of the world's surface in nine time zones from Kaliningrad to Kamchatka; there used to be eleven time zones, but the government recently eliminated two of them. Roughly 140 million people in Russia consider Russian their native language, putting it among the most-spoken languages in the world. Russian is spoken as a native or second language by millions of people outside Russia, too, including many in the former Soviet Republics of Central Asia, as well as Ukraine, Belarus, and the Caucasus. There are large communities of Russian speakers in every major European and North American city.

We come at last to the story about vodka. Well, there might be some truth to that one. Legend has it that Prince Vladimir of Kiev chose Christianity as the official religion of the Slavs partly because Islam prohibited alcohol. As the Prince put it, 'drink is the joy of the Russians.' On the other hand, not every Russian drinks vodka, but almost every Russian drinks tea. Tea is definitely the number one national beverage and tea-drinking the national pastime.

So if you're ready to start a new language, think about Russian. And the next time you hear someone speaking with a Russian accent, offer him a glass of tea. You might make a friend for life.

About the author

Benjamin Rifkin is Professor of Modern Languages and Dean of the School of Humanities and Social Sciences at The College of New Jersey. He is a past president of the American Association of Teachers of Slavic and East European Languages and is a long-standing member of the board of directors of the American Council of Teachers of Russian. He is also the author of numerous articles about the learning and teaching of Russian and instructional materials for learners at different levels. E-mail: rifkin@tcnj.edu.

Suggestions for further reading

In this book

Other chapters on individual languages include 52–55 and 57–65. Opportunities and requirements for professional use of language abilities are discussed in Chapters 22 (bilingualism), 39 (America's language crisis), 45 (language-related careers), 46 (dictionaries), 47 (interpreting and translating), and 49 (forensic linguistics).

Elsewhere

Billington, James. *Face of Russia* (TV Books, 1998). A review of Russian culture.

Massie, Suzanne. *Land of the Firebird* (Hearttree Press, thirteenth edition 1980). A review of Russian culture.

Rzhevsky, Nicholas. ed. *The Cambridge Companion to Modern Russian Culture* (Cambridge University Press, 1999). A review of contemporary Russian culture.

www.russnet.org. Interactive (Web-based) materials for learning Russian. See especially the article 'Why Study Russian?' at http://modules.russnet. org/why.

http://slavica.com/teaching/rifkin.html. A review of materials available for the study of Russian.

57

What's exciting about Icelandic?

Pardee Lowe Jr.

Why do linguists love Icelandic? Is it related to English?

It's too bad the pop singer Björk does most of her songs in English, rather than her native tongue. Icelandic is a really interesting language, with sounds not heard in most of the major languages of the world. Icelandic and English *are* related—they're both Germanic languages, and speakers of Old English could understand Old Norse, the ancestor of modern Icelandic—but there have been so many changes over time that you'd have to be a linguist to spot the connection. One of the Icelandic sagas blames this loss of mutual intelligibility on the conquest of England in 1066 by 'William the Bastard' (William of Normandy—whom most of us know as 'William the Conqueror').

Of the two languages, it was English that changed more down through the centuries. Today's Icelandic isn't much different from the language the Vikings brought to Iceland in the ninth century. Think about that. We need a college course to get us through the thousand-year-old Old English poem *Beowulf*, and even Shakespeare's plays, only a few hundred years old, can be difficult going for us. But a modern Icelander can still read eleven-hundred-year-old stories from the Middle Ages with ease—and without a dictionary. The pronunciation of the language has changed through the years, but not much else has. Yes, and despite the changes in English, it's sometimes still possible to see the relationship between the two languages. For example, the Modern Icelandic sentence Það er klukka-n tólf (literally, 'That is clock-the twelve') is the equivalent of Modern English 'It's twelve o'clock.'

How is it that the past is still so accessible to modern Icelanders? Well, they lived for centuries in relative isolation, not much influenced by changes happening in other languages. One way languages change is that the endings of words can disappear. Think of how English lost the '-st' verb ending in phrases like 'thou hast'. That happened to Swedish and Norwegian, too. They're sisters of Icelandic, but their grammar is quite streamlined. Icelandic grammar, in contrast, didn't lose many of its early forms, and it remains rich and complex. This old-fashionedness makes Icelandic harder to learn if you're not an Icelander, but it's one of the reasons linguists love the language: Icelandic offers a window on the early Germanic past.

The Icelanders love their language too, and want to keep it just the way it is. Global communications media create pressure to modernize it, but Icelanders resist. Unlike the Germans, who by the late twentieth century had pretty much adopted modern international terms like Telephon (replacing its 'pure German' equivalent, Fernsprecher), the Icelanders continue to create new vocabulary from native words or parts of words. For example, a 'telephone' is talsími, that is 'speech wire', and 'telegraph' is ritsími or 'write wire'. They're constantly producing dictionaries to provide Icelandic terms for new words from abroad.

The language is also traditional in the way it handles personal names. Most Icelanders don't use surnames, that is, names that are shared through generations by all members of a family. Instead, each person has a given name and a patronymic, based on his or her father's given name. For example, a brother and sister named Eiríkur and Þórdís, whose father's name was Haraldur, would be called Eiríkur Haraldsson and Þórdís Haraldsdóttir. Tryggvi, the son of Eiríkur and grandson of Haraldur, would be called Tryggvi Eiríksson. And when you look them up in the phone book, you'll find Haraldur, Eiríkur, Þórdís, and Tryggvi alphabetized under their *given* names.

Maybe because of their long winter nights, Icelanders read more books per capita than any other people in the world. Their ancient (Old Norse) poetry, known as the Eddas, and their ancient prose, the Sagas, are where much of the early history of the country is preserved. They're also among the sources Richard Wagner drew on for the Germanic myths he wove into *The Ring of the Nibelungs*.

The Eddas include one of Iceland's most famous poems, 'Völuspá' (The Song of the Sybil), which is worth listening to for its beauty, even if you need a translation to understand the words.

The Sagas exist in several series, but two are particularly note-worthy: the *Sagas of the Kings of Norway* tell how and why the fiercely independent earliest Icelanders left Norway and its kings to migrate to Iceland. The *Sagas of the Icelanders* tell of the families who settled the island and what became of them. Probably the most famous of these is *Njal's Saga* (see the bibliography below).

One of the reasons you might want to read the Sagas is that they record the first discoveries of America, which the Vikings called Vinland. Read 'The Saga of Leif Erikson' or 'The Saga of Erik the Red' for details. No, Columbus wasn't the first to discover America. To be honest, the ancient Icelanders may not have been either. But they were the first to write the discovery down! And now those accounts are out in paperback.

There also exists a rich and varied literature in Modern Ice-landic. Halldór Kiljan Laxness won the 1955 Nobel Prize for his novel *Independent People*, about hardscrabble peasant life in early twentieth-century Iceland. Among his many other works is *Under the Glacier*, which Susan Sontag has called 'one of the funniest books ever written.' Prize-winning Icelandic detective thrillers available in English include *Jar City* and *Silence of the Grave*, by Arnaldur Indriðason, and *Last Rituals*, by Yrsa Sigurðardóttir. How many other cultures can offer you a thousand years of litera-ture with so much variety?

About the author

Pardee Lowe Jr., of Falls Church, Virginia, has a Ph.D in German with Linguistic Emphasis from the University of California, Berkeley. He is a specialist in foreign language proficiency testing and an independent scholar and writer. He has taught Ancient Icelandic (also known as Old Norse) and has long enjoyed the delights of Icelandic language and literature.

Suggestions for further reading

In this book
Icelandic's historical role is an example of processes also discussed in Chapters 6 (language relationships), 8 (language change), 13 (grammar), 44 (U.S. dialect change), and 51 (origins of English). Other chapters on individual languages include 52–56 and 58–65.

Elsewhere
Smiley, Jane, with introduction by Robert Kellogg. *Sagas of the Icelanders: A Selection* (Penguin Books, 2001). This 782-page paperback offers an excellent selection of nine sagas (among them the Vinland Sagas about the discovery of North America) and seven Old Icelandic tales. Appropriate titles for further reading include the following:

Brønsted, Johannes. *The Vikings* (Penguin, 1960).

Cook, Robert, translator. *Njal's Saga*. (Penguin, 1997).

Forte, Angelo, Richard Oram, and Frederik Pedersen. *Viking Empires* (Cambridge University Press, 2005).

Hjálmarsson, Jón R. *History of Iceland: From the Settlement to the Present Day* (Iceland Review, 1993).

Larrington, Carolyne, translator. *The Poetic Edda: A New Translation by Carolyne Larrington* (Oxford University Press, 1996).

Sturluson, Snorri, translated by Jean I. Young. *The Prose Edda: Tales from Norse Mythology* (University of California Press, 2001).

58

What's the difference between Hebrew and Yiddish?

Neil G. Jacobs

Are Hebrew and Yiddish the same language? Why would Jews need to know both of them? Why do people confuse the two languages?

When someone asks you what you do, and you answer, 'I teach Yiddish,' prepare to be told in no uncertain terms what Yiddish 'is': 'the language of the Old Testament', or 'just Jewish slang words you can mix into whatever language you're speaking', or 'German without a grammar', or 'another name for Hebrew'. None of these ideas are right. Even a quick glance at basic vocabulary and sentence structures will make it clear to anybody that Yiddish and Hebrew are very different languages. Here, phonetically transcribed, is how you say 'He read the book,' first in Yiddish, then in Modern Israeli Hebrew:

Er hot geleyent dos bukh.
Hu kará et ha-sefer.

So why do people—usually non-Jews, but not always—confuse the two languages? That's an important and interesting question.

One reason outsiders can be confused is that significant Jewish speech communities have used both languages over long spans of time. Another is that both are written today in what's often called the 'Hebrew' alphabet. ('Jewish' would be a more accurate term, historically speaking.) So somebody who doesn't know that alphabet has no way of telling a document or street sign in Hebrew from one in Yiddish. A third possible cause of confusion is that the two languages have a sizeable shared vocabulary (primarily Hebrew words and phrases that have become part of Yiddish).

A final complication is that the interactions between the two languages have differed from one Jewish community to another and from one historical period to another. In the millennia-long history of the Jewish people as a whole, more Jews have *read* Hebrew, over a longer period of time, while more Jews have *spoken* Yiddish, for a longer period.

Hebrew is a member of the Semitic family of languages, closely related to Aramaic (the language spoken by Jesus) and somewhat more distantly to Arabic. (Modern Israeli Hebrew is very different from the Classical Hebrew spoken in biblical times, and both are very different from Rabbinic Hebrew, the scholarly language of the centuries in between; but those are topics for another essay.) Yiddish is more difficult to classify genetically. Its basic grammatical structure derives from Germanic, as does most of its vocabulary (usually estimated at about 70 percent). The remaining 30 percent comes from Hebrew, Aramaic, and Slavic languages, which have also left various imprints on Yiddish grammar.

Given these diverse sources of vocabulary, some people have viewed Yiddish as a hodgepodge of linguistic scraps from donor languages, rather than as a language in its own right. The great twentieth-century Yiddish scholar Max Weinreich has described it, more accurately, as a 'fusion language' that incorporates vocabulary elements of diverse origin into a grammar that is uniquely its own. This kind of fusion is common when one language borrows vocabulary from another. English, for example, has adopted the Yiddish word *glitsh* ('slippery area; a slip-up') to refer to mechanical or electronic malfunctions. In Yiddish, the plural would be *glitshn*, but English speakers have 'naturalized' this borrowed word with a regular English plural: 'glitches'.

Linguistic coexistence like that between Hebrew and Yiddish has a very long history in Jewish culture. Even before the Romans destroyed Jerusalem's Second Temple in 70 CE, the everyday spoken language of most Jews was their own version of Aramaic, although they still used Hebrew for religious purposes. Over the centuries, scattered Jewish communities of the Diaspora, influenced by the spoken languages of their non-Jewish neighbors, developed new vernacular languages (common speech) of their own: Judeo-Persian, Judezmo (sometimes called Ladino), Judeo-Arabic, and others. At the same time Hebrew (or Judeo-Aramaic) continued to be used, not only for religious purposes but also for important documents, and as a lingua franca for maintaining connections with other Diaspora communities. A kind of multilingualism became the norm for Jewish civilization: everyday life required the ability to navigate appropriately back and forth between Hebrew/Aramaic and a Jewish vernacular, and often between that vernacular and the languages of nearby non-Jewish populations.

Yiddish arose in Europe between the tenth and twelfth centuries, in much the same way as earlier Jewish vernaculars had arisen in the Middle East. Medieval Jewish communities along Germany's Rhine river evolved into a new branch of the Jewish people—Ashkenazic Jewry, with a new language of its own, influenced by German. At its maximum extent, around the nineteenth century, the home territory of Yiddish in Central and Eastern Europe occupied the second-largest geographic expanse of any European language/culture area (after Russian). The number of Yiddish speakers worldwide on the eve of World War II is estimated at eleven to thirteen million, making Yiddish the fourth or third most widely spoken Germanic language at the time. Of the six million Jews murdered in the Holocaust, five million were Yiddish speakers.

Yidish (which is the Yiddish word for 'Jewish') is a relatively new name for the language among its speakers. In earlier periods, Jews typically called Yiddish 'our language' or *mame-loshn* ('mother language') to distinguish it from Hebrew/Aramaic, which was called *Loshn-koydesh* ('the language of sanctity'). There was a rather fixed division of labor between the two languages in traditional Ashkenazic religious study: sacred texts were first read aloud in the original Hebrew or Aramaic, then discussed in Yiddish. Coexisting within a single cultural space, Hebrew over the centuries continued to exert influences on Yiddish, and Yiddish patterns, not surprisingly, sometimes found their way into Ashkenazic *Loshn-koydesh*. Until the modern period, the status of Hebrew prevailed; books published in Yiddish earlier typically bore a title in Hebrew.

The modern period in European history has been noteworthy for the successful struggle of vernaculars like Yiddish to become national languages, used for academic discourse, journalism, national literatures, and more. Interestingly, the early twentieth century saw Hebrew, too, re-established as a flourishing national language. Even outside the domains of spoken Hebrew and Yiddish, the two languages each continue to play roles in the ethnography of Jewish speech today—such as in American Jewish English—continuing a linguistic complexity in Jewish life that stretches from the ancient past to the present day.

About the author

Neil G. Jacobs is Professor in the Yiddish and Ashkenazic Studies Program of the Department of Germanic Languages and Literatures at The Ohio State University. Widely published in the area of Yiddish linguistics, he is author of *Yiddish: A Linguistic Introduction* (2005/2009). His other areas of teaching and research include post-Yiddish Jewish ethnolects; Jewish cabaret; Jewish geography; and the Sephardic Jewish Papiamentu of Curaçao. He is active in the Society for Germanic Linguistics, and has twice been elected as its vice-president.

Suggestions for further reading

In this book
Chapters connected in various ways with themes discussed in this one include 6 (language families), 7 (language of Adam), 9 (lingua francas),

28 (language rescue), and 59 (Arabic). Other chapters on individual languages include 52–57 and 60–65.

Elsewhere

Fishman, Joshua. 'The sociology of Yiddish: A foreword', in Joshua Fishman, ed., *Never say die! A Thousand Years of Yiddish in Jewish Life and Letters*, pp1–97 (Mouton, 1981).

Glinert, Lewis, ed. *Hebrew in Ashkenaz: A Language in Exile* (Oxford University Press, 1993).

Weinreich, Max. 'The reality of Jewishness vs. the ghetto myth: the sociolinguistic roots of Yiddish', in *To Honor Roman Jakobson: Essays on the Occasion of his Seventieth Birthday, 11 October 1966* (Mouton, 1967), 3: pp2199–221.

Weinreich, Max. 'Internal bilingualism in Ashkenaz', in Irving Howe and Eliezer Greenberg, eds., *Voices from the Yiddish* (University of Michigan Press, 1972), pp279–88.

59

Do all Arabs speak the same language?

Jerry Lampe

What is Arabic like? Should we be studying it? How hard is it to learn? What can you do with it?

Arabic is all around us these days. On news broadcasts we hear words like *mujahideen, intifada* and *al-Qaeda*. Middle Eastern foods like hummus and falafel are considered gourmet delights. And, if you look closely you'll see small ads in Arabic script—for some reason often on the sports page—seeking people who can read and speak the language.

It has an exotic sound to Western ears. But we'd better get used to it. Because it's not just for linguists and gourmets anymore. It promises to be part of our lives for a long time to come.

Arabic is spoken by more than 250 million people in an area extending from the Persian Gulf to the Atlantic Ocean. It's the language of the Qur'an, the holy book of Islam, so more than 700 million people have it as a spiritual component of their daily lives. The governments of twenty-two countries list Arabic as their principal language, and the U.N. made it one of its official languages in 1974. By any of several measures, Arabic is one of the most important languages in the world.

And yet it's been pretty much neglected in countries that should know better. A prime example is the United States. You've probably heard that the FBI and other government agencies—more than eighty of them—have huge needs for Americans proficient in Arabic. And that military and civilians serving in Iraq don't have the language or cultural skills to deal with the Iraqis. Arabic is now the foreign language most critical to U.S. national security, but nowhere near enough people with Arabic skills are available to fill the multitude of job vacancies: translators, interpreters, diplomats, business consultants, market analysts, intelligence analysts, and, of course, teachers and researchers.

You've probably heard it said that Arabic is hard to learn. What's the hard part? Well, the writing system takes a little getting used to, because words and sentences are written from right to left, meaning that what you might think of as the back of a book is actually the front. The alphabet has just twenty-eight letters, with a few extra dots that float above and below them. I've heard the letters described as a collection of 'worms and snails', and to the Western eye they can look, well, vermicular. But they're really quite beautiful, and they, in fact, constitute the principal form of art in the Arab and Islamic worlds. And it doesn't take more than a couple of weeks to learn them if they are studied systematically.

Also, Arabic pronunciation can be tricky in spots, because there are a number of sounds that we don't have in English; some in the back of the throat remind me a little of German.

Probably the most challenging thing about Arabic is that you have to learn two variants of the language to get along well. One is Modern Standard Arabic, known as MSA, which is the language of literature and media throughout the Arab world. In addition to that, you need a colloquial variant of Arabic, a dialect, which is the language used in everyday talk in a given country. Most people learn either the Egyptian dialect or the Levantine dialect because they are the two variants most often taught in the West, and most American and European students of Arabic attend study-abroad programs in Egypt and the Levant.

Why do you need both Modern Standard and a dialect? If you speak only MSA, you'll be understood by most Arabs, who hear it in formal situations and in films or TV. But many Arabs don't speak it on a daily basis, so you won't understand them unless you learn the dialect of the country you go to. In fact, local speech varies so much from country to country in the Arabic-speaking world that even Arabs may not always understand one another when they travel.

So yes, it takes some time and dedication to learn Arabic. But it's well worth doing. Arabic is a centuries-old language and is part and parcel of a very rich culture. Learning it is a truly enriching, mind-opening experience, and the diligent study of Arabic can lead to exciting careers in a variety of fields. Shouldn't the non-Arab world be teaching it more often in schools?

About the author

Jerry Lampe is an independent consultant who taught Arabic and Islamic Studies for more than thirty years. His current projects include serving as Senior Academic Advisor to the (college-level) Arabic Flagship Programs; working to develop online Learning Objects in Arabic for high school students; and working with federal government colleagues through the Interagency Language Roundtable to devise skill level descriptions for Competence in Intercultural Communication. A draft of this document can be reviewed on the ILR's website, www.govtilr.org.

Suggestions for further reading

In this book

Other chapters on individual languages include 52–58 and 60–65. Opportunities and requirements for professional use of language abilities are discussed in Chapters 22 (bilingualism), 39 (America's language crisis), 45 (language-related careers), 46 (dictionaries), 47 (interpreting and translating), and 49 (forensic linguistics).

Elsewhere

American Association of Teachers of Arabic (AATA), www.aataweb.org. See the following sections: About Arabic, Manuscripts, Arabic Programs, Arabic Software, and General Links.

Brustad, Kristen, et al. *Alif Baa: Introduction to Arabic Letters and Sounds* (Georgetown University Press, 2001).

Brustad, Kristen, et al. *Al-Kitaab fii Ta'allum al-'Arabiyya: A Textbook for Beginning Arabic, Part One* (Georgetown University Press, 1995). These are the textbooks most widely used in the U.S. for beginning Arabic.

Nydell, Margaret. *Understanding Arabs: A Guide for Modern Times* (Intercultural Press, fourth edition 2005). The most popular guide for people who want to know more about the Arabs, their language, and their culture.

National Foreign Language Center (NFLC), www.langsource.umd.edu. A database composed of brief reviews of some of the best resources for learning/teaching the Arabic language and culture.

60

Is Swahili the language of Africa?

Donald Osborn

What languages do people speak in Africa? Are they all related, like the European languages? Are they less complex and advanced than European languages?

'Say something in African.' That's a question you might hear from a college freshman talking to an African exchange student. But of course there is no single 'language of Africa'. According to *Ethnologue*, the widely cited reference on languages, there are 2,110 separate tongues on the continent. Some are spoken by very small groups of people, maybe in only one village; others are spoken by millions. The thing to remember is that Africa, especially south of the Sahara, is one of the most multilingual regions in the world.

But what about a shared 'language of Africa' like Swahili? Well, a large number of people do speak Swahili, but it's limited mostly to east Africa. Africa is a vast continent and even the most widely spoken languages cover only sub-regions.

Because of the sheer number of African languages there's a lot that we're still learning about them. Since most are only spoken tongues, with an oral tradition but no written record, they're not easy to document. And to what extent are they related? It wasn't until 1963 that the linguist Joseph Greenberg, building on earlier work such as that of Diedrich Hermann Westermann, suggested that they fall into just four separate families: a huge one of over

1,300 languages spread across most of sub-Saharan Africa; a north African family that includes Hebrew, Arabic, and Amharic; a group in the middle around Chad and Uganda; and a small group called Khoisan, near the Kalahari desert.

So what are these languages like? Because of their diversity, no language represents them all. You've probably heard an occasional word like *harambee*, from Swahili, meaning 'pulling together', which was a rallying cry in Kenya. Or maybe the songs of Miriam Makeba or Ali Farka Touré. Or dialogue in the film *Amistad*, in which actors portraying enslaved Africans speak Mende, a language of present-day Sierra Leone. Perhaps the most exotic to the ears of English speakers are the clicking sounds used as consonants in some southern African languages. You can hear them in the recent film version of Bizet's opera *Carmen*, spoken and sung entirely in Xhosa.

The sounds and grammar of African languages are often very different from what we English speakers are more familiar with. For instance, many of them, such as Yoruba in Nigeria, use *tones* to distinguish meaning of words, much as Chinese does. These tones, by the way, are what permits the famous 'talking drums' of the region to convey messages.

And the structures of some African languages are quite intricate. We might think of German as complex, with three genders to classify nouns; but the Fulani language of West Africa has over *two dozen* noun classes. In this case, however, the noun endings and the indicative particles harmonize so that learning them is actually simpler than remembering, say, the gender of an object or abstraction in a continental European tongue.

Other languages have unique sounds, such as that click in Xhosa, which linguists believe was borrowed from neighboring Khoisan tongues. It has been suggested that the clicks are surviving remnants of the earliest sounds our human ancestors made in communicating—which would make these languages some of the oldest ones we know in terms of their phonetics.

Old, yes, but in no sense primitive. Many non-Africans still believe that African languages are less capable of expressing complex thought than European tongues. It was in reaction to such attitudes a half-century ago that Senegalese scholar Cheick Anta Diop translated an explanation of Einstein's theory of relativity into Wolof, a language of Senegal and Gambia.

And what about writing? It is often said that African cultures are oral, but this is an oversimplification. A number of African languages have also been written for a long time: a few in indigenous scripts like the one used for Amharic and Tigrinya in Ethiopia and Eritrea, several in west Africa as well as Swahili in Arabic script (though this is less common today), and many in the Latin alphabet, sometimes with added letters to represent additional sounds used in these tongues. However, the number of people actually using the written form of their language tends to be limited.

Now, with all those different languages, how do people communicate? The answer is: they find a way. Close to home, Africans commonly use more than one language in daily life. Further away, they may rely mainly on a *lingua franca* like Swahili, English, or French—or maybe a pidgin language.

But this answer hides another set of questions—how distinct are all these languages, or how many are there really? Many of the over 2,000 languages *Ethnologue* counts in Africa are in fact very closely related—some groups of them might alternatively be categorized as dialects of one language. For instance, the Mandinka of *Roots* author Alex Haley's ancestor Kunta Kinte is similar enough to languages called Malinke, Bambara, and Jula that fluent speakers of one can understand the others to varying degrees. On this basis some suggest that Africa is not really the tower of Babel it seems to be.

Nevertheless, with population growth and social change, the multilingual situation, already complex, becomes even more so. African languages are in flux, especially in cities, where diverse peoples come together. Some that are no longer taught in schools— or never were—are losing speakers. Economic incentives favor English or French. But African tongues are firmly part of the daily life, cultural identities, and economic activity of the continent. So what's the future of 'saying something in African'? There are probably as many answers to that as there are languages in Africa.

About the author
Donald Osborn is an independent scholar who works in the Washington, D.C. area. He also runs Bisharat, a small initiative to facilitate use of African languages on computers and the Internet. Dr. Osborn is a specialist in environment, agriculture, and development, who has studied and speaks two African languages, and has published a lexicon of one of them, Fulfulde. He has lived and worked for twelve years in west and east Africa.

Suggestions for further reading

In this book
Other chapters on individual languages include 52–59 and 61–65. Chapters on how groups of language are related include 6 (language families), 51 (origins of English), and 52 (Native American languages).

Elsewhere
Batibo, Herman M. *Language Decline and Death in Africa: Causes, Consequences, and Challenges* (Multilingual Matters, 2005). An introduction that focuses on endangered languages in Africa.

Childs, G. Tucker. *An Introduction to African Languages* (John Benjamins, 2004). An introduction to African languages and linguistics.

Heine, Bernd and Derek Nurse, eds. *African languages: An Introduction* (Cambridge University Press, 2000). A compilation of eleven articles by noted linguists expert in the study of different aspects of African languages.

Webb, Vic and Kembo-Sure. *African Voices: An Introduction to the Languages and Linguistics of Africa* (Oxford University Press, 2000). A compilation of articles on African languages and their importance to African societies.

Osborn, Donald. *African Languages in a Digital Age: Challenges and Opportunities for Indigenous Language Computing* (HSRC Press / IDRC, 2010). A pioneering look at efforts to help multilingual Africa to take full advantage of information technology.

61

Do you have to be a masochist to study Chinese?

Barry Hilton

*Was Chinese (as some Western missionaries felt) invented by
Satan 'to keep the gospel out of China'? Is it the most difficult
language in the world? Is it worth the trouble?*

If you ask professional linguists questions like these, most will
probably say that every language is complex in some ways and
simple in others, and that they average out to around the same
level of complexity. But that's probably not the kind of answer
you're looking for. If we rephrase the question, though, and ask
which major language is *hardest for native English speakers to learn*,
well, yes, a pretty good case can be made for Chinese. (Background
note: the name 'Chinese' refers to at least half a dozen regional
languages that are closely related but as different from each other
as French, Spanish, and Italian. What I have to say applies to all of
them, especially to the one most widely spoken, called 'Mandarin'
by foreigners. It is the official language of both mainland China
and Taiwan.) Let's look at some of the reasons.

One difficulty is that Chinese is unrelated to English. When you
study a cousin of English in the Indo-European language family,
like Spanish, Russian or Hindi, you find plenty of cognates—

related words, similar in sound and meaning—to use as stepping-stones. To learn Chinese you have to acquire a vocabulary that is totally new, except for a few borrowings like 'typhoon', 'gung ho', 'coolie', and 'kowtow'.

As a second obstacle, Chinese has a phonetic feature that can be difficult for English-speaking learners to hear and reproduce. Like English words, Chinese words are made up of consonant and vowel sounds, but each Chinese syllable also has an *intonation* pattern that's *not optional*. Mandarin syllables come in five patterns: (1) high level (think of a cartoon opera singer warming up: 'mi-mi-mi'); (2) rising (like answering a knock at the door: 'Yes?'; (3) dipping-and-rising (like a drawn-out, pensive 'we-e-ll'); (4) sharply falling ('Stop!'); and (5) toneless or unaccented (like the second syllable of 'cattle'). The Chinese word $lyou^4$ (falling tone) means 'six'; $lyou^2$ (same consonant and vowels but rising tone) means 'remain'. $Ying^2mu^4$ means 'tent'; $ying^1mu^3$ means 'acre'; jya^4jr^5 means 'value'; jya^3jr^1 means 'artificial limb'. Learners of Chinese who get tones wrong can sound as odd—or incomprehensible—to native ears as learners of English sound to us when they mix up the vowel sounds in words like 'fit' and 'feet', or 'hall' and 'hull'.

Now, many other languages—like Hungarian and Arabic and Indonesian—have no cognates for English-speaking students to rely on. And some, like Vietnamese, Thai, and various African languages, are also tonal. But there's another obstacle that puts the difficulty of Chinese on an entirely different level: its writing system.

If you've ever done volunteer work in a literacy program, you know what a frustrating handicap illiteracy is, and how empowered an adult learner feels as he or she masters the 'code' that links familiar sounds with the few dozen squiggles that represent them on paper. People learning Chinese have a very complicated 'code' to master, which impedes not just their ability to read but their ability to broaden their vocabulary and develop other linguistic skills.

The squiggles the Chinese writing system uses—usually called 'characters'—don't represent simple consonant and vowel sounds, the way English letters do. Each one stands for a whole one-syllable word or word element, combining sound *and meaning*. For example, if a Chinese-like system were used to write English, the word 'unbearable' might be written with three squiggles, one for 'un', one for 'bear', and one for 'able'. And *that* 'bear' squiggle would be different from the squiggles representing the same sound in 'polar bear', 'childbearing', and 'the right to bear arms'—to say nothing of 'barefoot', or 'Bering Strait'. That adds up to a *lot* of squiggles for learners to memorize—several thousand characters instead of a couple of dozen alphabet letters. Not surprisingly, illiteracy is a major problem in China.

And when you meet a new character (or one whose sound and meaning you've learned and forgotten), how do you look it up? There are hundreds of Chinese dictionaries, and almost as many different systems for arranging characters. Without alphabetical order, tracking down an unknown character is much more labor-intensive than flipping pages while silently mouthing the ABC song. Even when you find the character, you won't necessarily know—without still more dictionary research—whether it's a stand-alone word or part of a compound like 'unbearable'.

I hope these comments serve less to discourage than to challenge people interested in learning Chinese. Learners can take heart from the fact that the *sound* system of Chinese is pretty simple except for the tones; and Chinese grammar—unlike, for example, Navajo grammar—poses no real difficulties for English speakers. Even the writing system, devilish as it may seem, has fascinated foreigners for centuries, and offers a key to understanding the classical literature and modern economic vitality of one of the great civilizations of the world.

About the author

Barry Hilton is the Associate Editor of this book and was a member of the review board of the radio series from which it was adapted. He is a freelance writer/editor and independent scholar living in Maine and working as a marketing specialist for a small publishing company. He is an honors graduate of Harvard College who, after graduate studies at Cornell, Yale, and George Washington Universities, and the Foreign Service Institute, has travelled extensively and lived in both Europe and Asia. In a variety of U.S. government assignments he has made professional use of Vietnamese, Chinese, Japanese, French, and German. He describes himself as an 'armchair philologist and recovering polyglot'.

Suggestions for further reading

In this book
Other chapters on individual languages include 52–60 and 62–65. Writing systems are also discussed in Chapters 11 (scripts), 12 (history of writing), 58 (Hebrew and Yiddish), 59 (Arabic), and 62 (Japanese).

Elsewhere
Kratochvil, Paul. *The Chinese Language Today* (Hutchinson University Library, 1968). Although some of the vocabulary examples are very dated by their political flavor, as a brief introduction to Chinese for the serious general reader this book has not been superseded.

DeFrancis, John. *The Chinese Language: Fact and Fantasy* (University of Hawai'i Press, 1984). The grand old man of Chinese instruction in the U.S. (1911–2009) authoritatively debunks a number of myths about Chinese—particularly about the writing system—in a highly entertaining style.

McCawley, James D. *The Eater's Guide to Chinese Characters* (University of Chicago Press, 1984). There are any number of lightweight 'teach yourself Chinese characters' books on the market, some of them superficial to the point of being potentially misleading. McCawley's guide provides sound practical exercises in reading and looking up Chinese characters, while limiting itself to the useful aim of showing general readers how to find their way around a Chinese menu.

Moser, David. 'Why Chinese Is So Damn Hard', www.pinyin.info/ readings/texts/moser.html. An accurate and amusing detailed account of the difficulties of Chinese, which almost in spite of itself serves as an invitation to potential learners: 'The more you learn about Chinese characters, the more intriguing and addicting they become.'

62

Is studying Japanese worth the effort?

Blaine Erickson

Is Japanese really the world's hardest language? Is it related to Chinese?

No one language is the 'world's hardest', but any language takes longer to learn the less it has in common with your native tongue. By that measure, Japanese is one of the hardest languages for English speakers.

However, not everything about Japanese is difficult: its *sounds* pose little problem. Many of them are much like English, though as you probably know, Japanese has only a single sound corresponding to both 'l' and 'r' in English—so that comedians imitating Japanese-accented English get cheap laughs by simply reversing the two sounds. On the downside, Japanese is absolutely unrelated to English, so you don't get a free startup vocabulary of cognates, as you would if you were learning, say, German or French. While Japanese has borrowed plenty of words from other languages, you might not recognize them. For example, the name 'Smith' becomes *Sumisu*, and *kuruunekku seetaa* is a crew-neck sweater.

Japanese grammar isn't too complex, but it's definitely un-English. For example, English sentence order is usually subject, then verb, then object. Japanese sentences put verbs at the end, and subjects and objects, especially words for 'you' and 'I', are often left out. Japanese sentences also sometimes end with mini-words that can change a statement into a question, or make a sentence more emphatic, or seek agreement.

Interestingly, some of these mini-words are used only by men, others only by women. Male/female speech differences, while not as strong as they used to be, are noticeably greater than in English. In fact, male and female vocabularies are different enough that dialogue between a man and a woman in a Japanese novel can omit 'he said' and 'she said'.

Besides using 'female' words, women usually speak more politely than men, demonstrating another un-English aspect of Japanese: an elaborate system of polite, respectful, and humble speech. When you talk to superiors or strangers, you refer to them and their actions with 'respectful' words, like *irassharu* for 'go' and *ossharu* for 'say'; for your own going and saying you use the 'humble' *mairu* and *mooshiageru*. (This is part of why 'you' and 'I' can be omitted.) When you talk with friends and family you can use 'neutral' words like *iku* and *yuu*, no matter whose actions you're referring to. How do you know when to use respectful or humble language? Well, it's not easy, even for the Japanese, who get exposed to it as they grow up. Japanese college graduates, newly hired by big companies, are often sent off for training in polite speech—so don't worry if you can't quite master it overnight.

Another thing sometimes bewildering for foreigners is that the Japanese so often seem to cut linguistic corners. They talk about 'that' without ever mentioning what 'that' refers to, and even leave verbs, subjects, objects, and even entire phrases out of sentences, once everyone knows what the topic of conversation is. To an outsider, a social conversation can be as cryptic as a Mafia telephone call.

Still, these are all things you can master with a reasonable amount of time and effort. It's the Japanese writing system that gives learners fits. By some accounts, it's the most complex writing system in current use.

Like many other Asian peoples, the Japanese were enormously influenced by China. When they began writing their own language—which is not at all related to Chinese—they adapted

Chinese characters. They took a system already challenging for learners—thousands of characters to memorize—and added a new difficulty: they used one character for several different words. If English were written using Chinese characters in the Japanese way, the same character (let's say the one used to write 'horse') might appear as part of the written versions of 'chivalry', 'cavalier', 'horseman', and even 'knight'. The reader would have to deduce from context which of those the writer meant. It's not as hard as it could be, though. The Japanese commonly use only about 2,000 characters (as opposed to 3,000, 4,000, or more for Chinese), and they spell out quite a few things phonetically. But just to keep you on your toes, they do it with two different homegrown systems, plus the Roman alphabet! Even for people born in Japan, it can become confusing.

The Japanese sometimes seem to take perverse pride in the obstacles their language poses, but the fact is that foreigners can and do learn it—some even become Japanese celebrities. Learning it well will take more study than a European language, but the effort is really worthwhile. Japanese has 127 million native speakers, which makes it the eighth most-commonly spoken language in the world, ahead of German, French, and Italian.

The time is long past when the Japanese were feared as an imperialist power or the label 'Made in Japan' was thought to mean cheap imitation goods. Today, the world beats a path to Japan's door to do business, buy its products, and enjoy its culture, including pop music and animation—everything from sushi to sumo. The gateway to understanding and appreciating that fascinating culture is the Japanese language.

About the author
Blaine Erickson is an Associate Professor of Japanese at the Defense Language Institute Foreign Language Center at the Presidio of Monterey, California. He was educated at the University of Oregon, Waseda University (Tokyo), the Chinese University of Hong Kong, the University of Tokyo, and the University of Hawai'i at Manoa. He specializes in

both modern and historical Japanese phonology and morphology, with additional interests in historical Chinese, modern Cantonese, and modern and historical English. He has lived in Yokohama, Sapporo, Kanazawa, and Kumamoto, and has traveled in many other regions throughout Japan. His favorite food is unagi (broiled freshwater eel), though basashi (raw horse meat), a Kumamoto specialty, is a runner-up.

Suggestions for further reading

In this book
Other chapters on individual languages include 52–61 and 63–65. Writing systems are also discussed in Chapters 11 (scripts), 12 (history of writing), 58 (Hebrew and Yiddish), 59 (Arabic), and 61 (Chinese).

Elsewhere
Miller, Roy Andrew. *The Japanese Language* (University of Chicago Press, 1967). While this book is old, it is a classic. It covers a wide range of topics, some of which are of more interest to specialists than to general readers. It's still a good read.

Shibatani, Masayoshi. *The Languages of Japan* (Cambridge University Press, 1990). More recent than Miller's book, it covers not just Japanese but also Ainu, a nearly extinct language spoken in northern Japan. Again, some topics may be too specialized for the general reader, but it is still accessible.

McClain, Yoko Matsuoka. *Handbook of Modern Japanese Grammar* (Hokuseido Press, 1981). An excellent reference for the student of Japanese, with topics logically divided by grammatical pattern and type.

Haig, John H., ed. *The New Nelson: Japanese–English Character Dictionary, based on the classic edition by Andrew N. Nelson* (Tuttle, 1997). The definitive reference work for those who are serious about learning to read Japanese.

63

What's the language of India?

Vijay Gambhir

How many languages are there in India? What's the role of English there? Does everybody in India speak Hindi? What's the difference between Hindi and Urdu?

India's language situation is hugely complicated. Where a country like Japan or Sweden has a single language that unites and defines it, India has *hundreds* of languages and dialects. The 2001 census asked citizens what language they learned from their mothers as children. The tabulated responses identified 1,635 distinct speech communities, 234 of which had 10,000 or more speakers. Indian experts classify those 234 communities as speaking dialects of 122 languages. Of those 122 languages, 22 are spoken as mother tongues by some 95 percent of India's population, and their major role is explicitly recognized in the nation's constitution.

These 22 languages vary widely. Hindi, the most widely spoken language in the country, belongs to the Indo-European language family, like English; so do Assamese, Bengali, Dogri, Gujarati, Kashmiri, Konkani, Maithili, Marathi, Nepali, Oriya, Punjabi, Sanskrit, Sindhi, and Urdu. The Dravidian language family, unique to south India, is represented by Kannada, Malayalam, Tamil, and Telugu. Two of the 22 languages, Bodo and Manipuri, are part of the Sino-Tibetan family, like Chinese. Santali, spoken mainly in border areas near Bangladesh, Nepal, and Bhutan, belongs to the

Austro-Asiatic family, like Cambodian. And it seems that not all of India's languages have yet been counted. Just recently, in 2008, National Geographic's 'Enduring Voices' project discovered a previously unreported language called Koro, in the Himalayan region.

For practical reasons, this vast linguistic diversity is reduced to two 'official' languages, Hindi and English, with Standard Hindi as the primary one. Not everyone in India knows Hindi; but it is widely used, and most people in urban centers can speak it. Although people in non-Hindi regions may not have functional knowledge of it, Hindi is spreading rapidly because of internal migration for jobs and business opportunities. The Indian film industry, popularly known as Bollywood, has also popularized Hindi throughout the country. The linguistic profile of cosmopolitan cities like Mumbai (Bombay), Kolkata (Calcutta), and Bangalore (the Silicon Valley of India) has changed significantly in recent times. Although the regional languages of those cities are Marathi, Bengali, and Kannada respectively, Hindi functions as a bazaar language or *lingua franca* in all three.

Although Hindi is primary, keep in mind that India is also the world's second largest *English*-speaking country. English came to the subcontinent with British colonization in the early 1800s, and has played a role there ever since. As the language of colonial rulers, it was shunned by freedom fighters like Mahatma Gandhi during India's struggle for independence. But it was eventually adopted as an official language because of rivalry among the many Indian languages. After serious linguistic riots against Hindi in the mid-1960s, the government declared that English would continue as an official language for an indefinite period.

English is the language of higher education. And globalization has created rapidly growing demand for English training at all levels, since proficiency in English is seen as a ticket to a high-paying job. English is compulsory in India's middle and high schools under the so-called 'three-language formula', which requires that students be taught in Hindi, English, and a regional language. Many working-class Indian parents send their children to private English schools as opposed to government schools. College graduates are rushing to English coaching centers to improve their conversational skills.

For all that, only a small fraction of Indians actually have working proficiency in English. Their English often has a distinctive flavor of its own, which some monolingual Americans seem to find amusing, but which gets the job done. (And the English of Indian-staffed commercial call centers is rapidly improving.) Hindi speakers frequently mix English words and phrases into their colloquial speech, producing a mixed variety of Hindi known as Hinglish. For example, *I told you ke vo aayegaa* ('I told you he would come'). Hinglish is becoming a 'cool' style for the younger generation. Because Hinglish seems less intimidating for non-Hindi speakers in India, it is also shrinking the gap between the language of elites and non-elites, and is being used as a tool for reaching Indian consumers by multinational companies such as Coca-Cola and McDonald's.

And what about Urdu? Although it's a tricky political question, any discussion of Hindi has to include the principal language of Pakistan, since Hindi and Urdu are close enough to be dialects of the same tongue. Although they share a common origin and have almost the same basic vocabulary, grammar and sound system, they are treated as different languages in India and listed as separate languages in the Indian Constitution. One reason is that they have different writing systems: Hindi uses Devanagari (the same as Sanskrit script), which is written from left to right; Urdu uses Nastaliq (Perso-Arabic script), written from right to left. But the main reason is that speakers of Hindi and Urdu have distinct socio-religious identities, and they borrow their literary and formal vocabularies from different sources. Hindi borrows mostly from Sanskrit; Urdu from Arabic and Persian. The spoken varieties of Hindi and Urdu are mutually comprehensible, but the languages grow widely apart at the literary and formal levels.

There was a time, not so long ago, when Hindi was limited to a narrow part of the globe and rarely studied outside India. No more. Hindi speakers are found in large numbers in places such as Suriname, Singapore, Dubai, England, Canada, Australia, and America. The language is taught in almost a hundred American colleges and universities across the U.S.—and even in some elementary schools. Its influence is on the rise, and it can fairly be said to have joined the ranks of 'world languages'.

About the author

Dr. Vijay Gambhir is a retired professor of South Asian languages and linguistics from the University of Pennsylvania. Her areas of interest include Hindi syntax, language acquisition, assessment, and heritage language learning. She has published several articles in professional journals and is editor of the book Teaching and Acquisition of South Asian Languages. She is also guest editor of 'Teaching and Learning Heritage Languages of South Asia', the first volume of the online journal *South Asia Language Pedagogy and Technology*. She has co-authored a popular video series for learning Hindi: *nayii dishaayen naye log* ('New Directions, New People').

Suggestions for further reading

In this book

Other chapters discussing multilingual societies include 9 (lingua francas) and 21 (language conflict). The importance of Hindi is a theme of Chapter 39 (America's language crisis), and a Hindi grammatical example is cited in Chapter 18 (language and thought). The relationships among languages are discussed in Chapters 4 (dialects) and 6 (language families). Other chapters on individual languages include 52–62 and 64–65.

Elsewhere

www.lib.berkeley.edu/ANTH/emeritus/gumperz/gumptalk.html

Gumperz, John J. *Crosstalk* (broadcast on BBC television, 1979). One of a series of ten programs entitled *Multi-Racial Britain*, which deals with workplace miscommunication among British and Indian immigrants.

www.indiaeducation.net/UsefulResources/Maps. Shows the distribution of major languages of India across different states and union territories of India.

Kachru, Braj, Yamuna Kachru, and S. N. Sridhar, eds. *Language in South Asia* (Cambridge University Press, 2008). Introduction discusses the linguistic impact of Sanskrit, Persian, and English on South Asian languages. Part 2 of the book discusses the status of South Asia's major, minor, and tribal languages.

Rai, Amrit. *A House Divided: The Origin and Development of Hindi-Urdu.* (Oxford University Press, 1984) Focuses on the origin of Hindi/Urdu and the separation of modern Hindi and Urdu into two separate languages.

Schiffman, Harold F. *Bilingualism in South Asia: Friend or Foe?* (www. lingref.com/isb/4/163ISB4.PDF, 2005). Provides an insight into India's linguistic conflict in the post-Independence era and the role of English.

64

Whatever happened to Esperanto?

Arika Okrent and E. M. Rickerson

Whatever happened to the idea of a universal language?
Is Esperanto still alive? And if so, who speaks it?

Wouldn't it be wonderful if everyone in the world spoke the same language? Or wouldn't it be almost as good if everyone could speak their own language at home but agree to learn the same *second* language for international communication; a language that didn't belong to any one country; and so easy you could learn it in just a few weeks?

If you like that idea, you're in good company. Starting as early as the seventeenth century with philosophers such as Bacon, Descartes and Leibniz, there have been hundreds of proposals for an international language—and people are still trying to create one. For a variety of reasons, however, the only one that had lasting success was Esperanto, invented in Poland in the late nineteenth century by Ludwig Zamenhof, an idealist who understood the power of language to unite or divide.

What kind of a language is Esperanto? People who have heard of it but never heard it spoken are sometimes led to believe that it is based on Spanish, which is not true. The name 'Esperanto' has a Spanish flavor, but the vocabulary of the language is a mix of European tongues; it includes Slavic and Germanic word roots, as well as roots from Latin and Romance languages. The name of the language is formed from the Romance root for 'hope' (*esper-*) and the endings *-ant-* (indicating that the action is taking place) and *-o* (making it a noun). It means 'one who hopes'.

The endings used to form Esperanto words are completely regular. Nouns always end in *-o*, adjectives in *-a*, present tense verbs in *-as*, past tense verbs in *-is*; once you know the endings, you know how to add them to any root to make a word. This means that with a minimal amount of memorization, you can be up and running pretty quickly. Esperanto is much easier to learn than natural languages, with their pesky irregularities and exceptions. It is not, however, completely predictable. There are expressions, idioms, and ways of putting phrases together that must simply be learned. The rules of Esperanto are defined, but not too well defined. This is one of the reasons it has flourished while hundreds of competitors never gained any traction. Esperanto allows room for change and growth, and for a community of speakers to define its standards through usage.

So whatever happened to Esperanto? It was created in 1887, got a big boost in popularity from the war-weariness of the 1920s, even became a serious candidate to be the official language of the League of Nations—and then seemed to fade away. But it did not, in fact, disappear. Although it had ups and downs throughout the twentieth century, the language quietly survived. And as the twenty-first century gets under way, Esperanto has emerged again, robust and gaining in popularity—in part because of the Internet. Where Esperantists once had to travel to meetings and conferences to find other people to speak with, now they can sit down at the computer to chat with their fellow Esperantists anywhere in the world.

That said, the meetings and conferences are still an important part of the Esperanto scene. While many invented languages have been presented to the world as mere useful tools for commerce, science, or international diplomacy, Esperanto gained its appeal by focusing on the wide range of other things that humans do with language. When Esperantists get together they perform Esperanto songs, comedy skits, and poetry readings. There are Esperanto novels and magazines. There's a translation of the Bible, as well as *The Lord of the Rings*. There are Esperanto jokes, puns, and swear words. There is even a feature-length film with a sound track entirely in Esperanto: *Incubus*, which stars a young, pre-*Star Trek* William Shatner.

There are also a few hundred people in the world for whom Esperanto is a native tongue. Since a native language is one you learn at your mother's knee, and Esperanto is a language *constructed* for people who already have a native tongue, you may wonder how anyone could speak it natively. Answer: mother and father meet at an Esperanto conference, but don't speak each other's native languages. So they use Esperanto with each other at home, and raise their children speaking it. These new native Esperanto speakers are *not* monolingual—they also speak the majority language outside the home. Their linguistic situation is not much different from that of children who grow up in a home where immigrant parents speak a language different from the majority language.

Esperanto speakers are dispersed, so it's hard to get an exact count of them. It's also hard to tell what level of fluency one should reach to be called an Esperanto speaker. But there are at least tens of thousands—50,000 seems a reasonable estimate—with some conversational ability. The annual Universal Congress—which is most often held in Europe, but has also taken place in China, Korea, Japan, Brazil, Australia, and Israel—usually has a couple of thousand attendees.

Esperanto is by far the most successful language in the long history of language invention. It isn't a universal language, and it's unlikely to become one, but it has become a living language.

About the authors

Arika Okrent received a joint Ph.D. in the Department of Linguistics and the Department of Psychology's Cognition and Cognitive Neuroscience Program at the University of Chicago. She has written about language for *The American Scholar*, *Tin House*, and *Slate*. In the course of writing

286 ARIKA OKRENT AND E. M. RICKERSON

her 2009 book *In the Land of Invented Languages*, she earned a first-level certification in Klingon.

E. M. ('Rick') Rickerson is the General Editor of this book. He is Professor Emeritus of German, Director Emeritus of the award-winning language program at the College of Charleston (South Carolina), a former Deputy Director of the U.S. government's Center for the Advancement of Language Learning, and an Associate of the National Museum of Language. In 2005 he created the radio series on languages (*Talkin' about Talk*) from which *The Five-Minute Linguist* has been adapted. He is currently retired in the mountains of North Carolina. E-mail: rickersone@bellsouth.net.

Suggestions for further reading

In this book
Other chapters on languages consciously created by humans include 26 (sign languages) and 65 (survey of artificial languages). Languages that have served as 'bridges' between groups that would otherwise be unable to communicate are discussed in Chapters 9 (lingua francas), 10 (pidgins), 53 (Latin), and 58 (Hebrew and Yiddish).

Elsewhere
Okrent, Arika. *In the Land of Invented Languages: Esperanto Rock Stars, Klingon Poets, Loglan Lovers, and the Mad Dreamers Who Tried to Build a Perfect Language* (Spiegel & Grau, 2009). A popular history of the many attempts to overcome Babel by creating artificial languages.

Richardson, David. *Esperanto—Learning and Using the International Language* (Esperanto League for North America, third edition 2004). Includes chapters on the history of Esperanto, a complete course in the language, an annotated reader, and a bibliography.

Jordan, David. *Being Colloquial in Esperanto* (Esperanto League for North America, second edition 2004). A complete overview of Esperanto grammar.

www.Esperanto.net. General information about Esperanto, in 62 different languages, with links to other relevant sites.

www.lernu.net. A multilingual site that will help you learn the language, free of charge.

65

Does anybody here speak Klingon?

Christopher Moseley

Why do people invent artificial languages? Can invented
languages be more scientific than natural languages?

With nearly seven thousand languages already in the world, what
possesses people to make up new ones? For some, the motive
seems to be idealistic, to create a single language to unite mankind
in mutual understanding. But there may be a flaw in that reason-
ing: some of the bloodiest conflicts in history have been fought
among people who speak the same language. Think of Vietnam or,
for that matter, the English civil war, the American civil war, and
the two British–American wars in-between!

Another motive seems to be to create an exclusive secret society. Children make up languages all the time to do that.

Then there are languages created as backdrops for fictional
civilizations. Good examples are the Klingon language in the *Star*
Trek television series, and the languages Tolkien devised for the
elves, dwarves, and other inhabitants of Middle Earth in *The Lord*
of the Rings.

Still another reason is that thinkers have been frustrated at
how imperfectly natural languages represent the world. Beginning
at least as early as the seventeenth century there have been attempts
to create a 'logical' language, using symbols—as in mathematics—
that could be understood regardless of what language the user

spoke. But while the invented languages were logical, they were also complicated, arbitrary, and hard for anyone but the inventor to learn.

The late nineteenth century saw a great flowering of attempts at a universal language, starting in 1880 with a language called Volapük. Then came Esperanto, and languages with names like Novial, Interlingua, and dozens of others. Almost all of them were based on western European tongues, usually German, French, English, or Spanish. And most of them are extinct. Once an invented language is launched onto the stormy seas of language *usage* it rarely survives the death of its inventor, no matter how clever or systematic it may be.

Of these idealistic nineteenth-century ventures, Esperanto became the best-known and the most widespread; it now has a body of literature of its own and still has many enthusiastic speakers around the world today. But there have been other artificial languages that have embodied more unusual concepts. Two of the most intriguing made-up languages are based on extraterrestrial or musical ideas. Even though it's fictional, Klingon is known even to non-linguists, and—like Esperanto—may be one of the rare languages that does outlive its creator. If you want to learn it, there are things to help, such as a grammar book and audio tapes, a multimedia Klingon tutor, and dictionaries—in Portuguese and German, as well as English. There are even some international societies that try to keep the language alive. All of this for a made-for-TV invented language of roughly 2,000 words, designed to sound as alien and harsh as possible, to capture the nasty nature of the Klingons.

The second language, which was one of those invented in the nineteenth century, reminds me of the film *Close Encounters of the Third Kind*. You may remember the scenes in which an alien spacecraft begins its efforts to open communications with Earthlings by teaching them to reproduce a haunting series of five tones. The invented language Solresol was based on a very similar principle: starting with the do-re-mi system used to teach singing, it created words by combining the seven notes of the scale in particular sequences. For example, *fa-fa-do-fa* was the word for 'doctor' and *fa-fa-do-la* meant 'dentist'. Solresol was relatively easy to learn, and what made the language unique was that it could be sung, played or whistled as well as spoken! It was popular for quite a long time.

There have also been languages created for a scientific purpose, such as Loglan, which was invented in 1960 to test whether grammar rules based on mathematical logic would make a language's speakers more precise thinkers. And a language invented in 1962 called 'BABM' (pronounced 'Bo-A-Bo-Mu'), with a writing system in which each letter represents a syllable. Or one from 1979 that uses a system of icons instead of letters to represent concepts and sounds. The list goes on.

Dr. Zamenhof's creation, Esperanto, and the languages like Ido and Novial that competed with it in the late nineteenth century were all created on the basis of natural European languages. European empires encircled the globe at the time, and it was only natural for Latin and its daughter languages to be taken as the basis for these languages. They are what linguists call 'a posteriori' languages—created out of a blend of languages already existing. Solresol, Klingon and a host of others, some using familiar alphabets, some with scripts of their own, are what we call 'a priori' languages—created from scratch.

There's a website called www.langmaker.com where, barring technical difficulties, you can find a lot of these languages— including the newest ones—either for fun or to further an ideal. Would you like to create your own language, better than the ones we already have? If so, join the club. Among people who like languages, it seems to be a universal urge.

About the author

Christopher Moseley (Chrismoseley50@yahoo.com) is a university lecturer, writer and freelance translator, editor of the *Encyclopedia of the World's Endangered Languages* (2006) and the *UNESCO Atlas of the World's Languages in Danger* (2009), as well as co-editor of the *Atlas of the*

World's Languages (1993). He has a special interest in artificial languages (and has created one himself).

Suggestions for further reading

In this book
Other chapters on languages consciously created by humans include 26 (sign languages) and 64 (Esperanto).

Elsewhere
Large, Andrew. *The Artificial Language Movement* (Blackwell, 1985). Large's book is the most comprehensive overview of this complicated story in one volume. If you want to explore the individual languages further, you must seek out the textbooks and manuals of their authors and propagators. These can be very hard to find; hardly any are still in print.

Okrent, Arika. *In the Land of Invented Languages: Esperanto Rock Stars, Klingon Poets, Loglan Lovers, and the Mad Dreamers Who Tried to Build a Perfect Language* (Spiegel & Grau, 2009). Less encyclopedic than Large's book, but academically sound; also highly readable and entertaining.

The www.langmaker.com site mentioned above is an excellent place to take a look at the lively competition to create languages today. As of *The Five-Minute Linguist*'s publication date, the main site is out of operation because of technical difficulties. Several sections of the site, however, are in operation. These include www.langmaker.com/base.htm, www.langmaker.com/conlang.htm, www.langmaker.com/mlindex.htm, and www.langmaker.com/outpost/ido.htm, among others.

Index

CPSIA information can be obtained
at www.ICGtesting.com
Printed in the USA
FSOW02n1625010717
35740FS